Philosophy of Religion

'Allamah Muhammad Taqi Ja'fari

Translated by
Mansoor Limba

Thoroughly Revised and Edited by
Beytollah Naderlew

Top Ten Award
International Network Inc.

2023

Published by: Top Ten Award International Network Inc.

Vancouver, BC **CANADA**
Email: Info@TopTenAward.Net
www.toptenaward.net

Ordering Information:
Quantity sales. Special discounts are available on quantity purchases by universities, schools, corporations, associations, and others. For details, contact the "Sales Department" at the above mentioned email address.

Philosophy of Religion, 'Allamah Muhammad Taqi Ja'fari, 1st Edition.
ISBN: 978-1-990451-93-5   Paperback

In the Name of Allah,
the All-beneficent, the All-merciful

Contents

Foreword

This work embodies Allameh Jafari's philosophical meditations on religion as a subject-matter of philosophical thought in general. Jafari's philosophy like those of other traditional Muslim philosophers is basically theologically grounded. To put the matter otherwise, philosophy in the land of revelation and prophecy has emerged as an essentially theocentric discipline. Muslim philosophers including Allameh Jafari seek to frame their philosophies around the key phenomenon of religion. It is in this very sense that Allameh Jafari's philosophy is a religiously minded philosophy.

Of course, this work is not a disciplinary study of religion a la modern and postmodern philosophers. Rather it is a genuine primordial and traditional assay of the key issues concerning religion both in the form of *Shariah* (formal practices conceived as the external framework of religion) and Tariqah (gnostical initiation reflecting the quintessence of religion). Jafari shows his brilliant knowledge of contemporary scholarship on the subject in all chapters of the work. The reader can feel it to the heart if gets engaged with the work in a sympathetic fashion. Allameh has expressed his mind on many issues regarding the key phenomenon of religion either in the form of essays devoted to independent subjects or participations in the interviews conducted by the scholars of the Institute of Islamic Thought and Culture in Tehran. Jafari has applied his vita logical philosophy of intelligibility to such problems as the nature of religion, the relationship of science, philosophy and religion and religious pluralism, not to mention many others. This serious engagement with philosophical enigmas regarding religion some of which dates back to the dawn of philosophical thought, shows Allameh Jafari's committed philosophical mind. He has broached some two hundred brilliant and groundbreaking questions about human scholarship in general that includes religion too. It suffices just to read these questions so as to understand how serious philosophy is for Jafari particularly when it comes to such fundamental reality like religion.

This work would have not seen the light of day if some kind of people had not assisted the Allameh Jafari Institute to publish this work. We are obliged by Mansoor Limba who undertook the herculean task of translating this work. Beytollah Naderlew who has already translated three key works of Allameh Jafari into English accepted to edit the work and revise the translation thoroughly. We would like to express our warm thanks for his sincere efforts. Finally we hope this work fill the existing gap in the scholarship and rebalances the current monological debates dominated by the western disciplinary narratives of philosophy of religion.

Allameh Jafari Institute
16, November, 2015

Preface

The present book contains five discourses by 'All¡mah
Mu¦ammad Taqī Ja'farī on the study of religion. Whereas it is a
new edition of 'All¡mah's treatise on the philosophy of religion,
as proposed and published as the first volume of a series of
debates on philosophy of religion by the Institute of Islamic
Culture and Thought in 1375 AHS (circa 1996), and includes
some new discussions which are published for the first time in
a book form, then, it is worthwhile to mention briefly the
manner of its compilation.

After a series of consultations and sharing the ideas with
the late 'All¡mah, it was decided to force the pace of some
fellow researchers in the Institute by asking them to present
'All¡mah with some questions concerning the issues of the
philosophy of religion so that he may author some essays on
the philosophy of religion. At the outset, definitions of religion
from various books were presented to the author. The
transcription of the discussions held with the 'All¡mah was
presented to him for review. Dr. Qar¡malikī arranged and
compiled the whole of 'All¡mah's discourses, and at the same
time, enriched them by his own occasional glosses. He has also
presented his course of action in the introduction. After
completion of the work, I proofread and corrected some parts
which were to be published then as "the definition of religion".

The second part is concerned with the scope of religion. Mr.
Mu¦ammad Ri¤¡ Asadī took the responsibility of propounding
of the relevant questions and arranging its contents. This part
was first published in 1378 AHS (circa 1999) by the Institute.
For the revised edition of the book, he gave me a copy of the
headings not published earlier. Mr. Asadī has added some
notes to 'All¡mah's discourses which are helpful in

understanding the subjects better.

The third part of the book concerns the relationship of religion and politics, which has been arranged under the title of "Secularism". It was first published as volume 25 of *Tarjumeh wa Sharh-e Nahj al-Bal¡ghah* [by the 'All¡mah] and is presented here with modified headings.

The fourth part is on the relationship of science and religion for which 'All¡mah has chosen the following title: "Science, Religion and Theosophy as Three Major Elements of Human Intelligible Life"." In this work the author has ,made important points about the relationship of science and religion, science and philosophy with the trans-physics, and the limits of science in knowing reality. This work was published through *Ittil¡'¡t Daily* during 'All¡mah's lifetime. The unavailability of the author's manuscript and the errors in the existing text caused enormous difficulties in arranging and publishing it. Anyway, its edited version with new headings is presented here.

The last part of this volume is a set of questions and answers about pluralism, first published in the 7-8 issue of the journal, *Naqd wa Na¨ar*. Since this issue is related to the philosophy of religion, it is also included in this volume.

It is noteworthy that the undersigned edited the abovementioned parts of the book, particularly Parts 1, 3 and 4, while taking into account the writing style of the author, and to a certain extent this edited version has simplified the intricacies in the text. No doubt, if the late thinker were alive, the work would have been presented in a more integrated form.

Abdullah Na¥rī
The Persian Editor

Part 1
Definition of Religion

Editor's Introduction

The discourse on the definition of religion includes the following steps: at the outset, there is a methodological introduction to the possibility of a definition in the various fields of social sciences and humanities, in general, and the study of religion, in particular, elucidated and elaborated by the editor. He has also appended some methodological questions to it. 'Allımah replied these questions which were all about the definability of religion in detail.

After the methodological introduction, it was agreed that major definitions of religion by leading intellectuals to be presented along with a brief analysis of the key notions of their intellectual systems according to original sources, so that 'Allımah could systematically assess those definitions based on the intellectuals' weltanschauung. This decision was not implemented except in two cases, viz. the definitions of James and Jung who were among the prominent and macro-theoretician psychologists in the modern study of religion, and then, due to 'Allımah's decease, it was not continued. Many other definitions had been inquired by the researchers of the Institute of Islamic Culture and Thought which all were cited and analyzed by 'Allımah. For the sake of faithfulness to the original text, there is no modification of any sort in 'Allımah's expressions which are also identified as such.

Chapter 1

A Methodological Introduction to the Definition of Religion

Introduction

The inquiry into the nature of religion is preceded by some logico-methodological debates:

- The necessity of probing into the definition of religion
- The objective of definition and its types
- The logical conditions of a methodically grounded definition
- The undermining factors involved in the disorders of definition
- The impediments and difficulties embedded in the way to definition of religion
- The taxonomy of definitions of religion

1) The Necessity of probing into the Definition of Religion

A common principle in the domain of sciences and knowledge is to give a clear and enlightening definition of the science and its relevant subject-matter, which identifies its issues to a great extent. The researchers, then, begin to proceed their studies under the light of that definition.

Exposition[1]

To recognize the fields of science,[2] Muslim logicians have

---

1. The introduction to the discourses and parts of the text under the heading "Exposition" are by Dr. Qar¡malik¢.

2. The doctrine of science (Wissenschaftslehre) is one of the significant issues dealt with Muslim scholars. They have four main approaches in

arranged the issues and objects of questions in every science according to six major questions, classifying them according to the following logical order:

1. Conceptual analysis (expression of "what-of-lexical-explanation");
2. The question of existence and emergence (expression of "simple whetherness");
3. Essential analysis (real "what");
4. The question of quality, properties and rules (expression of "compound whetherness");
5. The question of existential cause (The Why of an affirmation); and
6. The question of the reason for emergence (The Why of an objective fact).

A methodically grounded inquiry in every field of knowledge is dependent on the observation of logical sequence of objects of question. Thus, before dealing with the properties, effects and rules of every matter and even before embarking on the affirmation and negation of a matter, one must offer a clear and distinct definition of it. The lack of a clear and approved definition leads to critical disagreements on the issues related to undefined matter. For this very reason, without having a clear notion of a subject one cannot embark on its affirmation or negation, and speak of its properties, rules and outcomes.

The debate on the rise of proponsity for religion and its consequences is among the important issues discussed in various domains of religious studies including psychology of religion, sociology of religion, history of religions, philosophy of religion, theology, and modern philosophical theology. No doubt, one of the reasons of emergence of diverse and contradictory views concerning the analysis of these two issues is the lack of a clear and universal definition of religion. It is based on a universal definition that it becomes clear whether contradictory views pertain to the same subject or not.

Wissenschaftslehre.

If two mutually discordant theories on the consequences of religiosity have their origin in two different notions of religion, they are not indeed mutually discordant and their relationship is an amphibology of contradiction, not real contradiction.

The Muslim logicians' emphasis on the primacy of definition of the subject as a [guiding] principle in every debate or dispute has been much welcomed today by analytic philosophers. The analytic philosophers' maxim "explain the notions first and clarify the meaning of concepts included by the claim so that we would then turn to the truth and falsity of the claim," basically implies the logical primacy of definition over other issues.

Generally speaking, the prerequisite for every debate on a subject is its clear and universal definition. For instance, as long as there is no clear and distinct definition of determinism (*jabr*) and free will (*ikhtiyjr*), we cannot hold a dialogue on this issue. It often happens that a scholar speaks against free will while other scholar offers proofs in favor of it, and yet there is other thinker who considers its refutation and demonstration impossible. Having said this, despite the amphibology of contradiction among these three views, due to these scholars' different notions of free will, there is no real contradiction among their views as they do not have the same subject under study, indeed.

Then, before propounding the issues of the philosophy of religion and jumping into the unending disputes of religious studies, it is necessary to turn to the definition of religion in the light of critical evaluation of the existed definitions. When one asks of the relationship between religion and freedom, religion and ideology, religion and art, and religion and development, s/he has to be retorted, "What do you mean by 'religion'?" When one speaks of religion, for example, in terms of exclusivism, ecumenism or pluralism, it needs to be inquired, "What is the theoreticians' notion of religion?" Since without a clear definition, the debate turns deceptive and erroneous and is always overshadowed by homonymy. Providing a definition, particularly in the domain of multidimensional and sophisticated phenomena, is far from easy. The difficulties lied in definability, however, cannot be a reason to turn a brown eye to the issue instead of solving it and to turn a deaf ear to the call for definition and leave the audience in ambiguity and confusion.

2) The Objective of Definition and Its Types

The ideal of scholars in logic and philosophy is to offer the most comprehensive definition ever possible which is called **perfect definition.** *The perfect definition identifies the subject through its genus proximum and* **real** **differentia** *which represent the very essence of* **definiendum.**

And whereas, for certain reasons, our knowledge is not able to permeate through the essence of things, the definition has to be of such peculiarities which are closer to the essence so as to cover all aspects of the **definiendum** *and to ban whatever lies outside its essence as well.*

Exposition

Definition types are mutually correlated with their objective and what is expected from them. Thus, the purpose of definition is outlined. To begin with every definition is expected to distinguish the matter at hand from other matters. To make the *definiendum* both conceptually and extensionally distinguished from other notions and matters is the chief objective of definition.[1]

Logically speaking, distinction is of two types: (1) essential distinction or conceptual distinction, and (2) accidental distinction or distinction in terms of properties and requirements. The definition which expresses the essential

---

1. The "chief objective" here indicates the existence of other objectives specifically highlighted by modern logicians; for example, vocabulary expansion; prevention of linguistic ambiguities; clarity of the scope of application of the term; and behavioral effect. In this regard, see Irving M. Copi, Introduction to Logic (New York: McMillan Publishing Co., 1982).

distinction is called *"definitio"* and the definition which depicts the accidental distinction is called *"descriptio"*. If *definitio* is such that includes all the essentials and notions implied in the *definiendum*, it is called "perfect definition". Although perfect definition is the most credible one ever possible for the identification of a matter, it is either difficult or impossible to obtain as it is not an easy task to identify all the essentials of a thing. Then, scholars often content themselves with imperfect definitions.

Imperfect definitions have numerous varieties; both linear and accidental varieties. Linear variety refers to various definitions which are not of the same level, like definition by way of extension, definition by way of example, definition by way of the negation of contradiction, definition based on properties, as well as lexical, stipulative, ostensive, abstractive and recursive definitions.[1]

Accidental variety refers to various definitions of the same kind, such as a number of descriptions of a single matter. This variety stems from the diversity of requirements and properties of the phenomenon.

Definition variety has its origin in the diversity of the objectives and expectations implied in the definition. The objective is once merely the attribution of a certain meaning to a word. In this case one is required to offer a stipulative definition. Sometimes one's objective is to determine the semantic scope of an expression and to mention the examples to which the concept applies well. In such an occasion, ostensive definition is used. At times, the intention is to define the distinctive properties and being this the case, a descriptive definition is provided.

One of the general disorders of definition is

---

1. For more information on the linear variety of definition by modern logicians, see Muwahhid ®iy¡', W¢zhen¡meh-ye Taw¥¢f¢-ye Man§iq (Tehran: Institute for Humanities and Cultural Studies, 1374 AHS), pp. 27-28; Copi, Introduction to Logic; P. Suppes, Introduction to Logic (New Jersey, 1957); Richard Robinson, Definition (Chford, 1972).

misappropriation, i.e. by offering stipulative definition, for example, one would claim that s/he is propounding a descriptive definition. When one turns to definition s/he needs to know in advance that to which type of definition does her/his intended definition belong. This error has occurred in the definition of religion time and again. A complete picture of religion cannot be drawn from a mere ostensive definition. Every critical assessment of the definitions of religion has to take their status and scope into consideration. Accordingly, based on the point stipulated in the text,[1] we are not after an all-encompassing and perfect definition but its description. Having said these, definition type and those aspects of religion which it is supposed to explain have to be specified.[2]

3) The Logical Conditions of a Methodically Grounded Definition

The most basic condition of a sound definition is compresiveness and properness.

Exposition:

Definition variety has misled some to the belief that definition is essentially subjective and relative, and thus no critical rhetoric in this regard is ever allowed. However, it needs to be taken into account that definition as such is a methodically oriented effort which seeks to provide a new notion upon the synthesis of previous self-evident notions. The new notion has to be the notion of the very thing whose nature or essence is the subject of inquiry.

As it was mentioned earlier, every definition struggles to throw new light on some aspects of the *definiendum*. This claim must be critically assessed in terms of its strength, perfection and defect. Is the proposed definition capable of laying the

---

1. It refers to 'All¡mah's claim that: "For certain reasons, it is impossible for our knowledge to permeate through the essence of things." In this regard, see 'Al¢ ibn S¢n¡, Ris¡lat al-°ud£d, pp. 74-75; Shaykh al-±£s¢, As¡s al-Iqtib¡s, pp. 441-442.
2. The nature/aspect error can be discussed along with these definitional errors.

necessary distinctions? Whether these distinctions are general or they only cover some aspects?

For this very reason, logicians seek to lay down some logical conditions and rules in the logic of definition[1] so as to distinguish between the sound and unsound definitions. The stipulated conditions in the science of logic can be reduced to two major conditions: one of which is concerned with concept while the other pertains to extension. Definition has at least two basic conditions: (1) conceptual clarity and (2) extensional conformity. Firstly, the definition has to be totally clear. Ambiguous definitions are inadequate as they provide us with no definite knowledge and clear notion. Secondly, the definition must be such that the *definiens* would perfectly represent the *definiendum*. To put the matter otherwise, the totality of extensions of *definiens* and *definiendum* has to be balanced. Almost all logical conditions of definition are reducible to these two conditions.[2]

The definition of man as "a complicated machine" stands for an example of inadequate definition, as it lacks conceptual clarity and extensional conformity. This is partly due to the semantic ambiguity of the very notion of "complicated" that makes the latter *complicated*! And it does not give a clear picture of the issue. On the other hand, it covers not all extensions as the totality of extensions of man does not match that of machine.

---

1. It refers to a branch of logic, which deals with the nature of definition, its types and the logical rules and conditions of each of the types of definition. In Aristotelian logic, this part of Avicennian logic is drawn up as a distinct part. See Far¡marz Qar¡malik¢, "Al-Ish¡r¡t wa 'l-Tanb¢h¡t: Sar¢gh¢z-e Man§iq-e D£ Bakhsh¢," ¡yineh-ye Pazh£hesh, p. 24.

2. In the words of °ak¢m Sabziw¡r¢,

The extensionally equal is clearer/ Don't you see it is called the explaining word

4) The Undermining Factors Involved in the Disorders of Definition

Some factors cause the definition to fail to satisfy the abovementioned conditions:

Exposition:

Definability follows certain logical rules. Any neglect in observation of these rules leads to a major disorder in definition. The undermining factors involved in the disorders of definition are of two types: (1) factors that cause ambiguity in the definition and (2) factors that lead to extensional incompatibility between *definiens* and *definiendum*. Apart from these two factors that are lexically, conceptually or extensionally related to the definition itself, there are also some other factors pertaining to some affairs which lie outside the definition.

1. Linguistic factors: Ambiguity in definition can be caused by linguistic factors, as propounded below:

The Undermining Facors (continued)

The first factor is the inclusion of concepts irrelevant to the subject, e.g. to define "wise" one would refer to "beautiful voice" as part of the definition! Or in the definition of "water" the beauty of vessel would be taken as part of the definition.

Exposition:

One of the most important instances of ambiguity in definition, as logicians would say, is the semantic superfluity of definition (*ḥadd*) as compared to the defined (*maḥdūd*). The inclusion of anything essentially alien to the *definiendum* leads to ambiguity in the definition. To tackle such an ambiguity, logicians have suggested that an ideal definition is semantically lucid and conceptually parsimonious. Description and explanation are different from definition as such. To explain a phenomenon, one can resort to its rules, peculiarities and countless characterizations; while to define it, one has to merely seek to indicate its essence.

The Undermining Facors (continued)

The second factor refers to verbal disputes. As a famous anecdote goes, once a Turk, a Persian and an Arab wanted to eat something together. They had a quarrel over what they would eat. "Let's eat ʙzьm ("grape" in Turkish) for lunch today", said the Turk. "What is ʙzьm? We have to have angūr ("grape" in Persian) today, retorted the Persian". "I want neither nor angūr. The best meal is 'inab ("grape" in Arabic), said Arab." Someone who was familiar with all three languages jumped into this baseless dispute and said, "Give me the money I'll buy and bring whatever you want to eat for lunch." He took the money and brought grapes for them all, and they realized the quarrel was baseless and caused by their ignorance of the other two languages.[1]

Exposition:

One of the logical conditions of definition is to avoid using unfamiliar and strange words. Clear and accurate language is the most important condition of definition,[2] since strange words trigger verbal dispute.

There are other linguistic factors involved in the disorders of definition which can be briefly outlined as follows:

- "Definition by the unknown" or definition by notions which are more complicated and sophisticated than the *definiendum* itself;
- "Circular definition" or definition by notions which owe their conceptual clarity to the *definiendum* and are defined by the latter; and
- The application of consecutive signification (indication per nexum), homonymy, metaphor, allegory, and any expression which blurs the intended meaning.

    Homonymy (equivocation) always obstructs (the understanding): the similarity between the infidel and the

---

1. Rumi's *Masnavi*, Book 2. See Reynold A. Nicholson (trans.), The Masnavi of Jalalu'ddin Muhammad Molawi (Tehran: Soad Publisher, 2002), Book 2, pp. 187, 189. [Trans.]

2. 'Alₑ ibn Sₑnᵢ, Al-Ishᵢrᵢt wa 'l-Tanbₑhᵢt, ed. Maˈm£d Shabᵢnₑ (Tehran: University of Tehran, 1339 AHS), p. 35.

true believer is in the body (alone).[1]

Most of the errors in definition are rooted in psychological and personal factors, which impel a person to adopt defective definitions. Among these factors comprise:

The Undermining Facors (continued)

The third factor is the encroachment of pre-cut principle or principles on definition. For example, the definition of man as a beast of prey, which is rooted in Hobbesianism[2], the motto of which reads "Man is a wolf to [his fellow] man."[3]

Exposition:

Every man is touched by his studies and presumptions. However, a dogmatic encounter with phenomena and seeing them through the prospect of one's own theories is erroneous. Numerous instances of this type of error can be detected in the analyses of religious matters like "religious experience" by Freud,[4] Marx[5] and others. According to Jung,[1] in all his

---

1. Reynold A. Nicholson (trans.), The Masnawi of Jalalu'ddin Muhammad Molawi (Tehran: Soad Publisher, 2002), Book 6, line 649, p. 75. [Trans.]

2. Thomas Hobbes (1588-1679): English political philosopher, who sought to apply rational principles to the study of human nature. In Hobbes' view, humans are materialistic and pessimistic, their actions motivated solely by self-interest, thus a state's stability can only be guaranteed by a sovereign authority to which citizens relinquish their rights. Leviathan (1651), his most celebrated work, expresses these views. [Trans.]

3. See the dedication to his work De cive (1651). [Trans.]

4. Sigmund Freud (1856-1940): The founder of psychoanalysis who founded the International Psychoanalytical Association in 1910 and whose view on psychoanalysis was reached through his study of the effect of hypnosis on hysteria. Among his numerous and well-known works are The Interpretations of Dream, The Psychopathology of Everyday Life, Introductory Lectures in Psychoanalysis, Humor and Its Relation to the Unconscious, The Ego and the Id, The Problem of Anxiety, and The Future of an Illusion. [Trans.]

5. Karl Heinrich Marx (1818-83): a German philosopher, political economist, historian, political theorist, sociologist, and communist revolutionary, whose ideas played a significant role in the development of modern communism and

definitions, Freud was ensnared by his theory of Oedipus Complex[2] and he would see everything within that framework.[3]

The Undermining Facors (continued)

The fourth factor is the justification of a definition based on scientific intents in the domain of a science, such as the definition of the "earth" according to an agricultural intent, which is different from the definition of the earth upon civil intents.

> *O enlightened friend! He who seeks one thing*
> *Cannot see anything except what he intends.*[4]

Exposition:

The selective nature of current studies in empirical sciences makes every scientist to look through his own point of view and consequently, to know just a particular dimension of the subject. This methodological exclusivism got prevailed particularly after the emergence of modern science and positivism, and its outcome was the new fallacy of taking an aspect of a thing *for* its nature, or in modern terminology, the fallacy of reductionism. Interdisciplinary study, which is a sort of methodological pluralism, is the cure to this fallacy.

Methodological exclusivism has yet other dimensions which are dealt with in the fifth factor involved in the disorders of definition.

The Undermining Facors (continued)

The fifth factor is the difference in scholarship, taste and skill in recognition of subjects and problems of science which certainly leads

---

socialism. [Trans.]

1. Carl Gustav Jung (1875-1961): a Swiss psychiatrist, an influential thinker and the founder of analytical psychology. [Trans.]

2 Feelings of a sexual desire that a boy has for his mother and the jealous feelings towards his father that this causes (English Editor)

3. Far¡marz Qar¢malik¢, "Tahl¢l-e Far¡s£-ye Raw¡nshin¡kht¢-ye Freud az D¢n," Qabas¡t, Issue 3.

4. Rumi's *Masnavi*, Book 4.

to intense disagreements on the defined realities. An example is the difference of opinion between a classical physicist who would define matter as "a body which occupies space", and a modern physicist who is engrossed in quantum mechanics.

Exposition

The difference of perspectives that leads to the difference in definition is of two types. One is the linear difference like the one stated in the fourth factor. The difference of perspectives between the physicists and the chemists in analyzing a single phenomenon gives rise to the difference in opinions. The other difference is a matter of the heirarchical difference of the multiple levels of reality. Everyone embarks on definition according to the depth of his or her experience of reality. In a conventional and ordinary experience, nature has an independent existence, while in an *other* experience, its relational identity gets revealed.

The Undermining Facors (continued)

The sixth factor consists of the effects that give rise to sensitivity (acute allergy) or sympathy toward the subject of definition; like the rejection of religion after wittnessing its abuses or the hyper-sensitivity about pure science which usually results in individual emotions, which deprive the man from touching the truth of affairs. Anger and carnal desire derange the psychological balance, and as a result deprive the man of knowing the real nature of things.

> *Anger and carnal desire make the man squint-eyed,*
>
> *Metamorphosing the soul upon their resistance.*

This truth has also been indicated in authentic tradtions: "One's passion for something makes him/her blind and deaf." Those who approach realities with specific mindset distance themselves from their [true] nature. This issue is particularly of great significance in the definition of religion. People, like Freud, who have considered religion a bulk of superstitions, can never come up with a sound definition of religion, since the prerequisite of understanding of the truth of something is neutrality. When one's understanding of a matter is imbued with hostility, aggression and negative feelings, s/he will not fulfil but what s/he intends.

> *O enlightened friend! He who seeks one thing*
>
> *Cannot see anything except what he intends*

The seventh factor is ignorance or insufficient knowledge concerning the causes of definiendum. Most of the definitions of religion which we will turn to here suffer from this disorder.[1]

The eighth factor concerns the partial knowledge of the nature of definiendum. We need to take all dimensions of the object which is supposed to be defined into account, not just one or two of its dimensions, as far as we can, if we seek to reach an integrated and fair definition of it. This is the major disorder inflicted modern understanding of religion in secular West.

As this research will demonstrate, almost the majority of these definitions of religion have sketched a blurred outline of one or a number of limited aspects of religion, and put it against science, wisdom, philosophy, politics, and civilization. Accordingly, this sort of definition lacks academic value and should never be taken as the basis for any positive or negative discourse on religion.

Unfortunately, after the triumph of mechanical theories over all realities of the world including man and nature, these very defective and sketchy definitions have clouded all social sciences and humanities under the pretext of discovery and production of life amenities based on mechanical laws, insofar as today we can say that only very few things are defined upon the consideration of their real nature. For instance, we can briefly cite the following examples:

1. In view of human mental state, the correct definition of freedom is supposedly to be like this: "freedom implies ego's supervision and control over the positive and negative sides of an action", while the current definition reads: "freedom connotes one's ability to do or not to do a thing", which is a very simple-minded notion of freedom. It goes without saying that to understand the true connotation of freedom as just defined, we have simultaneously to take both pre- and post-freedom stages into consideration. The pre-freedom stage refers to "emancipation" which only removes the shackles of oppression. The stage of normative acquisition of freedom refers to volition or freewill.

2. If one seeks to know the definition of politics in current sense of the term, s/he will see that its key idea is the administration of social affairs upon politician's power, taste and orientation. However, the real definition of politics consists of the due

---

1. In fact, this factor can be reduced to the fifth factor.

administration of human lives through preparing the ground for realization of citizens' positive talents for fulfillment of material and spiritual felicity.

Exposition:

The definition's inclusion of all dimensions of *definiendum* is among the conditions of its perfection. To begin with, however, one needs to distinguish between essential and accidental dimensions, for the definition's inclusion of all dimensions and aspects of the *definiendum* is not possible today. Secondly, in those cases which the *definiendum* is a multidimensional matter or a complicated phenomenon, it is very difficult and almost impossible to deal with every essential level, dimension and element of the *definiendum*.

Those who have made efforts to suggest a definition of religion admit that a perfect definition, which includes all aspects of religion, is impossible.[1] For this very reason, it is said that this condition has to be met *as far as we can*. What is of great importance in this moment is the 'fallacy of taking aspect for the nature' or as it is called in the West, 'fallacy of generalization'. If one focuses only on some particular dimensions of *definiendum* for any reason whatsoever, and then takes whatever he observes for the *definiendum*'s whole identity, s/he indeed commits the fallacy of generalization. But if s/he mentions that this definition is only true as to certain aspect of the *definiendum*, his/her definition will be acceptable as an official definition provided there are logical rules as it has been done by William James[2], not as most people have done.

5) The Impediments and Difficulties Embedded in the Way to Definition of Religion

Religion is among those phenomena which are not easy to define. Due

---

1. William James, Dçn wa Rawįn, trans. Aˡmadç Qį'inç (Tehran, 1362 AHS), pp.2-3.
2. William James (1842-1910): a pioneering American psychologist and philosopher trained as a medical doctor. Among his best-known works is The Varieties of Religious Experience. [Trans.]

to the difficulties hindering one from achieving a clear and distinct definition of religion some scholars have considered it undefinable. The problem is that in spite of the great efforts of religious scholars in the past two centuries, a comprehensive and universal definition of religion acceptable to all religions is yet to be attained.[1] In his The Meaning and End of Religion, W. C. Smith[2] says, "It is perhaps not presumptuous to hold that no definition of religion so far proposed has proven compelling, no generalization has come anywhere near to adequacy."[3]

Exposition:

It is to be analyzed in a convincing manner whether the inquiry on the definition of religion is productive or futile? Can a comprehensive and distinct definition of religion be ever proposed? The answer to these questions hinges on the clarification of certain leading methodological issues on the definition of religion:

I) Is the method of definition of religion logical or empirical? To put it otherwise, should we proceed through empirical study of world religions and take their shared aspects as universal nature of religion? Being this the case, can we arrive at any shared aspect, or as John Hick[4] argues, "Perhaps a single specific feature of the different phenomena which are called 'religion' does not exist, but rather it is better to believe in a set of 'family resemblances'" and take it as the *definiens* of religion? Moreover, which criterion does help us to identify 'religion' through our

1. See Norman Geister, Philosophy of Religion (Michigan: Ondervan Corporation Grand Rapids, 1997), p. 14.
2. Wilfred Cantwell Smith (1916-2000): a Canadian professor of comparative religion who from 1964-1973 was director of Harvard's Center for the Study of World Religions. His best known and most controversial work is The Meaning and End of Religion (1962) in which he notably and controversially questioned the validity of the concept of religion. [Trans.]
3. Wilfred Cantwell Smith, The Meaning and End of Religion (New York: New American Library of World Literature, 1964), p. 16.
4. John Hick (1922-): philosopher of religion; edited The Myth of God Incarnate. [Trans.]

empirical studies? Whereas there we have also religions in which there is no room for the worship of a supreme being, such as Theravada Buddhism, then a definition has to be adopted which could include such religions too. Does the method which is applied in the definition of religion represet a logic that offers the so-called arbitrary definitions? That is, just as a term is considered to have a certain meaning in the beginning, the same is also incorporated into its definition. Examples are the definitions based on phenomenology, some psychological definitions (like the definition of William James), and some sociological definitions (like the definition of Parsons[1]).

Having said these, where should one begin to define religion? Should one first present a definition upon a priori concepts of religion and then assess through it the authenticity of whatever is called 'religion', thereby distinguishing true religions from the false ones? Or, on the contrary, should one first explore whatever is called 'religion' and then by studying all of them, extract the special common feature as the essence of religion, or based on the theory of 'family resemblances', should one propound a series of descriptions and seek to uncover the definition of religion in their light?

---

1. Talcott Parsons (1902-79): an American sociologist who served on the faculty of Harvard University from 1927 to 1973. [Trans.]

The Impediments and Difficulties (continued)

To answer this question, we need to offer an explanation of logical and empirical methods. Some scholars have recently claimed that the logical method of definition refers to reasoning through a series of proven or self-evident universal premises which have to be applied to particular propositions (cases and extensions) if one seeks to reach a conclusion. Take, for example, these premises: "There is a reality beyond perception." "A whole number is either odd or even," and "The whole is greater than the part." This method is called reasoning upon universal premises for proving particular proposition.

The empirical method is the very method of inspection, inductive reasoning and experimentation of particular cases in order to reach a universal conclusion.

If we closely examine the empirical method, we shall conclude that this method (of inspection and induction) does indeed lead us to a universal premise which is drawn from particular cases and premises, and it is this very universal premise which is applied to particular cases in reasoning. For instance, we conduct an inductive research and experimentation on animals and see that every animal has a sense of self-defense or conatus, and reproduces. Upon these observations, we infer a universal premise which reads, "Every animal defends itself and reproduces." Both methods, then, take advantage of a universal premise to demonstrate the intended conclusion. The difference lies in the fact that in the logical method the universal premise is taken for granted in advance and it no longer requires to be proved, while in the empirical method the universal premise is reached through observations, experiments and inspection of cases and concrete extensions and then applied to them. That some scholars have set these two methods against each other, calling one 'logical' and the other 'empirical', is definitely wrong as both methods can be considered 'logical'. One sets the universal premise its point of departure and proceeds to demonstrate the intended particular premise, while in the other begins from the concrete cases and extensions and draws the universal premise and applies it to its desired particular premise. There stands still a difference between the two types of universal premise, which is required to be discerned to the effect that when the universal is taken as the point of departure, the universal turns to be general in the sense that it is applicable to all cases like "The whole is greater than the part" while when one inspects the concrete extensions to draw the universal it would fail to cover all cases on the ground due to the inadequacy of observations and experimentations. Having said this, the logic of science requires the percentage of application of empirical observations in this inductive method to be noted say the premise X covers 90% of the cases.

II) When one seeks to define religion, its extensions or applications turn very crucial, whether the definition sets them its point of departure, or the definition is applied to them in an a priori fashion. But what is the criterion upon which one can discern whether that which is called 'religion' is a true extension of religion or not? Which religion does really fit into our definition of the term? How can one consider a non-monotheistic and non-revealed religion an application of the term?

It is needless to say that not only in religion but rather in all realities which have a bipolar existential fulfillment (subjective vs. objective), the observation, examination and inspection of objective extensions and cases are as crucial as introspection and subjective notions like beauty, justice, conscience, escalated love and affections, and the like.

Another issue which requires to be closely inspected is: "What is the criterion upon which one would discern whether that which is called 'religion' is a true extension of religion or not?"

There is a general notion which can serve as the intended criterion and reads "religion means taking a step beyond the self and having the belief that above the bestial selfishness and ordinary natural demands, there are truths in this life to which one must approach as the supreme telos of life", like 'nirvana' in Buddhism, and similar things in other religions. For this reason, this truth has a certain sort of sanctity and luminosity, and any struggle toward its fulfillment gives pleasure and delight to the believer, saving him or her from a sense of futility or absurdity. It goes without saying that this very notion of religion has its origin in a noble vision of life that represents a salient feature of religion as such, although it cannot include all aspects of religion due to turning a blind eye to God Almighty with all His Sublime Attributes as mentioned in formal religions.

III) Should the definition of religion be sought from religion itself, or does it belong to extra-religious studies? Whether one should turn to revelation and religious text for achieving an understanding of the truth of religion or s/he needs to resort to extra-religious tools and methods like empirical or logical methods? If these two methods are inseparable or they belong to two separated domains?

To answer these questions one need to distinguish between two issues:

The first issue: religion's nature involves its own special features, properties, tools, and methods.

The second issue: any proof for demonstration of the necessity of religiosity leads to petitio principi and proves nothing. However, to prove whether the tools and methods of religion are extra-religious or intra-religious depends on whether these are religious in nature, or secular and rational? If they are of a religious nature, such as the conditionality of ablution (wuḍū') and the purity of the body and clothes in the ritual prayer (Ṣalāt) and the necessary amount of alms (zakāt) for which one has to consult the religious text, there is no doubt that they are intra-religious. And if they are of a secular or rational nature, like almost all matters, it is clear that their definition and the knowledge about them lie outside religion. Religion itself refers people in many cases to common sense and rational facts. By the same token, two types of methods can be discerned here:

1) Extra-religious and 2) Intra-religious methods. The method of affirming religious laws which depends on the use of religious proofs and rational thinking, and not any personal or specific taste, such as emotions, imaginary premises, unproven hypothetical questions, and the like, is intra-religious. On the other hand, since the very ways of attaining knowledge and a sound mind are personal matters, they directly involve relying on extra-religious matters. Relying on them also has an intra-religious dimension from a general perspective, taking into account the spirit of *"Allah does not task any soul beyond its capacity."*[1]

IV) Should one expect a definition of religion to involve all dimensions of religion, or suffices it to refer to the basic methods of religion? What does distinguish the main from the correlative parts? There is no doubt that the more a definition is comprehensive and meticulous the more scholarly and convincing it turns to be and it will serve the higher causes in more efficient ways, but as one would witness throughout history, in the realm of science and philosophy, such an ideal has not been achievable, particularly in those human issues which had to do with the soul, self, personality, mind, and spirit. The inaccessibility of this ideal, however, has never resulted in the decline, interruption or retrogressive movement of humanity in advanced sciences, philosophy, industry, art, and dynamic cultures. The ancient tradition of sciences, worldviews and other realities requiring definition and proof shows that man

---

1. Sฅrat al-Baqarah 2:286. In this volume, the translation of Qur'anic passages is adapted from Sayyid 'Alฺ Qulฺ Qarฺ'ฺ, The Qur'an with a Phrase-by-Phrase English Translation (London: Islamic College for Advanced Studies Press, 2004). [Trans.]

has struggled to mobilize every available possibility to obtain more knowledge about his/her quadruple ontological relationships, viz. his/her relationship with God, his/her relationship with him/herself, his/her relationship with the world, and his/her relationship with his/her fellow human individuals. S/he has not subjected her/his efforts for getting benefitted from a reality to acquiring perfect knowledge of its every internal and external dimension as well as its ever-changing dynamics and having all relevant judgments as to it proven. In the whole course of human history, you cannot find even a single mathematician who suspended his activity and efforts in mathematics due to his/her unfamiliarity with the true nature of number. By the same token, a physicist would never postpone his researches until having the nature of causation in physical events known, defined and proven. In the same vein, do you know of any psychologist who, under the pretext of lack of dependable knowledge of the truth of mind, self, intuitive knowledge (self-consciousness), personification, and tens of similar psychological facts, abandons his work and turns to another job?

Upon these empirical observations, we reach the conclusion that one needs to content oneself with the principal elements in his/her studies of the nature of religion. There is, however, a difference here that makes religion distinguished from other realities, i.e. one's knowledge of the principal elements of religion and his/her deep-seated belief in them leads to his/her spiritual advancement. Then this amount of knowledge would either place the believer in a state of spiritual mirth and growth, or even lead to gradual religious enlightenment.

> *Be wary of Allah and Allah shall teach you.*[1]
>
> *As for those who strive in Us, We shall surely guide*

---

1. S£rat al-Baqarah 2:282.

them in Our ways.[1]

O, you who have faith! If you are wary of Allah, He shall appoint a criterion2 for you.[3]

***

Put the step forward and say naught
The path shall show you how to tread it.

6) The Taxonomy of Definitions of Religion

Due to the multidemonsionality of religion and also by virtue of plurality of world religions, religion has been defined in different ways. The most logical way of dealing with numerous definitions is to classify them. Based on various academic motives, different taxonomies of the definitions of religion have been proposed.

The taxonomy which has been followed in present treatise goes as follows:

1. General definitions which seek to offer universal definition based on universally approved notion of religion or common features of world religions
2. Essentialist definitions which analyze the essence of religion
3. Psychological definitions
4. Sociological definitions
5. Teleological definitions
6. Ethically informed definitions

---

1. S£rat al-'Ankab£t 29:69.

2. That is, a knowledge which will enable you to distinguish between truth and falsehood. [Q. Trans.]

3. S£rat al-Anf¡l 8:29.

Chapter 2

General Definitions of Religion

Introduction

To come up with a comprehensive and all-encompassing definition of religion, many scholars of religious studies have tried to examine world religions and discern those common features which can serve as a basis for the intended comprehensive definition. Typologically speaking, this method is basically different from the current methods which are applied to offer an abstract and philosophical definition of religion. Of course, there are various logical ways to acquire the common feature. Using Wittgenstein[1]'s notion of 'family resemblance' is one of these ways. John Hick, for example, seeks to come up with a general definition of religion based on 'family resemblance', and regards the salvation theory of religions as their common feature.[2]

The major point of ambiguity in this type of definitions is the lack of distinction between the constitutive elements of religion and its secondary features. Many religious decrees are common but they are not constitutive of the essence of religion. We shall discuss and assess four general definitions of religion which base themselves on the common features of religions.

Metaphysical Definition of Religion

---

1. Ludwig Josef Johann Wittgenstein (1889-1951): an Austrian-born philosopher who inspired two of the century's principal philosophical movements, viz. logical positivism and ordinary language philosophy. [Trans.]

2. John Hick, Philosophy of Religion, trans. Behzįd Sįlikȼ, p. 2.

Some philosophers of religion catagorise every school of thought which includes the following three principal elements of belief as religion:

1. There is a world beyond the world of sensible objects
2. Natural world is purposeful
3. Cosmos has a moral basis

The third element can be analyzed into two propositions: 1) cosmos has an understanding of moral good and evil and 2) cosmos rewards and retributs moral good and evil.[1]

Assessment

Some complementary and critical remarks are due here as to this definition:

I) As to the first belief, one needs to add that man is also a reality which has occurred on the borderline of the natural and supernatural worlds.

It is indeed you who have tied together/ the ends of two poles of existence tight

Human religious, scientific and philosophical efforts in this borderline area are intended to get his/her supernatural capital flourished. Having said this, the more s/he acquires knowledge of realities and laws of nature the more flourished s/he becomes in supernatural realm.

II) The belief in purposefulness of nature has its origin in another principal belief, i.e. the world of creation depends on the All-Wise God to whom futile action is an *impossibility*.

III) This definition has propounded the question of God in ambiguous terms. That there is a world beyond the world of nature and sensible objects is an extremely general statement as it would refer to a world in which there is no place for God like the world of myths and fairytales.

IV) The belief that cosmos rewards and retributs moral good and evil leaves it unclear if cosmos here refers to this world or it includes the otherworld as well?

---

1. °awzeh wa D﹎neshg﹎h Journal, issue 3, p. 68.

If it refers only to this world, then good deeds are not all rewarded in this world as due to this world's ontological limitations, the criminals cannot be duly punished for all their crimes. Of course, we have the law of causation, or action and reaction in this world but the capacity of this world is not enough to compensate all human actions. Unless the eternal world is accepted, one cannot determine reward and punishment for moral goods and evils.

V) Some creeds particularly mystical schools include all three aforementioned dogmas without having any claim of being religion.

VI) Every moral system is not necessarily religious. The moral system whose foundation is God, in the sense that the criterion for good and evil in it lies in the Divine commands, has religious dimensions. The foundation of what is morally good and evil in religion is revelation which is immune to error and deviation.

If "cosmos understands moral good and evil" implies that it has the ability to do so, then it is acceptable from a religious perspective as religion offers that all parts of cosmos are continuously in a state of glorifying, prostrating and remembering God. And if it suggests that cosmos contains the same epistemic capabilities that one finds in human individuals it is not a religious necessity.

That "cosmos rewards and retributes moral goods and evils" can be interpreted in two ways: one would claim that cosmic rewarding and retribution is among the laws which God has prescribed for this world. It is the very law of causation whose enactment and implementation is like other laws of God. While another one would say that God the Glorious has directly enacted and implemented this law to warn His creatures. One needs to know that this action/reaction law is only bewaring human individuals that: *"Every soul is hostage to what it has earned."*[1] Otherwise, divine justice can only be implemented in

---

1. S£rat al-Muddaththir 74:38. [Trans.]

the eternal world due to the limitations of this material world. One can say that in this definition, three subjects which are of immense importance for religion have been touched in an acceptable manner. However, it has not paid enough attention to religious obligations and rights and their difference as compared to moral codes. On the other hand, there has been no categorical and decisive statement regarding the Sacred Being of God, His control over creation, Attributes of Perfection, and the Resurrection.

Aston's Definition

W.G. Aston, a contemporary philosopher of religion, presents the following as the common features of religions:

1. The belief in supernatural beings
2. The sacred/ the secular dichotomy
3. Rites which concern certain objects
4. A set of moral codes whose implementation is guaranteed by a God or gods
5. Specific religious feelings (such as fear, reverence, sense of guilt, and gratitude) which are expressed before sacred things or during the performance of rites
6. Worship and other forms of communication with God or gods
7. A universal perspective of the world as a whole and human place in it (weltanschauung)
8. A relatively comprehensive organization of human life based on such a perspective (ideology)
9. A united social group supported by the abovementioned elements (community or church).

Assessment

I) These scholars appear to have allergy to the word 'God', as they talk about 'supernatural beings'. One should not forget that it was this very allergy that caused some Western countries to use the term 'supreme being' instead of the word 'God' in their constitutions!

Religion is essentially founded on the belief in the existence of God, not merely supernatural creatures. Of course, the belief in supernatural entities such as the angels and evolved souls who have reached the lofty station of immateriality, eternity, and the truths pertaining to them, is a part of religious beliefs.

II) The secular/ the sacred dichotomy is not necessarily part of every world religions.

III) Object centered rites are related to primitive religions. Rites exist in religions with divine origins which are not centered on certain objects, but which are held as a form of worship, linking the most trivial to the All-Significant. Anyway, the rites of early times, whether they are in the form of totem, taboo, or any other form, have nothing to do with the global Abrahamic faith.

IV) In revealed religions, God is the very basis of moral codes not merely an entity who guarantees the implementation of laws.

V) Having certain religious sentiments is one of the effects of belief in God. Religious rites and rituals make a person experience particular spiritual states. One needs to take it into earnest consideration that in some creeds and so-called religions one comes across rituals which are superstitious which cannot be compared with the rites of religions with divine origins, as it was mentioned earlier.

VI) Religion fosters unity among individuals. This is one of the requirements and consequences of religion not the religion itself. Of course, the 'united community' (*ummatan wāḥidah*) which is realized through religious conviction cannot be compared with organizations formed by groups, because the goal of religion is to let human beings move as a single caravan toward the Supreme Origin. The unity of a religious community is not like a racial, geographical, or political organization formed for a particular purpose, such as defense against an enemy. Rather, as stated in Islamic sources, the believers are like a single body; if one part experiences pain, all parts will experience the same. The souls of believers are like a single soul, and the believers' spiritual tie with God is stronger than sun beams' tie with the sun.[1]

VII) There is no doubt that cosmic affairs are connected with sacred truths, which are sometimes distinct from secular matters. One can say, however, that in Islam they are related to the world of creation and, all parts of the world of creation, whether they are inward or outward, are divine signs. *"Soon We shall show them Our signs in the horizons and in their own souls until it becomes clear to them that He is the Real"*[2] and *"So whichever way you turn, there is the face of Allah!"*[3] It follows then, that in a sense, the entire universe has a sacred dimension.

VIII) One needs to answer if by "the rites which concern certain objects" one means the presence of a set of rites in every religion? It is correct but the taboo rites must be distinguished from rites of worship and other intelligible tendency towards the supernatural.

IX) One is required to explain what does s/he imply by "the guarantor of the implementation of moral rules is God or gods"? There are some probabilities here:

First probability: It means that God helps human beings to successfully observe the moral codes. Of course, one can infer from the sources of Abrahamic Faiths (Judaism, Christianity and Islam) that Divine Justice and Grace make it necessary that He guides His servants to the path of material and spiritual prosperity.

Second probability: "The guarantor of the implementation of moral rules" means control and stimulation of the pure conscience and not deterministic factors that control actions.

---

1. Al-U¥£l min al-K¡f¢, vol. 2, p. 166.

2. S£rat Fu¥¥ilat 41:53. [Trans.]

3. S£rat al-Baqarah 2:115. [Trans.]

Third probability: "moral rules" refer to religious laws, obligations and rights in respect of their attribution to God. To put it otherwise, these moral cordes are considered in view of the fact that God enacted them and He is supervising human individual and social interactions. If this is the intended implication it seems more probable than the other probabilities.

X) Specific religious feelings (such as fear, reverence, sense of guilt, and gratitude) which are expressed before sacred objects or during the performance of rites:

On the one hand, such sentiments are not confined to religion, for when a rational person sees himself in front of a Real Being higher than him/her, s/he experiences a sense of cautiousness imbued with hope, a sense of awe. When a rational and wary person with a sound mind learns of the majesty of cosmos and its infinity and orderliness, he definitely experiences astonishment (not primitive bewilderment, doubt and skepticism). By the same token, anyone who does something against the law—provided he has a sound mind and personality—will feel ashamed, and this feeling is the result of committing a sin, although he may not use the same terms. Moreover, gratitude or thanksgiving in times of joy caused by material and spiritual favors in life, which is not attributed to mere luck, is a common phenomenon. All these phenomena can have a religious bent when they are brought about through human relation with God.

XI) As to "worship and other forms of communication with God or gods," one should say that in Abrahamic monotheistic religions (Judaism, Christianity and Islam) 'gods' are not objects of worship or other religious communications. There is no 'gods' in these religions at all.[1]

---

1. For further information, see Jafari, M. T. Jafari, *An Interpretation, Review and Analysis of Rumi's Masnavi*, vol. 10, pp. 63-73.

XII) A universal perspective of the world as a whole and human place in it (weltanschauung):

This perspective reads:

- Cosmos is a creation of God
- Cosmos has been created based on divine providence and will for a Supreme Telos

As an indispensible part of this world, man is a significant entity of various talents by which he can have interactive relationship with all levels and dimensions of the world in which he lives, and the scope and quality of his perfection depend on such a relationship.

Man can enjoy two types of dignity:

1) Inherent Dignity:

> *Certainly We have honored the Children of Adam, and carried them over land and sea, and provided them with all the good things, and given them an advantage over many of those We have created with a complete preference.*[1]

All human individuals possess this dignity and honor, if they do not deprive themselves of it by committing treachery (*khiyịnah*).

2) Acquired Dignity:

> *O mankind! Indeed We created you from a male and a female, and made you nations and tribes that you may identify one another. Indeed the noblest of you in the sight of Allah is the most God-wary among you.*[2]

XIII) A relatively comprehensive organization of human life based on that perspective (ideology):

This is the very human relationship with the world which comprises the third type of quadruple ontological relationships which all revealed religions seek to organize: (1) human relationship with him/herself; (2) human

---

1. S£rat al-Isrị' (or Ban¢ Isrị'¢l) 17:70.

2. S£rat al-°ujurịt 49:13.

relationship with God; (3) human relationship with the world; and (4) human relationship with his fellow human beings.

Therefore, there will be no objection if we say, "a relatively comprehensive organization of human life based on the abovementioned quadruple ontological relationships".

XIV) A united social group supported by the abovementioned elements (community or church):

In this part of the definition of religion, two significant issues have to be assayed:

1) The social organization as such is not among the constitutive elements of religion's identity, for even if only one person or a few people believe in religion in this world, he or they will still constitute a community (*ummah*). As such, the Noble Qur'¡n introduces Prophet Ibr¡hīm (Abraham) (*'a*) alone as a community:

"Indeed Abraham was a nation."[1]

Of course, as the number of individuals and communities that follow the religion increases, the social organization of those who believe in religion (*ummah*) also becomes larger.

2) *Ummah* refers to a group of people who believe in a particular religion, or if we really broaden its meaning, it refers to the group of people that cling to a given ideology, whether it is religious or not.

Like mosque, and other worship places built on earth, church means a center for collective worship and devotion, unless the original meaning of it is changed into another one.

Shariati's Definition

Dr. Ali Shariati [2] enumerates the common features of religions

1. S£rat al-Na¦l 16:120.

2. 'Al¢ Shar¢'at¢ (1933-77): an Iranian revolutionary and sociologist who

as follows:

1- Religion declares existence as meaningful

2- The world has an ultimate goal

This is the case if by meaningfulness of the world one means its association with God and the sublime wisdom and will of the Sacred Essence. This condition depends on the belief that the world has an Ultimate Telos. Similarly, the latter condition requires the meaningfulness of man and history. If the intended telos is not limited to the creation of the world, at least it can be regarded as one of its highest goals. Therefore, Sharī'atī might have possibly stated the first two points as one.

3- The duality of human existence in all religions: If this 'duality' refers to the physical and spiritual, the dispositional and the behavioral, the outward and the inward, the intrinsic and the extrinsic, it is correct.

4- Mundane consecration; this concept can be viewed from two perspectives. The first perspective is that the world relies upon Divine Providence and Will, and the notion of the world as a divine sign (*jyah*) (both within man and in the outside world) refers to this perspective:

> *Soon We shall show them Our signs in the horizons and in their own souls until it becomes clear to them that He is the Real.* [1]

According to the second perspective, this world has the power and potential to prepare man and urge him towards the Supreme Perfection as the Ultimate Telos of life the heated desire of which exists in the hearts of all people who are immune from selfishness. This cause has been refered to by Imam 'Alī ibn Abī Talib ('a), in his reply to someone who rebuked the world:

> *O' you who abuse the world, O' you who have been deceived by its deceit and cheated by its wrongs. Do you accuse it or should it accuse you? When did it*

---

focused on the sociology of religion and considered one of the most influential Iranian intellectuals of the 20th century. [Trans.]

1. S£rat Fu¥¥ilat 41:53. [Trans.]

> *bewilder you or deceive you? ... Certainly, this world is a house of truth for him who appreciates it; a place of safety for him who understands it; a house of riches for him who collects provision from it (for the next world); and a house of instructions for him who draws instruction from it. It is a place of worship for the lovers of Allah; the place of praying for the angels of Allah; the place where the revelation of Allah descends; and the marketing place for those devoted to Allah.*[1]

5- **Everythibng is divided into tangible and intangible;** this division is not a distinctive feature of religions though it is embraced in religions as an undeniable fact (the division of all things into tangible and intangible).

6- **Religion as the social spirit;** This issue is also not a distinctive feature of religions, for collective life—whether motivated by the need for division of labor among people, kinship through sexual reproduction or racial unity, or the natural demand for their civility—is a salient feature of human life in the sphere of coexistence.

7- **The global nature of the characteristic features of religion;** This issue needs to be examined closely as all revealed religions can be divided into two major groups:

First group: ethnic religions which belonged to limited groups in the history of religion. The prophets of these religions were not among the Arch-prophets (*ūlū'l-'azm*) and were limited to their respective time or group.

Second group: the world religions like the ones associated with Prophet Ibr¡hīm ('a) and whose messengers were the *ūlū'l-'azm* or Arch-prophets, viz. Nūh (Noah), Ibr¡hīm, Mūs¡ (Moses), 'Īs¡ (Jesus), and Mu¡ammad ibn 'Abd All¡h ('a). If it is not so, then the phrase refers to the common features of all religions like the belief in God, eternity, religious duties and rights, and the like.

8 & 9- **"The unity of man and nature" and "the unity of man, nature**

---

1. Nahj al-Bal¡ghah, Maxim 131.

and the spirit of being"; these two issues have a very broad implication and are not restricted to 'religion'. There are philosophers who philosophically acknowledge this unity. Sufis and mystics also believe in this unity and something even higher. They believe that, man, nature, the spirit of the entire universe, and even God are a single being (theory of the unity of being). The stoics and a group of Indian philosophers and mystics believe in this theory. Therefore, these issues are not exclusive to religion.

10- Apprehension, struggle and desire for union (itti¥¡l); this issue is also ambiguous. The possible implications of this issue are as follows:

- Human scorching desire, struggle and aspiration to be in union with God are like those of the droplets seeking to join the sea. This possibility is not concievable in monotheistic religions, for the Sacred Essence of the Lord is higher than a creature that He created or originated, to be part of His Sacred Essence.

- Human primordial desire to "become" divine through getting oneself qualified with Divine Attributes that already exist in man in the same potential form. If by this qualification one means human limited assimilation into Divinity, it is possible according to monotheistic religions.

- Union in this context implies exposing oneself to the radiation of Divine Perfection. In this station, the person can become an embodiment of Divine Lights, but never reach the Sublime Station of Lordship. This is the best possible implication among others.

Note: The word 'apprehension' which implies agitation along the way to perfection is not correct. Instead, scorching desire, serious endeavor and persistence, called kad¦ (کدح) in Arabic, are more accurate than the terms 'apprehension' and mere 'desire'.

11- The belief in dominance, progress, exaltation, and movement; 'dominance' requires to be explained here. If 'dominance' implies acquiring power to organize the quadruple ontological relationships (human relationship with himself, God, the universe, and his fellow human beings), then it is perfectly true as one can say that the Supreme Telos of religion is to provide the believers with such power. Acquiring power to organize one's relationship with oneself means self-control which puts one in the path of God-wariness (taqwᵢ)[1] or [moral integrity and] evolutionary self-preservation. And through this taqwᵢ s/he can touch the height of attraction to the Supreme Perfection. By acquiring power to organize one's relationship with God one can keep oneself away from sin, selfishness and self-centeredness, and undertake the ideal movement. By acquiring power to organize an intellectual, perceptive and interactive relationship with the cosmos, one will succeed to build oneself.

12- The notion of responsibility.

13- The denial of chance and futile deeds.

14- The belief in the principle of contradiction and a type of dialectical vision.

15- causality: logical analysis of the world.

16- The principle of survival.

17- The expansion of worldview.

18- Redemption from what is, i.e. from the captivity of isness; if this refers to disconnecting oneself from whatever exists and severance of relationship with whatever is, then it is forbidden in religion. Turning one's back to the world which is in turn part of the fundamental quadruple relationships is self-denial, indeed. Needless to say, self-denial is foreign to pursuing one's perfection, which emanates from God's boundless wisdom and favor. The world of being is the passageway for its progress and the Beatific Vision (liqᵢ' Allᵢh) in eternity is its ultimate goal and objective. One needs to take it into consideration that getting oneself benefitted from *the world*, which in the words of Imam Alī ('a), is the pantheon for the men of consciousness, has nothing to do with world-denial a la Buddhism.

19- The notion of protection and preservation of man, life and society; this implies nothing but protection of man, life and society from taints, degradation, fall, and backwardness. This

---

1 One can feasibly translate this key word of Moslem weltanschauung to Sorge or Care in Heideggerian fashion as the term is of the same existential spirit (Editor).

point is perfectly approved by religion, but religion seeks to go beyond the notion and fulfill it practically.

20- Knowledge, curiosity and employing curiosity [for a higher cause]; knowledge promotion, inquiry and research to increase one's understanding of the self, God, the world, and fellow human beings, and employing knowledge and learning for evolutionary "becoming" are among the essentials of religion.

21- Beauty and art; by beauty Sharī'atī should have meant the desire for sensible and intelligible beauties which serve the soul as a platform to bring her to the threshold of Absolute Beauty whose mundane radiations have made human long course to divinity shorter. Moreover, 'art' in this context refers to undertaking artistic intellectual or psychological activities and setting purely constructive artistic works at the service of spiritual growth and enhancement of human talents, and not the beauty and art which always exist for all people in various cultures of human society.

22- Love and worship; definitely, love refers to the highest degree of feeling, passion and craving for Supreme Perfection, which is the totality of beauty and glory, and one can feasibly consider it among the characteristics of religion. However, what is called 'metaphorical love' or mere love without its attachment to the Supreme Perfection (which is definitely what Sharī'atī intended to mean) is not part of the salient features of religion, in fact, religion is inimical to it. One's engagement with 'virtual love' will exhaust all his life's assets and capital, for

> *Love which based on just a pretty face/ Is not true love and it ends in sheer disgrace.*[1]
>
> *Everything, besides the love of Glorious Lord/ If turns to be eating sugar is agony of spirit indeed.*[2]
>
> *You know why the lovers've moaned in grief/ Since they've opened their eyes to Divine Threshold.*[3]

---

1. Rumi's *Masnavi*, Book 1, line 205 [Translation by Jawid Mojaddedi, Oxford World's Classics Series]

2. Rumi's *Masnavi*, Book 1, line 3686 [Trans.]

3. Rumi's *Masnavi*, Book 4, line 229 [Trans.]

However, worship of God the Glorious, after knowing Him, is the purest essential feature, rather the pillar, of religion.

23- The ideal, ideal man and utopia; this point can be analyzed into two issues: (1) the ideal means that religion is the very ideal goal of human individuals or human ideal lies in the religion; (2) it is religion that moulds the ideal man. Both issues are undoubtedly true, but 'utopia' (*madīneh-ye fj¤ileh*) in which individuals and social groups engage in social life with all their positive potentials, is obviously the principle feature of religion in the domain of human social life.

24- Expectation, protest against the status quo and moving towarc the ideal; Taking into account the fundamentals of Sharī'atī's ideology, expectation (*inti¨jr*) implies looking forward to behold the emergence of the best society and struggling for its realization. Its perfect form will be possible with the advent of the Master of the Age ('atfs).[1] Of course, it must be borne in mind that *inti¨jr* is not identical with protest (*i'tirj¤*) against the status quo. It actually stems from the feeling of disgust and anguish for the undesirable condition which stands in the way of a perfect collective human life.

However, protest against the status quo can be interpreted in two ways:

1. Protest against the status quo has its origin in the consecrated dissatisfaction with every condition which goes against human ideal felicity. In view of the high and reformist potential of human beings, it is a common phenomenon that exists in all communities and nations with rational cultures. This consecrated dissatisfaction with the status quo has been even described as one of the strongest moving factors in history.

---

1. Wal¢ al-'A¥r, literally, "Master of the Age" is one the titles of the 12th Im¡m Muhammad al-Mahd¢ ('a), the others being Wal¢ al-Amr (Master of the Affair), Im¡m al-Zam¡n (Im¡m of the Time), etc. The abbreviation, "'atfs" stands for the Arabic invocative phrase, 'ajjalall¡hu ta'¢l¢ farajahu'sh-shar¢f (may Allah, the Exalted, expedite his glorious advent), which is invoked after mentioning the name of Im¡m al-Mahd¢. [Trans.]

2. Protest implies dissatisfaction with anything that causes degradation, like mankind steeped in ignorance, poverty and human rights violations, and making efforts to change the direction of life's movement toward its lofty goals and means.

25- Nature's self-consciousness; this is a corollary of "the unity of man, nature and the spirit of being". This can also be inferred from the Quranic verses that indicate glorification (tasbih) and prostration (*suj£d*) of the creatures in the world. To prove the self-consciousness of nature, some thinkers have resorted to the law of 'action and reaction'.

> *The world's a mountain, actions like a shout/ Your echo will return to you, watch out!* [1]

Sharī'atī has not mentioned three very important salient features of religion:

I.   The religious laws, rights, obligations, and manners as well as worshiping the Supreme Origin (God) and belief in the Resurrection (*ma'¡d*) should have been stated more clearly and elaborately. The odds are that he has contented himself with previous statements. However, as it is expected from every sound definition, it would have been better if he had stated the above points more clearly and elaborately.

II. The ultimate answer to the sextuple fundamental questions on life – Who am I? Whence have I come? Where have I come? With whom am I? Where am I heading to? Why have I come? – can only be provided by religion.

III. True prosperity and virtue and sacrifices embedded in the way of lofty human values, such as, keeping one's promise and covenant, defending right, committed freedom, justice, and the like. Without religion, the world is nothing but a place for pastime, sleeping and eating where if one uses not all his possibilities and powers in the way of selfishness

---

1. Rumi's *Masnavi*, Book 1, line 215 [Translation by Jawid Mojaddedi, Oxford World's Classics Series]

and self-interest, he will lose miserably.

The world, galaxy, and stars all turn to playthings / If this long day of the terrestrial had no tomorrow.[1]

Geisler's Definition

Geisler[2] defines religion in its most general sense so as to include every alleged religion. He regards religion as having two basic characteristics: (1) awareness of the transcendent and (2) utter loyalty and devotion. The elements of this definition are mentioned as follows:

I. Awareness: one considers oneself a believer when s/he is aware of or acquainted with something other than her/him.

II. The Transcendent: one thing is transcendent when it transcends the ordinary and precedes one's direct awareness. Thus concieved, even in unconsciousness, transcendent ego, other minds and Kantian noumen are categorized as the Transcendent. Moreover, the Transcendent transcends one's empirical data.

III. It is a matter of utter loyalty and devotion. Religion comprises something which is beyond mere manifestation; something unconditional and ultimate; something to which people devote themselves with utmost sincerity. Said differently, it includes not only awareness of the Transcendent, but the Ultimate and utter devotion too. Of course, in the words of Ian Ramsey, this devotion must be simultaneously *whole* and *thorough* – related to the world as a totality.

Assessment

Some significant issues in Geisler's definition require to be examined:

I- It is true that from the totality of Geisler's remarks, it can be inferred that "the Transcendent" which is the object of awareness, total devotion, ultimate affection, and yearning

---

1. Ni¥ir Khusr£, D¢wįn-e Ash'įr, Elegy 241.

2. Norman L. Geisler (born 1932): a Christian apologist and philosopher noted for his philosophical approach to theology. [Trans.]

is no other than God, the Perfect and the Absolute, whom all religions have referred to, whether in explicit terms or as something essential to the ideological text. However, due to the sensitivity of definiendum, its name has to be stipulated. If it is argued that not all religions call it 'God', the reply is that an ambiguous reality, even if it is described as 'the Transcendent', cannot be considered the foundation of religion, because He must be the Creator of all beings and should have created them according to His supreme wisdom and will.

This analysis makes it clear that such remarks as "one considers oneself a believer when s/he is aware of or acquainted with something other than her/him" have been made somewhat inaccurately because the concept of God, Exalted is His Station, who is Perfect and Absolute in all aspects, is not clear in the above mentioned remark ("something other than her/him"). Similarly, arguing that "something is transcendent if it goes beyond" is not unambiguous as *going beyond* is a notion of wide use, so one must say "a thing is transcendent if it transcends everything."

II- "...and precedes one's direct awareness": This is an excellent point discussed in various expressions in Islam; for example, Prophet Moses ('a) is reported to have said to God, "How can I reach You?" In reply, God said:

As soon as you intend to reach Me, you reach Me.

Of course, this understanding is something more than being direct or without mediation. Even in knowledge by presence (self-consciousness) in which man perceives his own *ego* directly; one has to begin with the denial of not-ego though in a passing and brief fashion. While percieving God only needs intention. This is what Geisler means when he argues, "the Transcendent transcends one's empirical data." And in the jargon of Western philosophers, it is *a priori* upon which the philosophy of Kant, in particular, relies.

III- "Religion comprises something which is beyond mere manifestation; something unconditional and ultimate; something to which people devote themselves with utmost sincerity", Geisler argues. This is also a very subtle point noted as religion is not reduced to getting oneself familiarized with God. Rather after knowing the Divine Presence one is told to follow the primordial scorching enthusiasm for *becoming* that exposes one to the radiations of Divine Essence.

IV- Ian Ramsey's remark that "this devotion must be simultaneously *whole* and *thorough* – related to the world as a totality" needs to be revised as being delighted by knowing the world is other than devoting oneself to it. What religion offers is the former not the latter. To put it otherwise, it is delight caused by the fact that the universe has been created according to Divine Wisdom and Will and witnessing the celestial splendor of the universe that persuades one to pay ultimate devotion to God, and not just submit to the universe and surrender himself to it. A majestic element of the universe or one of the lofty aspects of this universe gives rise to devotion to the Creator. Man is not supposed to surrender to the universe. Instead, with utmost cheer and confidence, he must consider it a springboard for his own spiritual flight.

> *I am cheerful in the world as the world is cheerful with Him / I am in love with the entire world as the entire world is from Him.*[1]

---

1. Sa'd¢, Maw¡'ï', ghazal 13.

Chapter 3

Essentialist Definitions of Religion

Introduction

Traditional definitions, based upon Aristotelian logic of definition, seek to reveal the nature of religion. To state the matter otherwise, they struggle to show to which category does religion belong? What are its constitutive elements and essential components? Some definitions have stuck in a type of perplexity and confessed to their inability of touching the core identity of religion. Others have regarded it a set of principal articles of faith, morality and rules.

In this chapter a number of essentialist definitions have been discussed and examined. The definitions of Spencer, Max Mьller, Bonheoffer, Havelock Ellis, Spengler, Shakul, Tyler, D'Holbach, Santayana, Otto, Cassirer, Sartre, and Dewey are among those mentioned.

Spencer's Definition

Spencer,[1] the celebrated English philosopher, regards religion as belief in the presence of something absolute, or the absolute presence of something beyond investigation. In other words, he argues, religion implies plunging into an ocean of secrets.[2]

---

1. Herbert Spencer (1820-1903): an English philosopher, prominent classical liberal political theorist, and sociological theorist of the Victorian era who developed an all-embracing conception of evolution as the progressive development of the physical world, biological organisms, the human mind, human culture and societies. [Trans.]
2. Bunyįdh¢-ye Dįn wa Jįmi'ehshinįs¢ [The Foundations of Religion and Sociology], p. 37.

Assessment

This definition points to one of the basic pillars of religion, but it contains many ambiguities, the most important of which are as follows:

I- There are secrets in religion but not everything in religion is mysterious, because it concerns both the physical/ created ('ilam-e khalq) and the metaphysical world, which is the World of Divine Imperative ('ilam-e amr).

Since the World of Divine Imperative is above that of creation and our cognitive faculties are limited, any information about it is substantiated by revelation or undifferentiated intuition. It is not like pieces of information about the world of creation which are based upon sensory perceptions, experience and speculative thought. The most majestic Reality and perfect Being who created both worlds is God. Having said this, one can still perceive Him through inward purification and refinement. As in reply to Dhu'lab al-Yamịnī, who asked him, "Have you seen your Lord?" Imam 'Ali ('a) said,

> *I do not worship a Lord whom I cannot see [with the eye of my heart].*

Spencer's definition represents an average understanding of reality and he has to distinguish between plunging into noble perplexity, which has its origin in the intuition of the majesty and magnificence of the world of being by the enlightened men of ideas, and immersing into the ocean of secrets in a way that yields one nothing but darkness.

II- It is not clear what does Spencer mean by "the presence of the Absolute"? Does it mean human presence before God? Is He present in the universe? Is He present in human hearts?

III- This definition does not explain why the 'Absolute' is beyond investigation. It is needless to say that most celebrated and promising scholars of the East and West have conducted researches on the Absolute Reality by studying the law of causation, order, sense of magnificence, innate ideas, sense of transcendent duty, argument from necessity and perfection, ontological argument, discovery of the secrets of nature, self-knowledge, and so on and so forth. Of course, because of the limitations of human cognitive faculties and activities, this investigation does not reach His Essence.

Said otherwise, 'The absolute that is beyond investigation' certainly refers to God, whereas God's existence and His Attributes can both be discursively discerned and perceived through inward intuition. I wish a considerable number of Western thinkers would acknowledge that they live in a world in which their knowledge and insight can never penetrate the real essence of things. Yet, through the same common knowledge and insight, they can acquire hundreds of thousands of facts in all aspects of their lives and through the advancements they have achieved, they can lead a life free of agitation. The following embodies some proofs of this claim: (1) in a set of compound items whose parts are related to one another, the existence of an unknown part is enough to falsify any claim of knowledge about the other parts; (2) it is impossible to distinguish the effects of perceptive elements on perceived things so as to inspect the reality 'as it is' from a scientific point of view. It goes also without saying that one can speak of reducing the effects of perceptive elements but no one would ever turn them to zero.

Spencer's Definition Reworded

> Religion is metaphysical in its essence and deals with entities and objects beyond the limits of our knowledge. The metaphysical world is a mysterious world whose nature is unknowable and incomprehensible. To put it in a nutshell, religion implies reflecting on something which goes beyond our knowledge and thinking.

Assessment

I-   This definition is also inaccurate. According to this definition, religion is unknowable let alone being acceptable and useful. The proponents of this definition have imagined that anything metaphysical is beyond human knowledge. There are many perceivable truths in religion. For example, religion talks about the purposefulness of cosmos a truth which can be grasped by human common sense.

This definition presents religion as something unknowable and inexplicable. If so, then all brilliant scholars of East and West should be seen as people who have struggled to know *the totally unknown*. Can one identify Khwⱼjah NaⱤïr[1] and Max Planck[2] as people who were after the totally unknown? Heisenberg[3] says that I cannot claim that I am a religious man; what I can assert instead is, that I am in the process of becoming religious. Does such an outstanding figure talk about the totally unknown? If Kepler[4] who after his discovery sat in his office and raised his hands, saying, "O God! I praise You for letting me read Your signs and for letting me use them in the way of serving Your servants" was talking about the totally unknown?

Generally speaking, there are universal knowledge and intuitive data in the realm of religion as to human quadruple relationships (human relationship with himself, God, the world, and his fellow human beings) that can answer the fundamental questions of Who am I? Where have I come from? Where shall I go? Similarly, religion makes use of pieces of knowledge supported by scientific observations; for example, in proving the existence of God, one can avail oneself of scientific propositions.

---

1. Muɭammad ibn Muɭammad ibn °asan al-±£s¢, better known as Khwⱼjah NaⱤir al-D¢n al-±£s¢ (597-672 AH/1200-73): a Persian polymath and prolific writer—an astronomer, biologist, chemist, mathematician, philosopher, physician, physicist, scientist, theologian, and marja' al-taql¢d (religious authority). [Trans.]
2. Max Karl Ernst Ludwig Planck (1858-1947): a German physicist, father of quantum physics, and winner of the 1918 Nobel Prize for physics. [Trans.]
3. Werner Karl Heisenberg (1901-76): a German theoretical physicist who made foundational contributions to quantum mechanics and is best known for asserting the uncertainty principle of quantum theory. [Trans.]
4. Johannes Kepler (1571-30): a German mathematician, astronomer and astrologer, and key figure in the 17th century scientific revolution. [Trans.]

Thus concieved, religion turns to be reflection on something beyond knowledge and thought. Those who believe in this definition of religion are like people who barely see the earth from a long distance and make remarks on the nature of the earth as well as millions of creatures living in it, arguing, "This is it and nothing else."

II- The belief in supernatural entities is an indispensible part of religion, but religion itself is not metaphysical in nature, for religion manifests itself in psychological states, actions, speeches, worldly life and acts of worship, in a physical form. By the same token, the prosperity and virtue which are fostered by religiosity become manifested in this very world just as they will be realized in the eternal world. Can one declare the following truths which originate in religion as metaphysical —peace of mind, inner delight, and adherence to the laws and principles prescribed in this world for the wholesome life of people?

III- One should seek to fathom the nature of religion in the belief in God, which is the most perfect metaphysical truth as well as the belief in other metaphysical truths such as the angels, souls, revelation, Resurrection, eternity and universal commitment.

IV- It is not intelligible to argue that religion deals only with beings and things which are beyond the limits of our knowledge, for the most majestic metaphysical truth is God, and through inner purification and spiritual refinement, and acting after the lofty principles which awaken the divine insight, one can perfectly feel the radiation of the Divine Light inside, as did Imam Ali, who said:

> I do not worship a Lord whom I cannot see [with the eye of my heart].

We have not seen the truth of beauty but we can observe its various manifestations, for the flower is a manifestation of beauty not its essence. A sweet voice is beautful. A waterfall, moonlight, good handwriting, a human face, and thousands of other beautiful phenomena are all manifestations of beauty. We can definitely perceive within ourselves the overall essence of beauty whereas it has no distinctive features of any of the beautiful manifestations and is different from the universal concept abstracted from the aforementioned distinctive features. The universal concept of man can be grasped through abstracting the characteristics of individuals like James, Richard, Robert and the like. This is because the universal concept of man can be equally applied to all human individuals as their ideal form. However, beauty as a universal concept cannot be compared with its different extensions. Beauty is an ananlogically graded reality and no one could discern it through its extensions in a unique fashion. Having said this, we can still apply the notion of beauty to beautiful objects in one way or another. In a nutshell, God is perceivable to us just as the absolute essence of beauty, justice, and wisdom is. The following questions must be posed to those who believe in the following lines of thought about religion—"religion implies reflection about something beyond our knowledge and thinking," "It is unknowable" and "It is incomprehensible":

1. If philosophical and ideological generalizations are made based on thought and science? Of course not for scientific and speculative generalizations are not so varied like those of philosophy and ideology as the latter are mostly documented to taste, conjecture and intuition.

2. Are discoveries and inventions in science the result of knowledge and thought? No, since regardless of their important contribution, it is clear that the most fundamental factors at the basis of every major innovation are intuition and inspiration.

3. Can all the socio-religious revolutions throughout the history, and all the sacrifices in the way of truth, freedom and justice with religious motives be considered imagination or illusion?

4. Do all religiously motivated struggles accompanied with so many hardships to overcome the selfishness and egotism in

the world, and promote the truth have their origin in the pursuit of the totally unknown? Obviously, the answer to such questions is negative.

Max Müller's Definition

Max Mьller[1] defines religion in following words: "It is an attempt to depict the undepictable, give expression to the ineffable, and a yearning for the Infinite."

Assessment

Mьller's definition is merely an expression of human inability to understand religion. Can one argue that millions of intelligent and conscious people have struggled and are still struggling after the impossible, and for that matter, millions of books authored on religion seek to state the ineffable? If the attempt to know truths like beauty which are not both concrete and agreed upon is an attempt to know something undiscernable? Is it logical to argue that the most serious and magnificent actions and sacrifices done *in the wake of* religion in the long course of history are related to something which can neither be portrayed nor stated?

Having said these, it is human understanding of religious truths and acting upon them which have conferred meaning on her/his others words and actions. Has nihilism been encountered in a feasible fashion but in religion? It is far too clear that this issue has been addressed only by religion. Now Mьller and his followers must answer this question: How can an indescribable illusion give meaning and wisdom to all realities in the universe? Figures like Newton,[2] Khw;jah Na¥īr,

---

1. Friedrich Max Muller (1823-1900), more regularly known as Max Müller: a German philologist and Orientalist, and one of the founders of the western academic field of Indian studies and the discipline of comparative religion. [Trans.]
2. Isaac Newton (1643-1727): an English physicist, mathematician, astronomer, natural philosopher, alchemist, and theologian whose best-known discoveries are the laws of motion and universal gravitation as expounded in his 1687 magnum opus Philosophiæ Naturalis Principia Mathematica (usually called the

Ibn Sīnį (Avicenna),[1] Max Planck, and all the past scientists who, in the words of Planck, are all religious scientists and men of learning haven't spent their lives in vain to delve into religion as inspiring source of knowledge!

Religion as a Set of Beliefs, Moral Codes and Rules

Some have defined religion by taking into account the major elements of its message. Thus, religion is sometimes defined as a set of beliefs, moral codes and rules necessary for administering the affairs of human society and training human beings.

Bonheoffer's Definition

Bonheoffer[2] refers to religion as "a metaphysical system according to which one can have a notion of the world."[3]

Assessment

This definition represents one of the popular definitions of religion. If this definition is supposed to be a comprehensive definition it would have been more comprehensive to define religion as a mere notion.

If "notion of the world" in this context refers to the purposefulness of the world then there is no objection. Religiously speaking, the world is a manifestation of Divine Wisdom and Will and it has a purpose and end. The purposefulness of the world is only one of the subjects discussed in religion. There are many other issues in religion

---

Principia). [Trans.]
1. Ab£ 'Alɛ al-°usayn ibn 'Abd Allįh ibn Sɛnį Balkhɛ, known as Ab£ 'Alɛ Sɛnį Balkhɛ or Ibn Sɛnį and commonly known in English by his Latinized name "Avicenna" (c. 980-1037) was a Persian polymath and the foremost physician and philosopher of his time. He was also an astronomer, chemist, geologist, logician, paleontologist, mathematician, physicist, poet, psychologist, scientist, and teacher. [Trans.]
2. Dietrich Bonhoeffer (1906-45): a German Lutheran pastor, theologian, and martyr. [Trans.]
3. Majalleh-ye Kalįm, issue 2, p. 69.

which have not been touched in this definition; for instance, 1-
the belief in an Omnipotent, Unique, Omniscient and Totally
Perfect God, 2- transcendent sense of unity, fraternity and
equality which makes human individuals to share their joys
and sorrows, 3- observing the rights and obligations to regulate
the quadruple relationships.

Ellis' Definition

For Havelock Ellis,[1] "Religion means intuitive knowledge of the
union with the universe."

Assessment

If the definition is supposed to utter just an astonishing fact
concerning the *definiendum* then this definition definitely spurs
wonder in the reader. This definition does not imply any
religious law, principle and issue. Of course, the
abovementioned case is worth reflecting. It includes the
following issues:

1. Man's union with the universe (man as part of the universe):
   this issue can be intuitively realized by every man of
   common sense from the laity to the most sophisticated
   philosopher. To put it otherwise, everyone appreciates this
   fact even with the minimum mental capacity.
2. Man is identical with the universe and vice versa: Shaykh
   Mahmūd Shabistarī[2] has elegantly poeticized this reality in
   the following words:

   > *Nothingness is the mirror the universe is the picture / and
   > man is the eye of picture in which the person lies hidden*

   > *You are the eye of the picture, and He is the light of the*

---

1. Henry Havelock Ellis, known as Havelock Ellis (1859-1939): a British
physician and psychologist, writer, and social reformer who studied human
sexuality. [Trans.]
2. Ma!m£d Shabistar¢ (1288-1340): one of the most celebrated Persian Sufi poets
of the 14th century whose most famous work is a mystic text called The Secret
Rose Garden (Gulshan-e R¡z) written about 1311 in rhyming couplets (*Masnavi*).
[Trans.]

eyes/ Who has ever seen the seen with the eye seen?

Man becomes the universe, and the universe turns to the man. / Can it be expressed in a way better than this? [1]

3. In Shabistarī's verses, 'He' or 'Him' refers to God. Then, the concept of God has played a critical role in the expression of "man's union with the universe", while Ellis does not include God as part of his definition.

4. If we seek to have a hermeneutical encounter with the definition proposed by Ellis one would find him a pantheist.

Spengler's Definition

According to Spengler,[2] "A lively and empirical metaphysical philosophy consists in taking something real which there is no access to, and to consider the supernatural real and the belief in the existence of a world far removed to touch, but still real."

This definition seems to offer that there is a strong rapport between religion and empirical metaphysics. However, religion has nothing to do with empirical philosophy. The other conceptual elements of this definition have been critically assessed through the debates on previous definitions.

Bursur Shatul and Tylor's Definition

Bursur Shatul is of the opinion that religion is nothing but submission to the world of secrets. To paraphrase it in clearer terms, Tylor defines religion as belief in strange spiritual creatures. The two definitions have common defects and lack focus on the major facets of religion.

D'Holbach's Definition

D'Holbach[3] believed that science must replace religion because

---

1.Shaykh Ma!m£d Shabistar¢, Golshan-e R¡z, part 8. [Trans.]

2.Oswald Manuel Arnold Gottfried Spengler (1880-1936) was a German historian and philosopher whose interests also included mathematics, science, and art. [Trans.]

3. Paul-Henri Thiry, Baron d'Holbach (1723-89): a French-German author, philosopher, encyclopedist, prominent figure in the French Enlightenment, and

the latter lacks a definite knowledge.[1] Knowledge is based on sensory perception, D'Hollbach argues, and this connotes that one has to replace science with religion as an outdated source of explanation. He views Christianity as a superstition propagated by priests.

Assessment

By replacing religion with science, D'Holbach wants to set religion aside, because religion does not offer definite knowledge.

D'Holbach must be asked: Why does religion not offer definite knowledge? Is there any knowledge higher than one that links us with God and sets a motion within ourselves? Secondly, science is of an essentially cognitive nature while religion seeks to mobilize cognitive elements towards human spiritual becoming and fulfillment of life's Supreme Telos.

To say that knowledge is based only upon sensory perception is not correct because apart from sensory perception we also have intellection (*ta'aqqul*). Moreover, we also have divine inspirations (*ilh¡m*) and mystical unveiling (*iktish¡f*) which are impossible without intuition (*shuhūd*). Thirdly, sensory perception implies having sensibilia tansferred to human mind and they are reflected in the mind as nothing but specific details; otherwise, mirror and limpid water which also reflect forms and shapes of bodies must possess knowledge. We must accept the existence of a force called mental abstraction or separation of general matters to deduce general laws in the form of knowledge. Thus, sensory perception cannot be regarded as the only source of human knowledge.

D'Holbach believes that whereas in past times phenomena were explained by means of religion, now they must be interpreted by means of science. That is, he argues, religion was in charge of explanation of reality and now it needs to pass the

---

best known for his atheism, and for his voluminous writings against religion, the most famous of them being The System of Nature (1770). [Trans.]
1. Dictionary of Philosophy and Religion: Eastern and Western Thought, p. 647.

position to science. Even if in past people used religion to interpret the universe, this does not imply that all religions interpret the universe from a devotional perspective. We can see that Islam has grounded itself on a scientific outlook and thanks to this approach at least Islam helped the science not to get extincted. Both science and religion have their own specific functions and one cannot replace the other; for religion is rooted deep inside humanity and nobody could ever put it aside. I wish D'Holbach and his fellows were also informed of Muslim societies and could see how Islam and its believers give foremost value to knowledge from the beginning of its spread, and how they saved science from extinction during the Middle Ages (third and fourth centuries AH).

When D'Holbach argues that science must replace with religion he is as though proposing to replace one's head with his/her feet. His view about Christianity as a superstition propagated by priests must be closely examined. Do D'Holbach and his fellows possess academic honesty? If they did, why did they not declare that apart from the practices in the name of Christianity, there are other realities and currents such as those of Islam? Under the pretext of their perceptions of Christianity and its leading figures, why did they implicate other religions?

Santayana's Definition

Santayana[1] regarded religion as a bridge between magic and science.

Assessment

If Santayana feels convinced with this short comment on the nature of religion (and I think it is very unlikely from an original philosoher), he should be asked to define his triad, i.e. religion, magic and science, one by one and then relocate them in the light of his definitions of these concepts. Our criticism of D'Holbach is also the case of Santayana. He must be told, "Mr.

---

1. George Santayana (1863-1952): a Spanish philosopher, essayist, poet, and novelist. [Trans.]

Santayana, you have no idea that magic and the like are strongly condemned and prohibited in Islam, and those who practice them are deemed infidle! On the other hand, do you know that no school of thought or ideology can ever parallel the religion of Islam in defending knowledge, reason and understanding?"

Otto's Definition

Like Ritschl[1] and Troeltsch[2], Rudolf Otto[3] followed a historical line in philosophy of religion and chose some particular concepts as his guideline.[4] After choosing his preferred concepts, he systematically developed them. Like his predecessors, he did not ground his notion of religion on the Absolute. His interpretation of religion revolves around the notion of sacredness.

Assessment

There are many issues that can be propounded as to this definition of religion but we shall only deal with some of them:

1. It goes without saying that from a human perspective, it is very useful to benefit from historical trends of every phenomenon and sometimes it is even undeniably indispensable. For example, if we want to completely understand the importance of economic issues, we have to refer to history and try to know whether economy has been discussed throughout history as an inalienable need for mankind. Of course, we have to distinguish between those phenomena of dualities like the interior and exterior, existence and appearance, and material and spiritual, and

---

1. Albrecht Ritschl (1822-89): a German theologian. [Trans.]

2. Ernst Troeltsch (1865-1923): a German Protestant theologian and writer on philosophy of religion and philosophy of history, and an influential figure in German thought before 1914. [Trans.]

3. Rudolf Otto (1869-1937): an eminent German Lutheran theologian and scholar of comparative religion. [Trans.]

4. We shall deal with the definition of religion by Ritschl and Troeltsch in chapter 5.

those which lack them. Take for example the case of the statue of an animal in a cave or a mountain with some statues of men around who are looking at it. No one could ever reveal the exact philosophy behind this setting as it is not discernable in concrete terms as a mental entity. So, by just observing that setting we cannot be absolutely certain about their real motive. For instance, are they merely looking at the animal? Are these people familiar with this animal? Do they consider it an intermediary between them and the metaphysical? Thus, by mere observation of phenomena and various events in history, one cannot be certain as to the specific motives behind its occurrence in a particular community or nation.

2. On which basis did Otto shuffled these concepts? Is his basis inalterable or alterable? Is it regional or local? Is it global or regional?

3. Taking into account the fundamental principles of religions, religion cannot exist without the belief in God and accepting commitment in life and a set of other religious principles. If we consider the concept of sacredness in the above definition, [we can realize that] its requisite is belief in the Absolute, and this contradicts Rudolf Otto's definition of religion.

Cassirer's Definition

Cassirer[1] viewed religion as a kind of relation essentially natural-metaphorical in contrast to symbolic thinking used in science.

Assessment

Those definitions that espouse conflict between science and religion, like Cassirer's, are marred with a fundamental problem which have no correct foundation.

---

1. Ernst Cassirer (1874-1945): a German philosopher who developed a philosophy of culture as a theory of symbols founded on a phenomenology of knowledge. [Trans.]

It is regrettable to note that they offer a definition of neither science nor religion. They discuss a subject which is of interest by the laity. Such writers must define religion by taking into account the principal and real elements of religion. Due to the vital significance of this point, we shall cite an example in order to see whether there are symbolic phenomena among them or they are all real, as presented to humanity on the basis of revelation, reason and pure natural intuition?

I. The universe is real and its coming into existence is real as well. So, the universe is not a mental construct and it has come into existence by the transcendent wisdom of divinity.

II. The creator of this universe is God who is One and Unique.

III. God has all the Attributes of Perfection of the highest order, such as knowledge, power, wisdom, forgiveness, justice, authority, absolute sovereignty over the universe, absolute self-sufficiency, supervision of the universe, preservation of the laws governing the universe, love for the creatures, and the like.

IV. God has created mankind for a supreme purpose, and that is exposing oneself to Divine Radiation.

V. One must live according to the rational principles and laws of divinity, both in the realms of 'isness' or 'oughtness'.

VI. Every human individual, provided that s/he has not spoiled his/her own primordial dignity through vices, treachery and crime, is like any other human individuals, a single soul in the sight of God.

VII. A man deprived of knowledge and learning—although it is possible for him to acquire them—is simultaneously deprived of acquired dignity.

VIII. To know the totality of his *existence*, one has to be in relation with oneself, God, the universe, and his/her fellow human individuals. By the same token, in order to know the 'oughts' and 'merits' of intelligible life, one needs to refer to revelation. To put it more precisely, the ultimate bases of all these things are ontological revelation and legislative revelation.

IX. The Resurrection and eternal life are real. The following poetical remark serves as a proof for this reality:
The world, galaxy, and stars all turn to playthings / If this long day of the terrestrial had no tomorrow.[1]
That is to say, denial of God, the Resurrection and eternal life involves the denial of all the 'oughts' and 'maybes' of life as well as the moral and cultural rules which manage selfishness and egotism.

X. Human growth and development know no limit. Through utmost efforts and struggle in organizing the quadruple relationships with himself, God, the universe, and his/her fellow human individuals, and preparing the theoretical and practical answers to the sextuple ontological questions (Who am I? Where have I come from? Where have I come to? Where am I heading to? What have I come for? Who is with me?), one can reach far beyond himself and expose oneself to Divine Radiation as the holy verse reads,

Indeed we belong to Allah, and to Him will we indeed return.[2]

Is a single one of these propositions of a metaphoric or symbolic facet?

Sartre's Definition

According to Sartre,[3] "Religion is man's project for becoming god."[4]

---

1. N¡¥ir Khusr£, D¢w¡n-e Ash'¡r, Elegy 241.
2. S£rat al-Baqarah 2:156.
3. Jean-Paul Sartre (1905-80): French philosopher, dramatist, novelist, political journalist, and leading exponent of existentialism whose writings reflect his vision of the human being as master of his or her own fate, with each life defined by a person's actions: "Existence precedes essence." [Trans.]
4. Sartre, Being and Nothingness, p. 760.

Assessment

This is also narrow-mindedness of the highest order of exaggeration and extremism. Since Sartre has drawn public attention by defining religion in a single interesting statement without actually defining religion itself, we can examine and assess this very statement.

There is no mention of "man's becoming god" in any of Revealed Religions, particularly, the three global Abrahamic Faiths, viz. Judaism, Christianity and Islam. They speak of joining "Divine Mercy", "exposing oneself to Divine Radiation", "reaching the ultimate perfection as far as it is possible for human individual" and "entering paradise where man can have whatever s/he wishes."

It is true that mystics and celebrated figures of religious tent speak of man's becoming god but it must be borne in mind that it means man's attainment of a majesty, which cannot be compared with any human greatness in this life. A quatrain reads:

> Pace the way to the point where the duality disappears/ if there is still duality you need to pace/ you can never become Him but if you struggle/ you can pace a path where you get purified of you.

Such remarks by mystics are always accompanied by the term 'heated iron' (al-ḥadīdah al-muḥammjt). Because of its contact with the fire, the iron becomes reddish, acquiring the color of the fire although its essence remains the same. Rumi[1] says,

> The colour of God is his deying vat:/ All things become one-coloured mixed in that/ If you tell one who's fallen in, arise/ Don't blame me, I'm the vat itself! He cries/ Just like the saint who "I'm the Truth" once said/ He was still iron but he burned bright red:/ The iron's colour is effaced by

---

1. Jalaluddin Muhammad Molawi (Rumi, 1207-1273): the greatest mystic poet in the Persian language and founder of the Mawlawiyyah order of dervishes ("The Whirling Dervishes"). He is famous for his lyrics and his didactic epic, *Masnavi* (Spiritual Couplets). [Trans.]

flames/ It's silent while the fireness makes claims.[1]

Dewey's Definition

According to John Dewey,[2] "Any activity pursued in behalf of an ideal and against obstacles and in spite of threats of personal loss because of conviction of its general and enduring value is religious in quality."[3]

Assessment

This definition does also lack many elements key to the nature of definiendum but generality. This generality most probably refers to heating desire for ideals in the form of general propositions like reaching perfection, maximization of spiritual benefits, and the like, while, considering the individual idiosyncrasies, most of them are deprived of these ideals. The flaw of this definition is that first of all, it has pointed out the extremely varied inclinations and desires of people with the single word 'ideal' which has a very broad connotation and it must not be used as it has no scientific value in definitions.

Secondly, there is no mention whatsoever of the principal beliefs of religion such as belief in God, the prophets, the Resurrection, and religious duties and rights. Thirdly, if by "personal loss", Dewey means failure of people to hit those ideals, i.e. ideals useful in this world and within the context of natural flow of events, then this term must be changed because the lofty goal of religion is to help human personality to get flourished in the path of eternity which is impossible without God-wariness (*taqwi*) or self-preservation. And we know for a fact that *taqwi*, which is protection of the self from taints of this worldly life and preparing it for getting exposed to Divine

---

1. Rumi's *Masnavi*, Book 2, p. 99, lines 33-35 (Translation by Jawid Mojaddedi Oxford Classics Series). See Rumi's *Masnavi*, Book 2, lines 1345-1349, p. 141. [Trans.]
2. John Dewey (1859-1952): an American philosopher, psychologist and educational reformer. [Trans.]
3. Dewey, A Common Faith, p. 27.

Radiation in the eternal life, requiring sacrifices and enduring difficulties, can be reached and practiced. If Dewey means otherwise, then it must be explained clearly.

One can paraphrase Dewey as follows: religion means the struggle to attain the general and fixed ideals which answer the inner desire of man to achieve perfection. Unfortunately, however, people are incapable of attaining those ideals, and at least, always under the threat of being unable to attain those ideals. If this is what Dewey means it can be retorted that if the religious beliefs of man are immune from error and his efforts for the lofty ideals are anchored in sincerity and God-wariness (sincere pursuit of moral integrity) and far from selfishness, the outcome of this approach will get manifested in three cases:

First case: objective ideal like the observance of hygiene and honesty in speech and thought that can lead to physical wellbeing of the person and righteous order of social life. This religious ideal is attainable and discernible.

Second case: desirable tranquility, optimism and constant mirth—a kind of joy higher than it cannot be imagined in this world. These ideals are attainable as well as discernible.

Third case: evolutionary perfection of the self and its gradual preparation for being exposed to Divine Radiation which cannot be imagined and discerned by the self-conscious mind except through momentary flashes in this world. As stated in religious sources and indicated by Ibn Sīnj, the outcome of fulfillment of this ideal can be understood and realized after [experiencing] separation of the soul from the body. Ibn Sīnj thus says,

> These occupations (in your lifetime), as you know, affect the soul while she is in contact with the body. And if these passions and affections continue to be established in human soul after the soul's separation from the body just as they are established in the soul in the course of life, they will remain fixed with the difference that during lifetime the soul was busy administering the body. So, the resultant pain and joy couldn't be felt but after the separation from the body, the soul is no more

preoccupied and it comes to itself, sensing all those things...[1]

Oxford Dictionary

According to the Oxford Dictionary, religion is man's acknowledgment of a superior unseen power.[2]

Assessment

This kind of definition – unfortunately held by numerous scholars in West – cannot be treated as a perfect definition of religion although it does mention some important elements of religion. One reason for untenability of such a definition is that most of the objections leveled by the shallow-minded critics against religion set this definition as their point of departure as it lacks integrity and depicts a one-sided portray of religion and turns a brown eye to the aspects that bear the answers to the objections. Even this important element—"man's acknowledgment of a superior unseen power"—has a very basic flaw, i.e. it limits man's relationship with the 'superior unseen Power' (God) to mere acknowledgment. Having said this, religion is not mere acknowledgment of God but rather serious acknowledgment of God in practice through exposing oneself to Divine Radiation, demonstrated by acting upon the duties and rights in relation to the quadruple relationships, and observing noble characters, which is the only way of curbing selfishness.

Jastrow's Definition

Jastrow[3] argues that religion consists of three elements: (1) confession to power or powers beyond the scope of our control; (2) sense of subjugation in relation to this power or powers; and (3) struggling to connect oneself with this power or powers.

He continues, "Religion means belief in a force or a number

---

1. Ibn Sęnį, Al-Ishįrįt wa 't-Tanbęhįt, vol. 3, p. 350.
2. Oxford English Dictionary, vol. 1, p. 410.
3. Most probably, it refers to Robert Jastrow (1925-2008), an American astronomer, physicist and cosmologist. [Trans.]

of distinct forces that control us." This belief gives rise to some social entities: (1) specific organization and laws, (2) distinct practices, and (3) particular systems that relate and connect us to this power or powers.[1]

Assessment

The first criticism to this definition is that there are certain powers in the cosmos, like atomic forces, which we accept but never regard religion as their basis. Not every power beyond human control is an element of religion. Belief in the Power which is infinite and possesses grace, justice, wisdom, creativity, absolute perfection and the like and is called 'God' is one of the pillars of religion.

The second criticism to this definition is that the sense of subjugation in relation to this power must be interpreted correctly. Man invokes God upon His infinite power and majesty, and feels overawed by His power, and it is not like the fear a weak anima goes through before a stronger predator. Jastrow disregards all acts of worship, supplication and communion with God, which are based upon affection, acquaintance, love, inclination and devotion to Him.

In religion there is a set of specific systems, which pave the ground for human perfection. Generally speaking, it must be stated that religious conviction starts with the first call of wakefulness, i.e. man's consciousness of being part of a purposeful universe that exists through the wisdom and will of the Divine Essence and extends to the celestial world which sets human life—individual and social—in the Axis of Lordly Station. Needless to say, such a phenomenon is of dimensions and forms that are extremely diverse.

---

1. Bunyịd-e Dẹn wa Jịme'ehshinịsẹ, p. 37.

Chapter 4

Psychological and Sociological Definitions of Religion

Introduction

Psychological and sociological approaches are quite popular in modern studies of religion and define religion based on social and psychic factors. Many definitions proposed by modern theologians are of psychological taste. For this reason, an examination of psychological and sociological approaches is of an immense significance.

The definitions offered by William James, Freud, and Jung the macro-theorist psychologists, and Schleiermacher, Samuel King, Karl Barth,[1] Frazer, and Kauffman the modern theologians are examples of these trends. As an archetype of modern psychological perspective, the definition proposed by William James[2] shall be discussed in more details.

Psychological Definitions of Religion

William James' Definition

1. His Philosophy

William James (1842-1910) the famous American psychologist and philosopher was a pragmatist philosopher and the founder of the functionalist school in psychology which was basically contrary to William Wudnt's[3] psychological school of

---

1. Karl Barth (1886-1968): a Swiss Reformed theologian considered one of the most important Christian thinkers of the 20th century. [Trans.]
2. William James (1842-1910): a pioneering American psychologist and philosopher trained as a medical doctor. Among his best-known works is The Varieties of Religious Experience. [Trans.]
3.Wilhelm Maximilian Wundt (1832-1920): a German medical doctor,

structuralism. The following lists some key works by James:

1. *The Principles of Psychology*, 2 volumes (1890): They form a classical piece of work that has connected philosophical psychology of the 19th century to the scientific psychology of the 20th century.

2. *The Varieties of Religious Experience* (1902): In this work, his psychological and philosophical inclinations coincide to explain religious life. He describes religious phenomena, and presents a philosophical analysis of the importance of these phenomena.[1]

3. *Pragmatism: A New Name for Some Old Ways of Thinking* (1907): This work contains a theory about the truth mixed with his functionalist psychology.[2]

In *Pragmatism*, James finds a way to fill the gap between science and religion arguing, the touchstone of all truths is experience and everyone's religious experience is a phenomenon that must undoubtedly be accepted as a reality. These ideas led him to pluralism in the personal and moral sense but not in the metaphysical sense.

According to pragmatism, every belief is judged based on the nature of change that it brings to one's personal life.[3]

2. His Definition of Religion

I. The variety in definitions of religion shows that 'religion' does not refer to a single subject or something specific or determined. It is rather general in nature and refers to a set of things.

II. From the outset, we must declare that we will not reach a

---

psychologist, physiologist, philosopher, and professor, known today as one of the founding figures of modern psychology. [Trans.]

1. Part of this work (six out of 20 chapters) has been translated into Persian. William James, D¢n wa Raw¡n, trans. Mahd¢ Q¡'in¢ (Tehran: IntIsh¡r¡t wa ¡m£zesh-e Inqil¡b¢ Isl¡m¢, 1372 AHS).

2. William James, Pragmatism, trans. 'Abd al-Kar¢m Rash¢diy¡n (Tehran: Intish¡r¡t wa ¡m£zesh-e Inqil¡b¢ Isl¡m¢, 1372 AHS).

3. Israel Skefler, Four Pragmatists, trans. Muhsin °ak¢m¢ (Tehran: Nashr-e Markaz, 1366 AHS), p. 134.

point where one finds the essence of religion but rather obtains its features and effects in context.

> It is for sure that I can explain one aspect of 'religion' for the reader, but cannot find a categorical definition of religion that is acceptable to both friend and foe. Thus, religion refers to the effects, feelings and events that take place in one's inward isolation, distant from all attachments, making him realize the connection between him and that which he calls 'God'. In this definition, religion is referred to as 'religious experience'.

> With this definition of religion we do not have many ideological differences. Possibly, there is difference on only one subject and that is on the term 'divine matter'.

Therefore, religion refers to 'human reaction to a set of things' — reaction which generally happens in life for someone (in contrast to temporary reaction).

Assessment

"From the outset, we must declare that we can not reach a point where one finds the truth or essence of religion..." It is impossible to know the essence of religion like a physical phenomenon as it is related to human soul which is connected to God, and both are not physical entities. We also know that the wide variety of definitions is not limited to religion. It includes all human aspects which are somehow related to the universe, human psyche, intellection and conscience; like, beauty, culture, happiness, the delight of justice, God-wariness, mystical unveiling (*iktishȧfȧt*), the sense of helplessness, oppression committed by others, injustice, ignorance, and the like.

It goes without saying that a scholar chooses that aspect of his/her issue at stake which fits his mental and environmental conditions. Definitions of 'culture' exceed 150,[1] according to

---

1. To be exact, Kroeber and Kluckhohn compiled a list of 164 definitions of culture. See Culture: A Critical Review of Concepts and Definitions (1952). [Trans.]

Alfred Kroeber[1] and Clyde Kluckhohn[2] and this is due to the same point we have stated. If we try to know religion only through inner human perceptions and define it accordingly, distinguishing these perceptions from illusions, imaginations and various religious motives is very difficult, if not totally impossible. For instance, to distinguish signs of selfishness from the scorching desire for perfection is indeed difficult, except by applying the pure conscience whose preservation in its pure state is, in turn, very difficult.

And if we limit ourselves to external phenomena, that appeared in the external world, under religious motives, signs or symbols, it is clear that the overwhelming majority of external phenomena have not categorically presented their causes, conditions and goals because they have numerous possibilities in view of the purpose of their Originator. This perfectly clear example, will explain this subject

According to history, our war with such-and-such nation happened at such-and-such period whose causes based on sensory observations were not mentioned so we cannot point them out as it is the case with the cause of war. Let us assume that we went along with war experts, and used every means possible in order to identify the causes of war and we did not find out anything except individual corpses and mass graves, remnants of warfares and weapons, and other physical manifestations of war. Needless to say, through these observations alone we could not understand the cause or motives of the war whether it was economic, territorial disputes, revenge, selfishness, or world conquest?

This is why we argue that our etiological knowledge of such wars does not go beyond conjecture and probability. In order to arrive at a definition of religion which is comprehensive and

---

1. Alfred Louis Kroeber (1876-1960): considered one of the most influential figures in American anthropology in the first half of the twentieth century. [Trans.]
2. Clyde Kluckhohn (1905-60): an American anthropologist and social theorist. [Trans.]

inclusive to a considerable extent, we have no option but to consider the two basic realms, inside and outside.

1- The inside realities which religious people accept whether through intellection (*ta'aqqul*) or intuition (*shuhūd*), and interpret and make sense of their lives through the motives behind those realities.

2- The outside realities such as acts of worship, discharging of duties and rights; these appear in the external world due to inward motives.

Let us consider the realities and activities in the inside world of religious people. Among them are traces of sound mind, primordial nature (*fitrah*) and pure conscience (*wijdįn*); the purposefulness of the universe, existence of God who is the Creator, eternal life, and pressing need for God and His will.

I-   Peace of mind, which has its origin in [the belief in] the purposefulness of the universe and its order

II-   Taking life seriously and purposefully

III- Agreement on the outlines of values, like the principles of moral statements, which are essential for removing defects and supplementing merits in life.

 IV- Providing convincing answers to the sextuple ontological *hauptproblems* (1. Who am I? Whence have I come? Where have I come? With who am I? Where am I heading to? What have I come for?)

V-   The general essence of the acts of worship is to establish contact with God the Glorious, and to expose oneself to His Divine Radiation.

VI-   Sacrifice and devotion based upon the Revealed Will (*irįdeh-ye tashrī'ī*) of God in fighting against oppression, ignorance, poverty, and violation of the rights of the oppressed.

VII- Approving of the unity of mankind by citing the bases of this unity, such as the unity of their Creator (God), the unity of goal pursued by everybody, the unity of the natural essence of their origin, i.e. dust, the unity of the Origin of their soul, and other common elements.

VIII-Sufferings and hardships do not cause psychic disorders, pessimism and mental agitation in religious people.

IX- Following a lofty goal in life along the path of "We belong to God and to Him we shall return," the true believer envisages himself in the presence of God.

X- One of the significant features of religion is that believers regard every affair in life as a form of worship as movement towards the aforementioned direction ("We belong to God and to Him we shall return"). A worker who toils to make products in a farm or a factory is indeed in the state of worship with that sense of movement. By the same token, every learner, student, scholar, or anyone who is engaged in an intellectual pursuit to establish connection with realities and set them for the use of people in material and spiritual life from the most basic level up to the highest, is in a state of worship. Then, the temples built for invoking God are supposed to be a place for worship and direct communion with Divine Presence, and not that they are the only places where one can speak to God.

XI- A true believer regards as trust every concession s/he acquires—from material things to the loftiest spiritual matters—as well as power s/he earns, that must all be utilized for the material and spiritual welfare of humanity.

XII- For a true believer, knowledge is the brightest lamp at his or her disposal for the discovery of realities and s/he must try his or her best to make this lamp as bright as possible.

XIII-Religion sees the art oriented towards 'Intelligible Life' an excellent means to set human life on the verge of a major progress.

XIV-Management and leadership as conceived by religion denotes administration of a set of members organized for the movement toward worldly and spiritual prosperity, and the manager or leader is like a perfect and sound man who is in charge of managing his or her limbs, faculties and natural potential.

XV- No school of thought but religion has ever succeeded to

take the final step to overcome human selfishness, which has drowned his account in tears and blood. Only having faith in Divine Presence and acting upon His commands are effective in curing this fatal disease (selfishness), and nothing else.

XVI- Most of the constructive movements and uprisings in human history which required a collective action and sacrifices have either been consciously religious, or were based on some categorical notions like prosperity, humanity, justice, freedom, and even homeland. If one didn't expect to reach the absolute in this path, he would not have offered his life for them.

3- The phenomena and events that occur in the outside world under the motivation of religion. Such phenomena and events can be classified as follows:

a) Objective phenomena like buildings which in turn are of different types:

I- Places of worship like mosques, churches, synagogues, Hindu and Buddhist temples, Zoroastrian temples, and the like: these buildings, built with their specific idiosyncracies, proves that their construction is motivated by religion. Whereas so many places of worship have been built on earth since the dawan of humanity, it will not be a mistake to understand that they have been built for worship and express religious tendencies.

II- Structures whose religious motive has been identified by means of special inscriptions and sketches on them. Since time immemorial up to now, there have been a lot of hospitals, water reservoirs, bridges, and other structures in which the religious motives of those who built them have been clearly recorded in their respective epigraphs or in handwritten works such as deeds of endowment and testaments. For example, the deed of endowment of

Sultan Qal¡wun[1] Hospital in which this line has been written: "This hospital has been built by Malik Man¥ūr Sayf al-Dīn Sult¡n Qal¡wun, sincerely for the sake of Allah."[2]

b) Special acts performed as a form of worship for the sake of seeking nearness to God. Because of the special importance given by people to religion throughout history, history has recorded the quality and quantity of most devotional acts performed with the intention of seeking nearness to God. Even today one can use statistics to record the quality and quantity of devotional acts pursued by individuals. The major goal behind human trend towards religion is to meet his existential needs and set her/him in the path to Divine Perfection. For these needs, he strives hard in both the inside and outside realms.

Yet, as to James arguing, "Thus, religion refers to the effects, feelings and events that take place in one's inward isolation, distant from all attachments, making him realize the connection between him and that which he calls 'God'", one would say that these feelings and affections are generally appreciated by believers and no one can make them personal as religious experience.

Carl Gustav Jung's Definition

1. Jung and His Ideas

Carl Gustav Jung (1875-1961) was the son of a pastor of the Swiss Reformed Church. He spent his life studying philosophy, anthropology, alchemy, and finally psychology. He founded analytical psychology or the Zurich School *versus* Freud's First School of Vienna, after he broke up with Freud. Maddi has described analytical psychology as a mixture of physical and

---

1. Sayf al-D¢n Qal¢wun al-¯¡li¦¢ (also Qal¡'£n or Kalavun) (c. 1222-1290): the seventh Mamluk sultan who ruled Egypt from 1279 to 1290. [Trans.]
2. Built by Sul§¡n Qal¡wun in Cairo, Egypt, this hospital was one of the most majestic hospitals during the Middle Ages, and it had been operational for about four centuries.

metaphysical psychology.[1] Since the most important element of analytical psychology is seeking to touch the infinite horizon of humanity upon philosophy and meta-science.

Discovering 'collective unconscious,'[2] Jung helped humanity achieve, what is possible through pure empirical knowledge.[3]

2. Religion

Jung talked more about religion as "undoubtedly the superior and most universal expression of human soul."[4] In his 19-volumes collected works, one barely finds a treatise not dealing with issues related to religion. Among his works on religion are the following:

Memories, Dreams, Reflections[5] (1965): this work has been regarded as his religious will showing contrasting portraits of him: religious experiences full of love for God and serious criticism of deities and the church.

Psychology and Religion (1938): it is a collection of his lectures on the relationship of scientific psychology and religion.

Paracelsica (1942): in this book, he deals with alchemy, psychology and religion.[6]

Psychology and Alchemy (1944): it contains his reconstruction of Christian thought and a new reading of the Lord's Supper.

Answer to Job (1952): It is a famous work containing Jung's contradictory statements on a theological issue.

---

1. Salvatore R. Maddi, Personality Theories: A Comparative Analysis, 6th ed. (Pacific Grove, CA: Brooks/Cole, 1996.

2. Collective unconscious: a term of analytical psychology, coined by Carl Jung, proposed to be a part of the unconscious mind, expressed in humanity and all life forms with nervous systems, and describes how the structure of the psyche autonomously organizes experience. See:

http://en.wikipedia.org/wiki/Collective_Unconscious. [Trans.]

3. In "Introduction to Jung's Theology," I have discussed in detail Jung and his ideas. This paper has been published in Qabas¡t, nos. 5-6, pp. 54-140.

4. Fu'¡d-e R£¡¡n¢, Tehran: Shirkat-e Sah¡m¢-ye Kit¡bh¢-ye J¢b¢, 1370 AHS.

5. Parw¢n Far¡marz¢ (trans.), Kh¡§ir¡t, Y¡dd¡shth¢ wa Ind¢shehh¢ (Mashhad: Ast¢n Quds Razav¢, 1376 AHS).

6. Parw¢n Far¡marz¢ (trans.), Paracelsica (Mashhad: Ast¡n Quds Razav¢, 1368 AHS).

Four Imaginal Forms: In this work, Jung discussed four possible figures; he examined motherhood, rebirth, soul, and guile. He allocated the third part to an analysis of *Sūrat al-Kahf* of the Noble Qur'¡n.

3. Jung's Definition of Religion

Jung prefers to start his discourse on religion with etymological remarks on the term. As its Latin root *religere* denotes, Jung argues, religion implies reflection in the wake of conscience and with total attention. It is what Rudolph Otto (1869-1937) duly called 'sacred and luminous thing'.

Thus conceived, religion refers to a state of watchfulness, remembrance and close attention to powerful elements to which man attributes overwhelming power and idealistically portrays them as spirits, devils, gods, laws, or imaginal forms (ancient figures).[1]

In fact, 'religion' signifies a particular state of the conscience, which changes due to the perception of the quality of sanctity and luminosity.[2]

Assessment

Like William James, in his definition, Jung reminds us that the focal point of religion is the establishment of contact with God that requires the quality of sacredness and luminosity.

However, this description cannot be considered a seamless definition of religion. It is not only because it excludes those affections and feelings included by William James in his definition of religion, but also because it disregards the second basic part of religion which is acting on the basis of connection with God and reaching the quality of sacredness and luminosity.

A general objection to this type of one-sided definitions is that it deprives humanity of its essential need for religion, for by knowing the unique advantages that religion offers through

---

1. Far¡marz¢, Paracelsica, p. 8.
2. Ibid., p. 9.

an intelligible and purposeful life, the caravan of humanity can enjoy a mirthful and splendid life.

Herder's Definition

Herder[1] was among the first to consider religion as something inward and personal that relies on mythology and poetry.

Assessment

Throughout history, many people have offered their lives for a cause. How can these people explain these sacrifices through poetry and mythology?

One can use poetry and myths to make sense of religion but it is different from treating poetry and mythology as the foundation of religion.

Secondly, if we construe the religious beliefs of some primitive people in terms of mythology and poetry (something which has not yet been proven), this does not prove that the religious beliefs and practices of so many people, with thousands of profound scholars, sages and thinkers who have founded civilizations, are based upon poetry and mythology. Should we regard the religious beliefs and practices of such enlightened minds as Avicenna, F¡r¡bī,[2] Averroese,[3] Bīrūnī,[4] Ibn

---

1. Johann Gottfried von Herder (1744-1803): a German philosopher, theologian, poet, and literary critic who was associated with the periods of Enlightenment, Sturm und Drang, and Weimar Classicism. [Trans.]

2. Ab£ Na¥r al-F¡r¡b¢ (known in the West as Alpharabius) (c. 872-950/951 CE): a Muslim polymath (in the fields of cosmology, logic, music, psychology, and sociology) and one of the greatest scientists and philosophers of the world during his time. [Trans.]

3. Ab£ 'l-Wal¢d Mu!ammad ibn A!mad ibn Rushd better known as Ibn Rushd, and in European literature as Averroes (1126-98): an Andalusian Muslim polymath; a master of Aristotelian philosophy, Islamic philosophy, Islamic theology, Malik¢ law and jurisprudence, logic, psychology, politics, Arabic music theory, and the sciences of medicine, astronomy, geography, mathematics, physics, and celestial mechanics. [Trans.]

4. Ab£ Rayh¡n Mu!ammad ibn A!mad al-B¢r£n¢ (973-1048): a Persian Muslim scholar and polymath of the 11th century. [Trans.]

Khaldūn,[1] Rūmī,[2] Mullị ̄adra,[3] Mīr Dịmịd,[4] from the East to West, as relying upon myths and poetry?

On the other hand, Herder's notion of religion reminds one of mistaking ancient Greek theory on body elements constituting water, fire, soil, and air, and the theories of great contemporary physicists on the extraordinarily basic foundations of nature, such as the studies on quantum mechanics, as being one and the same!

Thirdly, let us presume that religion in its personal form ends up in mythology and poetry (pleasant feelings based upon selection and elimination in the realities of the world). Is the relation of perfectly divine religion to mythology and poetry more logical than that of multidimensional perfect man to unicellular organisms?

You cannot expect to find the same biological, physiological, psychological and mental qualities of modern man with so many mindboggling talents in unicellular organisms. By the same token, you cannot find a religious spirit like faith, which catches every eye in the world with its existential capacity in a unicellular organism. Can you discern any aesthetic taste, which helps a man to see a thousand types of beauty in a single reality, in a unicellular organism?

---

1. Ibn Khald£n (Ab£ Zayd 'Abd al-Ra!mịn ibn Mu!ammad ibn Khald£n al-°aнram¢) (1332/732 AH-1406/808 AH): a versatile Muslim scholar considered to be a forerunner of several social science disciplines as well as modern economics. [Trans.]

2. Mawlịw¢ or Mawlịnị Jalịl al-Dịn R£m¢ (1207-73): the greatest mystic poet in the Persian language and founder of the Mawlawiyyah order of dervishes ("The Whirling Dervishes"). He is famous for his lyrics and his didactic epic, *Masnavi* (Spiritual Couplets). [Trans.]

3. ̄adr al-Dịn Shịrịz¢ (1572-1641), better known as Mullị ̄adr¢ or ̄adr al-Muta'allihịn: the foremost representative of the Illuminationist (ishrịq¢) School of Islamic philosophy whose magnum opus is Al-Asfịr al-Arba'ah (The Four Journeys). [Trans.]

4. Mịr Dịm¢d, known also as Mịr Mu!ammad Bịqir Astarịbịd¢ (d. 1631/2): an Iranian philosopher founder of the School of I¥fahịn noted as the Third Teacher (mu'allim al-thịlith) after Aristotle and Fịrịb¢, and foremost figure (together with his student Mullị ̄adrị) of the cultural renaissance of Iran undertaken under the Safavid dynasty. [Trans.]

Schleiermacher's Definition

Schleiermacher[1] connects religion with feelings, particularly feelings of attachment. He defines religion as the sense of absolute attachment.[2]

Assessment

Two key points in this definition require to be noticed:
I) it is true that the basis of religion should be sought in the sense of attachment to the absolute, but one needs to take it into consideration that this attachment does not perpetuate human weakness rather it helps one to extend *oneself*. It was with this very sense of attachment that theists have taken great steps in founding civilizations and spearheading human progress and development. This potent movement is the essential condition of all transformative activities throughout history. Thus, whenever man has taken a positive step forward, whether in law, politics, economics, ethics, or culture, s/he has initially adopted an *absolute* as his motto or goal, like humanity, perfection and progress in human prosperity. After proving the necessity of society's attachment to the absolute s/he has mobilized the whole society.

II) This thinker has also limited his own definition of religion to sense of attachment as the bedrock of religion, without mentioning anything about other aspects of religion.

Feuerbach's Definition

"According to Feuerbach,[3] religion is essentially the reflection of human qualities. Auguste Comte[4] and Feuerbach were in

---

1. Friedrich Daniel Ernst Schleiermacher (1768-1834): a German theologian and philosopher known for his impressive attempt to reconcile the criticisms of the Enlightenment with traditional Protestant orthodoxy. [Trans.]
2. Schleiermacher, The Christian Faith, p. 12; Religion, p. 275.
3. Ludwig Andreas von Feuerbach (180472): a German philosopher and anthropologist whose thought was influential in the development of Marxist dialectic. [Trans.]
4. Auguste Comte (1798-1857): a French philosopher and social theorist. [Trans.]

search of a new religion for humanity."[1]

Assessment

For Feuerbach, man magnifies the traits he has, such as compassion and love for a heavenly being. That is, 'God' is a product of man, and does not exist outside human mind and feelings.

This theory defines religion as a mere imaginary phenomenon and mental activity. No one can ever imagine that any man of idea in East or West would make such a 'God' for himself and worship 'Him'. Islam emphasizes that every creature perceives God with all His Attributes. It is true that the existence of God can be proved by observing the law and order in the universe, but a relationship with that Sacred Being is intuitive and not imaginary or mere mental reflection. Definitely, Feuerbach and his followers have not studied the proofs substantiating the existence of God and the intuitive ways of perceiving Him found in the words of the pioneers of knowledge and wisdom.

Kaufmann's Definition

According to Kaufmann,[2] religion originates in human aspiration to promote himself.[3] According to this view, man is an ape that wants to become 'God'. Whether he upholds [certain] ideals or strives to attain perfection, man is an inebriated ape of God.

Assessment

This definition has numerous problems. We shall mention some of them:

I- How did such an impressive concept find its way into an ape's mind? Has the concept of God as an Essence of infinite

---

1. Dictionary of Philosophy and Religion, p. 647.
2. Walter Arnold Kaufmann (1921-80): a German-American philosopher, translator, and poet. [Trans.]
3. Walter Kaufmann, Critique of Religion and Philosophy, pp. 354-359.

knowledge, power, life, grace, beauty, and glory, dawned to ape's mind in a seminal form through evolutionary process that ended up in *Homo Sapiens*? How do they prove this claim?

II- Has an ape with such traits existed in the generation of apes of the past millennia?

III- Mr. Kaufmann must be aware that

> We know very well that most paleontologists relate man's evolution to at least one million years ago; that is, to the fourth geological epoch. The newest discoveries in the paleontology of the human race, state that human origins are extremely complex and ambiguous.
>
> New discoveries, show numerous and multifaceted branches that came into being and existed for a while and faded away, and only a set of them survived and initially lead up to the Homo sapiens, or the rational man and precursor of today's human being. Prior to this, paleontology maintained that today's human being is from the species of ape-like humans or pithecanthropus that came into being by the evolution of the Neanderthal man and then the Cro-Magnon man. Today, after numerous discoveries in Europe, Asia and Africa, it has become clear that the obtained fossils do not belong to a specific single species but to, at least, four different species, and our ancestor, that is, in reality, the ancestor of the 'rational' Cro-Magnon man is not the human, Neanderthal or Heidelberg man. And we are neither from the ape-like pithecanthropus humans nor from sinanthropus up to the genus prior to the 'rational man', whose fossils are absolutely unknown and unidentifiable.[1]

IV- Kaufmann offers no explanation why out of tens, nay hundreds of religious precepts this ape has sufficed to the desire to become 'God'. Is there any observed phenomenon or gesture of apes, which indicates this desire to become

---

1. Pierre Rousseau, Tįrȼkh-e ‾anįye' wa Ikhtirį'įt (Histoire des techniques et des inventions), trans. °asan ‾affįrȼ, pp. 19-20.

'God'?

Samuel King's Definition

For Samuel King,[1] religion implies having faith in a supernatural or mysterious power caused by fear, awe and reverence.

Assessment

I. Like many other similar definitions of religion, this definition touches on the root and the motive behind professing religion, and not on religion itself.

II. Standing in awe of God, the Glorious, and His sovereignty over creation, including human beings, is not comparable with fear and awe like that of a weak animal, a cat against a remorseless preying beast that needs to kill the weak for its own food. This is because the fear and awe in latter case, as we have already said, are related to a strong being's need to a weak being. Meanwhile, revealed religions particularly those of Abrahamic origin regard God, the Glorious, as the fountainhead of existence of all creatures, who loves them, desires their perfection, and has provided them with the most excellent means of understanding, such as the intellect, the heart and the conscience. God is not the source of fear and awe. The source of fear, awe and terror is man himself, whose selfishness deprives him of divine grace.

III. There is no mysterious force whatsoever in Abrahamic Universal Faith (Judaism, Christianity and Islam). Such blind forces should be sought in mythology, magic and the like. Of course, one can say that there are metaphysical truths that cannot be understood with average human knowledge, and this lack of understanding can easily discerned about the nature of 'soul' (*rūh*) and even 'ego' and other fundamental truths like natural basic elements and etc.

---

1. Samuel King: a Presbyterian minister and one of the founders of the Cumberland Presbyterian Church. [Trans.]

This is also the case with Robert Louis Stevenson,[1] who regards religion as the natural spontaneous reaction to the extraordinary, mysterious and fearsome phenomena of nature.

---

1. Most probably, it refers to Robert Louis Stevenson (1850-94), a Scottish novelist, poet, essayist and travel writer. [Trans.]

Goldziher's Definition

According to Goldziher,[1] religion is a manifestation of human soul.

Assessment

This is one of the most general definitions of religion, but in view of the fact that the "manifestations of human soul" are so varied, this definition can not render any help in knowing religion. In fact, we can say that Goldziher refers to the manifestation of soul, which only appears in professing a connection with God's Absolute Perfection, not to every inward manifestation.

Rainach's Definition

According to Rainach, religion embodies the totality of temptations that takes the place of free application of our power and talents.

Assessment

This definition refers to the inner insinuations that prevent us from freely using our power and talents. If it is really so, we have no objection to it because the writer has presented his personal spiritual state in a scientific manner! It is such remarks that have rendered human sciences pointless and replaced them with technologies that sacrifice life for comfort. The following points are worth pondering over:

I- Were all the religiously motivated scientific advancements in the arena of science and technology in Muslim societies (from the second half of the second century up to the end of the first half of the fifth century, AH) and saved science from definite extinction, as acknowledged by a number of Western scholars, mere temptations?

II. Were all the campaigns waged by Islam against ignorance

---

1. Ignác (Yitzhaq Yehuda) Goldziher, better known as Ignaz Goldziher (1850-1921): was a Hungarian orientalist of Jewish heritage. [Trans.]

and savagery rooted in insinuation?

III. Were all the executions of justice by Islam, as acknowledged by Islamic history scholars (like Gustave Le Bon[1]), resulting in its astonishing advancement and spread, insinuations?

IV. Was the constant pursuit of sublime perfection by the martyrs, who offered their lives, selfish insinuations?

We wish Rainach and his followers would have spent a day studying the record of Islam and then attempted to define religion.

Rupele's Definition

Rupele defines religion as human life's dependence on a mysterious soul to which man wishes to be attached, feeling a sense of unity or oneness with it and expressing delight for this feeling.

Assessment

This definition expresses an important element of religion which is human life's dependence on a higher truth, however, taking 'mysterious soul' for God, is like taking the cause for the effect, and the soul does not necessarily mean 'God' although it is a truth of highest order.

If 'mysterious' in this context connotes 'something of an unknown nature', then there is no objection; for although human mind has great potential, it is incapable of perceiving that Sacred Essence. However, making sense of Divine Attributes and possessing Divine light following self-refinement and purification is possible and every enlightened individual has a share of it in one way or another.

Frazer's Definition

"By religion, then, I understand a propitiation or conciliation of powers superior to man which are believed to direct and

---

1. Gustave Le Bon (1841-1931): a French social psychologist, sociologist, and amateur physicist. [Trans.]

control the course of nature and human life", Frazer[1] argues. [2]

Assessment

This definition has highlighted human quest for perfection by cajoling greater truths and powers, which are above everything and administer nature and human life. Yet, it does not give any explanation about those powers, and in particular, about the Truth beyond all truths (the great power which is definitely God by Frazer).

Such a definition is like defining science as the relevance of discovery as compared to realities! Just as the latter does not give any clear definition of science, so does such a definition of religion.

Koestenbaum's Definition

In Koestenbaum[3]'s words, "Religion refers to man's endeavor to do something for his hopeless state of restraint."[4]

Assessment

It is for sure that religion can help one out of the hopelessness arising from one's existential limitations and defects. This, however, does not imply that through religion, man condoles with his defects and limitations in the world of imagination. In fact, life based on religion expands one's existential dimensions. Due to an attachment to Supreme Perfection, he is released from any form of defect and limitation.

---

1. Sir James George Frazer (1854-1941): a Scottish social anthropologist influential in the early stages of the modern studies of mythology and comparative religion. [Trans.]
2. James George Frazer, The Golden Bough (New York: Bartleby.com, 2000), chap. 4, "Magic and Religion," http://www.bartleby.com/196/9.html (accessed: January 2011). [Trans.]
3. Most probably it refers to Peter Koestenbaum, founder and Chairman of Philosophy-in-Business and the Koestenbaum Institute, who has applied his knowledge of philosophy to business, leadership, management, marketing, and strategic thinking. [Trans.]
4. Koestenbaum, Religion in the Fraction of Phenomenal, p. 18.

Freud's Definition

According to Freud, religion signifies human struggle to find heavenly consolations to help him overcome frightening events in life. He also views religion as a guile and applies his own personal experience as a contribution to suppress a general pandemic.[1]

Assessment

Here Freud highlights three points as the definition of religion:
First point: religion is a heavenly consolation helping man to overcome the fearful events in life. One needs to say that this is not the meaning or part of the definition of religion but rather, one of the requirements of religion.

> I'd rather have poision as the beloved bears the cup/ I'd rather hold the pain whose cure comes from her[2]

As Socrates drank the cup of hemlock without any fear or speculation and Imam Hossein passed the greatest tragedy of all human history in proud and joy. I wish Freud and his followrs had even a poor knowledge of Islamic literature.

> O' my heart! If the flood of annihilation destroys the whole world/ since you have Noha as your captain never feel sad of the flood[3]
>
> O' Sa'di! If the flood of annihilation destroys your life down to the scratch/ stand strong as He is in charge of keeping everything on[4]
>
> Days came to their ends in our grief/ days followed days after days/ if we missed the days tell no one cares/ suffices you stay as there is no one like you pure[5]

Second point: to assess Freud's definition of religion a general view of his motives and ways of reasoning is of immense

1. Sigmund Freud, The Future of an Illusion, pp. 57-58.
2. Sa'd¢, Maw¡'ï", ghazal 13.
3. °¡fï", Ghazaliy¡t, ghazal 255.
4. Sa'd¢, Maw¡'ï", ghazal 13.
5. R£m¢,

importance. Freud does not give importance and credence to personality and its defense against sexual instinct's force and activities, but interprets all human aspects on the basis of this instinct; its suppression or indulgence! After becoming a popular trend in psychology and acquiring a sort of religious sanctity after the coinage of 'Freudism', this theory turned useless. However, the weakness of this theory became known to all and sundry, and apart from classifying what is 'conscious', 'unconscious', and 'semi-conscious', which was a plausible pretext, the themes of this school were subject to serious criticism. Apart from this, which in itself has a long story, there is an extremely worthwhile quotation of its founder that demolished the foundations of all his theories about moral and religious questions.

> *I always find myself annoyed by propounding incommensurable issues and I always acknowledge this annoyance!* [1]

Now assuming Freud's allergy for moral issues and supera-quantitative truths, can one rely on his definition of religion? Or, can one consider his negative views about religion and other sublime supera-quantitative human values as having any scientific value?

Third point: the definition offered by Freud of religion— "religion signifies man's struggle to find heavenly consolations to help him overcome frightening events in life"—states only one advantage of religion, i.e. contributing strength to deal with frightening events, among others and not the major telos or purpose of religion. For Freud, there is no room at all for spiritual delight and sense of solidarity with other human individuals through religion, because he was afraid of propounding incommensurable issues! For Freud, there is no room for any constructive services that man has offered in the wake of religion for freedom, justice and realization of human rights throughout history, for propounding incommensurable

---

1. Edgar Pesch, And¢shehh¢-ye Freud (Pensee de Freud), p. 92.

issues would annoy him!

Bultmann

For Bultmann,[1] religion refers to human scorching desire to escape from the world by discovering a hypothetical realm beyond this world.[2]

Assessment

Some individuals do have such an enthusiasm, but this is an insufficient definition of religion as it is concerned with only one side of this multideminsional phenomenon. **Firstly**, this definition says nothing about the Supreme Telos of Lif, its relation to man and the domain of religious rights and duties.

Secondly, Resurrection does not have a clear place in the above definition.

Thirdly, it turns a blind eye to the quadruple human relationships (with himself, God, the universe, and his fellow human individuals).

Fourthly, there is no doubt that man has a scorching desire to establish an intelligible relationship with this world, which is a product of a sound mind or conscience that religion urges to make it real. Religion does not invite the believers to escape the physical world but rather it depicts it as a divine nomos which should be respected.

The belief in a world beyond this physical world embodies one of the articles of faith underlined by revealed religions. Similarly, there is no doubt that this world is the place of absolute freedom from physical constraints. However, escaping from this world, from struggle and evolution of personality, to that eternal, spiritual world is against divine wisdom and will. This world is like an observatory to look at the Infinite and strive for it. Granted that human enthusiasm to escape from this

---

1. Rudolf Karl Bultmann (1884-1976) was a German theologian of Lutheran background. [Trans.]
2. Rudolf Bultmann, Myth and Christianity, p. 50.

world to the other world is included in the definition of religion, still it is just part of the definition and not its totality.

Sociological Definitions of Religion

Sociological definitions refer to the definitions of religion that base themselves on social causes and effects and reduce it into a social phenomenon. We shall consider three major definitions of this type:

Durkheim's Definition

For Durkheim,[1] "A religion is a unified system of beliefs and practices relative to sacred things, i.e., things set apart and forbidden—beliefs and practices which unite in one single moral community, called a Church, all those who adhere to them."[2]

According to Durkheim, the original 'sacred' is social, because society nurtures the individual and generates the 'sacred' feeling in him.

Assessment

The defects of this definition are as follows:

I- The first part of Durkheim's definition of religion is that it is "a unified system of beliefs and practices relative to sacred things". This is a good explanation of the nature of the elements of religion; the systematic and unified organization of a set of beliefs and practices as duties related to sacred truths. However, it does not give any explanation about the identity of those beliefs and practices. For this reason, we can say that this is also one of the defective definitions of religion.

II. As to interpreting religion in terms of prohibitions like the following remark by Durkheim "[religion denotes] things

---

1. David Émile Durkheim (1858-1917): a French sociologist who formally established the academic discipline and, with Karl Marx and Max Weber, is commonly cited as the principal architect of modern social science. [Trans.]
2. Durkheim, The Elementary Forms of the Religious Life (1912), Book 1, Ch. 1. [Trans.]

which must be prohibited and set aside", one need to take it into account that in Islam, prohibition is limited to those matters that cause physical or spiritual harm, and has nothing to do with prohibitions observed in taboo moral systems[1] of primitive societies.

III. In Islam, a moral community or an assembly in a structure called mosque has no specific distinction. It is identified as an *ummah*. Thus, there is no specific country, place or structure for the religious activity.

IV. Another clarification needed in this definition is: What does it mean by 'beliefs'? In some religions, false beliefs have found ways of duping people. In revealed religions, there are some theological, moral and social precepts whose origin is divine revelation.

The problem with Durkheim is that he regards the Sacred Being, i.e. God, as a social principle, believing that the society is the cause of human trend towards God. Said otherwise, he believes that society gives rise to the belief in something sacred, belief in God. To put it in other words, Durkheim does not give any credence to the individual; he gives all credence to society and envisages no identity for the individual, whereas, it is not so. Man has some talents inside and society can tile the path for their realization.

Durkheim's theory takes the influence of society to the extremes. It is not farfetched to say that his theory considerably contributes to the emergence of the idea that, "man has history but not a nature", which is propagated by writers, like Sartre, in public. Durkheim has confused occasional causation with adequate causation. Finally, he must address the problems caused by the denial of human individual identity and talent, such as the following:

1. How to explain revolutions, that have frequently occurred in the course of history, and why they continue to appear contra the natural course of societies (otherwise, they would not be

---

1. It refers to those prohibitions that are not based on any logical cause or reason.

labeled 'revolution')?

2. The basic human sense of freewill and responsibility is nothing but an illusion according to Durkheim's theory. To assume that the individual is constructed by its own society implies that he must compulsorily accept the fatalistic construction of society.

3. How to interpret the discoveries and inventions presented for the first time in society, considering the incapability of society in bringing them into existence and even in determining most of them?

Feaver's Definition

In his book entitled *"Religion in Philosophical and Cultural Perspective,"* J. Clayton Feaver[1] has defined religion in this way: plainly speaking, the term 'religion' is the *content* or the *basis* of human experience. Sacred institutions, speech, beliefs, and writings can be easily reviewed. Moreover, most of religions claim that they are more than a set of empirical data. Personal comportments, values and fundamental approaches to life are also religious phenomena. Religion (or at least, most believers) asserts that it is more than a set of data among other data, and more than a certain type of experience among other experiences. Religion asserts that it is *the Truth*, and in their most advanced form, most religions claim to be the Ultimate Truth in close harmony with the Ultimate Reality. Religion does not certainly claim that it is purely a rational understanding of reality. Speculation might be secondary in the face of fellings and will as most of the religious instructors assert. To be more precise, religion implies reflection on the meaning of the world for a better human existence. Religion is taking into account the possibility that something lies at the heart of reality that responds to and satisfies human needs in life and realizes his destiny.

---

1. J. Clayton Feaver (1911-95): an American philosopher-educator and ordained Presbyterian minister from Oklahoma City. [Trans.]

Assessment

Certain points in this definition worth to be noticed:

I. Among the discussed definitions of religion, this definition is relatively more accurate and has greater merit.

II. That "religion is the content or the basis of human experience", is a valuable definition about religion because by saying this, Feaver specifies that "sacred institutions, speech, beliefs, and writings are reviewable." A reality exists in religion and must be indicated in the definition of religion. This is in contrast to those who say that religion is a connection with the mysterious or imaginary world!

III. The majority of religions claim that they are more than a set of empirical experiences. Personal comportments, values and fundamental approaches to life are also religious phenomena. The forerunners of revealed religions substantiate this claim with sound reflection. They regard secularism (exclusion of religion from the worldly life) a product of ignorance of the reality of man's physical and spiritual life and their relation to one another.

IV. "Religion (or at least most believers) asserts that it is more than a set of data among other data, and, more than a certain type of experience among other experiences". One should say that common experiences applied towards knowing realities, although prove very important and realistic, but their result is relative, temporary and dependent on sensory perceptions, mental activities, orientations, and stances taken during the experience. Having said this, religious notions are mainly based on absolute realities consisting of the basic foundations of human quadruple relationships (with oneself, God, the world and one's fellowmen). For example, the universe has a purpose; my existence has its own purpose and philosophy; there is God; human beings have duties and responsibilities; eternal life and the Resurrection are true. Since religion is grounded in these realities, it is the truth and the ultimate truth.

V. Religious notion of the world is a kind of flourishing of human soul and not merely a rational understanding of the reality or a notion of it. Thus, reflection can be a prelude to a secondary feeling or will.

VI. "Religion implies reflection on the meaning of the world for a better human existence." Of course, Feaver should have also added the element of acting upon and searching for "a better human existence", because mere reflection does not include 'searching', which is the goal of religion.

VII. "Religion is taking into account this possibility that something lies at the heart of reality that responds to and satisfies human needs in life and for the realization of his destiny."

The abovementioned remark has to be modified in this way: "religion implies the necessity of accepting the truth that there is something at the heart of reality that responds to and satisfies the needs of man for life and realizes his destiny." At any rate, this definition has mentioned numerous dimensions of religion and has extra points compared to the previous definitions.

Jefferson's Definition

Jefferson[1] (1743-1826) believed that the pure teachings of Jesus ('a) were concealed under a wrong early account as a conspiracy of the clergy and kings to control the people.

Assessment

Jefferson has not actually defined religion but rather mentioned the use of certain religious teachings (Christianity) by priests and kings.

The defect of Jefferson's remark lies in the fact that first of all, he mentioned what happened to Christian teachings at the hands of priests and kings, thereby keeping the essence of Christian hidden. Secondly, it has been a peculiarity of the powerful to always use the best means for the worst objectives.

---

1. Thomas Jefferson (1743-1826): the third President of the United States (1801-09) and the principal author of the Declaration of Independence (1776). [Trans.]

Needless to say, in studying a reality, its salient features must be taken into account. If we look more closely we would see that every great concept like freedom, justice, beauty, governance, human rights, or cultural element that exists in history has been once misused.

Chapter 5

Teleological and Moralistic Definitions of Religion

Introduction

In this chapter two types of definitions of religion shall be examined:

The first type covers the teleological definitions of religion. Since every phenomenon's telos explains it as such one can include that telos in its definition. Telos as the final cause, according to classic logicians, can be included both in definition and proof. The major point of 'ambiguity' in teleological definition is mistaking telos for utility. The definitions by Karl Barth, Ritschl and Troeltsch are good examples of teleological definitions.

The second type embodies the moralistic definitions of religion. It is far too clear that morality plays a critical role in religious teachings. However, confusing religion with ethics is a mistake committed by some scholars of religion when they turn to define religion. Three examples of moralistic definitions of religion by Kant, Whitehead and Paul Johnson, shall be examined.

Teleological Definition of Religion

Karl Barth's Definition

Karl Barth believes that religion refers to human quest for reaching God and it always ends up in touching God provided that, it is in accordance with human desire.

Assessment

Man's quest for reaching God is important to some extent. Religion concerns knowing God as well as moving towards

Him. However, searching for God according to human desire is not sound as it should be. Human desire cannot be the touchstone in this particular regard. This hypothesis can only be approved of if Barth refers to human primordial desire. To state the matter differently, man searches for a God to whom his/her primordial nature attests. If we delve into Barth's claim deep enough, we can say that if by human desire he meant the human natural desire shared by all human individuals, it certainly contradicts the reality, since no great theologian has ever claimed to have conceived God according to his own desire, nor does he ever ask God for his aspirations, according to human desire. Having said these, this definition also is not accurate enough as it does not deal with all dimensions of religion.

Ritschl's Definition

Ritschl and Troeltsch regard religion as possessing autonomy, insight, and rational power to exert influence. They approach Christianity as a historical phenomenon indeed. Nevertheless, Christianity has emerged as an absolute from the heart of history.

Assessment

There are some objections to this definition:

I.   It goes without saying that 'autonomy' in this definition must be modified if it implies intensification and expansion of the 'natural self' a la Hobbesian leviathanism. Not only does this goal or motive have no place in religion but divine religion categorically and decisively wages a campaign against such 'autonomy'.

If it means that religion struggles to help man to touch the highest point of perfection, then it is totally sound and indisputable. Yet, it is clear that touching the highest perfection is possible by setting aside all dimensions of self-centeredness and egotism.

II. One of the peculiarities of religion is that it assists one to acquire a "rational view of life" that in turn puts him in a position to have an influential *existence*. Acquisition of rational view of life to be an influential player is not an exclusive enterprise pursued by religion as every human individual seeks to make sense of the realities, and to have a strong will to exert influence. Then this rational view of life is sought in religion to equip man to regulate his quadruple ontological relationships and acquire human virtue.

III. That "Christianity has emerged as an absolute from the heart of history" is a limited approach, which can be regarded as an important defect in definition.

Tillich's Definition

Paul Tillich[1] interprets God as the "ground of being" and sees religion as human ultimate devotion.

He tends to interpret this total devotion as ultimate desire. Religion, Tillich argues, stands for an unconditional attachment to something that is taken serious by man to the extent that s/he is ready to toil for it and even face death. The Ultimate Desire has both objective and subjective dimensions. The subjective dimension denotes that the individual is unconditionally serious about something. The objective dimension is indicative of the objectivity of the ultimate desire, which Tillich called 'God'. In other words, 'ultimate devotion' implies 'worship', and in this sense, worship is an expression of admiration of something sublime, of which man is conscious.

Assessment

This definition indicates some elements as essential components of religion:

I. God is the "ground of being" (the Originator and Sustainer of the universe). This component is the most basic element of the definition of divine religion.

---

1. Paul Johannes Tillich (1886-1965): a German-American theologian and Christian existentialist philosopher. [Trans.]

II. "Human ultimate devotion": this total devotion is desirable by man. When this element joins the first component of the definition, i.e. God is the ground of being, it sounds wholly intelligible and clear.

III. "Religion stands for an unconditional attachment to something that is taken serious by man to the extent that s/he is ready to toil for it and even face death." As the third component of the definition, this point is also totally correct. One can say that quantitatively and qualitatively speaking, the religious martyrs are the most important of those who voluntarily offered their lives obeying the commandment of God with the ardent desire to meet Him in the eternal life. The abovementioned passage includes some ambiguous remarks. He says that the ultimate desire has an objective as well as subjective dimension. The subjective dimension denotes that the individual is unconditionally serious about something. The objective dimension is indicative of the objectivity of the ultimate desire, which he called 'God'. The ultimate desire is not indeed a subjective phenomenon; rather, after the concept of God and acknowledgment of His existence and Attributes, the ultimate desire penetrates through the outside layers of mind into its innermost depth, and as an active element, it manages man's ideal life.

Moralistic Definition of Religion

Everett Dean Martin's Definition

For Everett Dean Martin,[1] religion determines the allegorical value of existence with expressions that bespeak of man's interests and inclinations to egotism.

Assessment

This definition is also not free from ambiguity as:

---

1. Everett Dean Martin (1880-1941): American writer and lecturer on social philosophy and psychology. [Trans.]

1. It is not clear that to which category does this 'value' belong? Whether the interpretation, definition and knowledge of the 'universe,' 'self,' 'God,' and fellow 'human beings' are parts of the 'value' or they are only matters of epistemology?

2. It is stated, "...with expressions that bespeak of man's interests and inclinations to egotism." If it means materialistic interests and inclinations, then this point is not correct, because religion places man's goal above the realm of material things and attachment to them. But if it means perfection of personality in the sense of its blossoming and coming to fruition in preparation for the eternal life, then this point is correct. However, instead of the word 'egotism' a more appropriate word must be chosen.

3. This definition does also suffer from integrity disorder as it does not give a whole picture of the *definiendum* like previous definitions.

Kant's Definition

Kant[1] classifies religion into two, viz. natural religion and supernatural religion. Accordingly, natural religion refers to the religion whose principles are based on the principles of practical (moral) reason, while supernatural religion has its root in revealed word (revelation). It seems that in Kant's eyes morality and revelation together build the religion. In his discussion of natural religion on morality, he argues that natural religion is not a rule. It is a moral religion inspired by God... Morality and revealed word together make religion.

Assessment

This is a plausible interpretation of Kant's view on religion. And one can examine its plausibility upon his famous words on duty. He said,

> O' duty! The great and high is your name! You are not

---

1. Immanuel Kant (1724-1804): the German philosopher regarded by many as the most influential thinker of modern times. [Trans.]

pleasing and charming, but you ask people to obey, and manage to push the will to surrender to what it abhors. You do not frighten it, but you only enact a law, which permeates through the self, and even if we do not obey it, willy-nilly, we respect it. Though all human desires go against it they stand still in its presence. O duty! Where does lie your noble origin? Where should we search for it? Everything human owes its value to you. Man lives on earth and it makes him mundane but you give him a status which can only be fathomed by reason. You give him nobility which lies in inderpendent and free will in the face of nature.[1]

In fact, Kant interprets religion upon moral concepts whose limit is not confined to reason. Kant seeks to touch religion through morality. To state the matter otherwise, through the sense of duty, he struggles to clear his path to the Origin of duty. He puts morality within the spectrum of practical reason. In fact, he embarks on proving religion on the basis of morality. Doing so, he uses something to prove religion that in turn needs to be examined closely. In other words, it is human conscience or primordial nature that presents man and the world as meaningful entities. This very conscience and primordial nature proves the appropriateness of morality in intelligible life. Other elements can be discerned in religion as follows:

I. The final answer to the sextuple ontological questions which is not possible for any school of thought but religion that reads,

> **Indeed we belong to Allah, and to Him do we indeed return.**[2]

II. Substantiating higher values and virtues without which human life turns unjustifiable and so all sacrifices and services offered by enlightened souls to mankind appear foolish.

---

1. Mu!ammad 'Al¢ Fur£gh¢, Sayr-e °ikmat dar Ur£p¡, vol. 2, p. 169.
2. S£rat al-Baqarah 2:156.

III. The sense of cosmic magnificence which owes its meaning to God's existence. These proofs show the need to profess religion in this life, but which religion? The latter requires an independent discussion.

Whitehead's Definition

Whitehead[1] maintained that religion is a system of universal truths which if sincerely accepted and correctly understood, manifests the effect of change in one's personality and morality.[2]

Assessment

This definition highlights the effect and outcome of religion. That is, if religion is sincerely professed and understood by a person, his personality will be transformed. In other words, religion is a system of universal truths, which has positive effects on human personality.

Whitehead has a positive and extremely admirable view about religion. In some of his writings, he has propounded key points in defense of religion and the refutation of misunderstandings of shallow-minded despisers of religion. Then, one can say that he has offered the abovementioned definition to address an occasion.

Whitehead's definition was particularly necessary to rescue narrow-minded and credulous individuals from sophistries and fallacies of the actors in the theater of egotism.

Paul Johnson's Definition

Paul Johnson observed three basic effects of religion:
1) primordial hope for some values;
2) self-conscious attachment to the forces that maintain these values;
3) ingraining these values through the help of those forces.

---

1. Alfred North Whitehead (1861-1947): an English mathematician who became a philosopher. [Trans.]
2. Mu¦ammad Iqb¡l L¡h£r¢, Ihy¡-ye Fikr-e D¢n¢ dar Isl¡m, p. 5.

One of the basic principles of religion is the belief that human existence is not by accident; rather, a certain Force has determined it and one can feasibly attribute will and desire to that force. Such definitions encompass some important elements of religion:

I. Emotional factor: belief in a Force or forces that control human destiny, and the respect accorded to material and spiritual values needed by people, are a product of this conviction.

II. Factor related to feelings and affections: feeling of attachment to this Force or forces in various ways.

III. Acceptance: religion deals with actions and acceptance; for example, performing ritual prayers and acknowledging moral laws.

IV. Social factor: religion is a social phenomenon that symbolizes the collective action.

Assessment

Some abovementioned features about religion are true. However, 'forces that control human destiny' must be clarified. If it implies Divine Will that governs the world, then it is correct. Divine will does not contradict human freewill but grants it. This definition seems to offer that the notion of superforces governing the world is in conflict with human freewill but it is no so as without human freewill responsibilities, regrets, lofty moral values, and freewill turn meaningless.

"Sense of attachment to this Force or forces in various ways" is supposed to be interpreted in such a way that in religion man feels a sense of attachment to the Absolute Perfection. That is, man has a sense of yearning and inclination toward God.

This definition then discusses the existence of a set of laws and responsibilities, which is acceptable. Finally, the social dimension of religion has been highlighted; that is, the existence of duties and values that establish a social order. Sociologists define religion in such a way that it encompasses polytheistic beliefs as well as Hindu and Shinto rituals. They have combined the common features of different beliefs and presented it as the definition of religion!

Part 2
Scope of Religion

Chapter 1

Why Do We need Religion?

Before marking the limits of religion in respect of its enlightening role, it is necessary to have a short debate on the reason and emergency of one's need for religion as until it is not logically clarified that on which basis man needs to turn to religion one can not speak of the scope of religious enlightenment in a meaningful fashion.

Firstly, to understand why man turns to religion and what s/he sees in religion that can not be found in something other than it one needs to know both the meaning of life and religion. Generally speaking, life is divided into two major types: ordinary natural life and intelligible life[1].

Ordinary natural life is what one finds in the ordinary natural phenomena of life; for example, feeling, moving, choosing, thinking, reproducing, attracting sources of pleasure, and avoiding sources of displeasure as far as possible. It is the pure natural life which is shared by all animals—from the unicellular organism to human being with 75 trillion cells.

Life, in the first sense, not only needs no religion, but in some cases, it is even disturbed by it. This type of life that helps natural self with all facts and values can benefit from everything in whatever way it wants for its desires. In this life, knowledge, art, nobility, dignity, morality, religion, rights, politics, culture, civilization, and freedom, are all viewed from a Machiavellian perspective, serve to fulfill the desires of natural

---

1. For a detailed discussion on Jafarian philosophy of life see his seminal work entitled Intelligible Life (2011), translated by Beytollah Naderlew, Xlibris, USA

self.

Now let's turn to *Intelligible Life* as natural life's alternative and ask what does it mean? Intelligible life consists of a conscious course of human acitivity every step of which make one more enthusiastic to experience the next step. Human personality leads this activity; the personality which has its origin in eternity. This meaningful world is his passageway. His ultimate end is to become exposed to the radiations of the Absolute Perfection in eternity; the Absolute Perfection whose zephyr of love and glory mobilizes the universe and whose light brightens the tortuous path of material and spiritual perfection.

Now, we turn to define religion. Religion is consisted of two basic parts:

1) The belief in the existence of the One and Only God, the Absolute Overseer and Sovereign in the universe, above any passion and inclination, the embodiment of all Attributes of Perfection. He has created the universe in accordance with His sublime wisdom; through the two great guides; reason, *the guide inside*, and the prophets and their successors as *the guides outside*, He has set man in motion for perfection until the realization of the Divine Vision (*liqi' Allįh*). Belief in the eternal life without which life and the entire universe would be an unsolvable puzzle complements the belief in One God. These beliefs are documented to a sound intellect and primordial sense, free from blind imitation.

2) A plan of action toward the goal embodied by 'laws' and 'obligations'. These two essential parts are grounded in two things:

A) **Moral codes:** Laws which are ordained for the attainment of virtues, refinement of the soul and inner purification. Due to the innate and universal nature of virtues and values, most of these laws are intrinsic and not extrinsic.

B) **Juristic laws,** which can be classified into two:

I. **Primary laws:** Primary laws are based upon the fixed needs of human beings, and can never be changed or modified except in emergency cases and change of subject. For example, the compulsoriness of specific acts of worship, and organizing individual and social life economically, culturally and legally; the prohibition of killing, adultery and fornication, debauchery, breach of contract, and treachery. In reality, these laws are indicative of the fixed nature of man and the nature of his quadruple relationships: with himself, with God, with the universe, and with his fellow human individuals.

II. Secondary laws: These laws shall be prescribed, as needs of individual or social life arise, and are based upon secondary causes and motives. In such cases, the ruler (*h̩kim*) prescribes laws to address those needs. If those needs are removed, those laws shall also be abrogated. Since the issuance of the secondary laws is also based upon legal needs, these laws shall be also considered conditional and the changes in them related to a certain case.

In order to conclude the plan of action for reaching the goal of life, one point requires to be taken into earnest consideration: since God has entrusted human beings with identification of subjects, oughts and ought-nots and virtues and vices in relation to individual and social life. Thus, Islamic laws are prescribed on the basis of those very identified subjects; like the importance of farming for the community that makes it an indispensible activity. However, in some cases, the identity of the subjects is specified by the primary Islamic sources; for example, the ritual prayer (¥al̩t) whose actions and recitations are determined by the Islamic sources; foster care (ir¤i') which renders unlawful the marriage to a foster sister or a foster brother and the like.[1]

Now, in view of the definition we have just proposed of life and religion, we can briefly enumerate the causes of the need for religion in human life, as follows:

I. The definition we have offered of 'intelligible life' cannot be realized without professing religion.

---

1. For further information on the permanent and the variables, see Mu̩ammad Taq¢ Ja'far¢, Tarjumeh wa Tafs¢r-e Nahj al-Bal̩ghah, pp. 243-309.

II. It is impossible to provide an ultimate answer to the most basic questions of life, i.e. (1) Who am I? (2) Whence have I come? (3) Where have I come? (4) Who am I with? (5) Where am I heading to? (6) Why have I come?, without resorting to religion which addresses them in the following words,

> *Indeed we belong to Allah, and to Him do we indeed return.*[1]

III. If there is no necessity for religion in life, no virtue and value can be ever demonstrated.

IV. No one and no school of thought can face the school of *might-is-right* and *survival-of-the-fittest*, according to which life is only meant for the powerful, without relying on religion.

V. Ignoring religion in life leads to the decline of human transcendent feeling of the magnificence of the universe—a feeling which without an extra-mundane Wisdom and Will is meaningless.

VI. It is impossible to give an ultimate and profound interpretation of the sensible and intellectual beauties without religion.

VII. Religion intensifies the transcendent sense of duty and maintains it. This transcendent sense of duty is different from the rules required for human natural life and establishment of order. Without this pure feeling, man will be reduced into a beast devoid of feeling and intelligence.

Secondly, everyone is supposed to clarify the reason behind the need for religion in keeping with his knowledge of himself and the things around him. Since religion is a public phenomenon and does not merely belong to a specific social class say the intellectuals, then the debate on the reason why we need religion in life is a public issue.

Of course it goes without saying that as one's scope of knowledge of an issue determines his approach to it, one's answer to the question of why one needs to turn to religion is a function of her/his scope of knowledge of religion as a whole. If

---

1. S£rat al-Baqarah 2:156.

s/he has no knowledge whatsoever of religion's nature her/his answer to the abovementioned question will take the form of a blind prescription of the *totally unknown*. However, with even the least knowledge of oneself and the universe, it is possible for a person to entertain this question: "With my ideas, beliefs and usual skills I must have for the natural life, should I have other ideas, beliefs and activities in the name of religion?" This is the first degree of knowledge that prompts a person to ask about the reason behind the need for religion. As one's knowledge about himself, God, the universe, and society increases, the question about religion and the need for it gets more serious. However, when skepticism or a sort of selfishness intoxicates him he loses interest in concluding his knowledge.

Thirdly, whereas the most fundamental questions in life are raised by the primordial nature (*fitrah*) and common sense, and not by a speculative reason. If we consider these two important faculties as factors that turn us to religion — without considering the fact that religion has emphasized the two and their components — the question about the reason behind the need for religion turns out to be an extra-religious question; in the sense that It does not have its origin in religion or religious texts. As such, the answer to be given to it by reason must also be extra-religious, otherwise it would be [a fallacy of] begging the question (*petitio principi*).[1]

However, if we consider the primordial nature, common sense and their consequences as things religion has emphasized and called upon, it follows that the question on the reason behind the need for religion as well as the positive answer to it will be regarded as intera-religious issues. Thus, no one can claim with total certainity that the question of necessity of religion is an extra-religious question and its answer is certainly an intera-religious one.

---

1. If the answer to the question "does man need a religion?" is to be taken from religion itself, it follows that an answer is already prepared from that which is asked, i.e. religion. This is while religion (and the need for it) is yet to be proven, let alone providing an answer to the question.

If we proceed to demonstrate the necessity of religion in the wake of primordial nature and common sense, one can feasibly claim that this question has its origin in the basic fundamentals of religion itself. In this regard, two points are worth mentioning:

I. In our view, not only should those individuals, who have not yet chosen their religion, question the reason behind the need for religion, the believers can also ask the same question, and to do by no means contradicts devotion and religiosity, rather it is also regarded as one of the foundations of religion, because it is based upon axioms of primordial nature and common sense.

II. This question is a perennial one as until human education is incapable of achieving human perfection at once it will continue to be asked.

We should also take it inot consideration that reviewing the key questions and issues of intelligible life not only does have its own particular avails rather it is necessary. This is because a profound understanding is something essential for a discernible, justifiable and purposeful life. Relying on predecessors' beliefs and established proofs, no matter how brilliant they were, can not help one to have a truly purposeful life. For this reason, all Shī'ah philosophers, theologians, jurists, and exegetes maintain that belief in the articles of faith (u¥ūl al-dīn) must be based on reasoning and not imitation except for those who are incapable of reasoning and thinking.

Fourthly, in order to elucidate the reason behind the need for religion, one can use the empirical, deductive and intuitive methods (scientific, philosophical and mystical methods), but one needs to take heed of the realities in which movement is possible and can be followed through experiment, evidence, reasoning, unveiling, and intuition. Here we shall point out some of these realities as examples:

I. Refining human mind of influences that hinder the activity of the primordial nature, common sense and conscience. It is through this refinement that man will become ready to perceive the truth, whether this truth is related to religion or not.

II. Since the trend toward religion has its origin in human primordial sense of pursuit of perfection and purpose in life then one needs to demonstrate it through rational proofs and intuitive facts.

III. Proving the existence of an order and harmony in humanity and the world through scientific laws.

IV. Proving the interdependence of cosmic objects: such interdependence affirms their dependence on an independent and self-governing Truth. This is a rational rule:

> Everything which is occurring on something else requires a substance/ reason is a telling witness to our claim

V. A transcendent sense of consciousness; that is, this feeling:

The world, galaxy and stars would be a plaything/ if this long day of the terrestrial had no tommorrow.[1]

If there is really no Origin (*mabda'*) and Resurrection (*ma'¡d*), then not only are fate, stars, virtues, and values nothing but playthings of the natural and animal life, but this would also be a place of struggle for survival, and mastery of the powerful, in which one would not officially recognize anyone except himself. If there is really no Origin and Resurrection, all the sacrifices of the noble and pure-hearted for the sake of rendering service to human beings, whose existence has been willed by God, would become futile and useless. If there is really no Origin and Resurrection, to die for the sake of defending human rights and to refrain from sensual pleasures would be sheer folly.

VI. There has been no authentic and deep-seated factor throughout history like religion, which provides peace of mind to people.

It is not distorted, or infused with obsolete concepts, which are practically unfeasible in the context of natural life.

VII. Intuition of a type of transcendent magnificence in the

---

1. N¡¥ir Khusr£, D¢w¡n-e Ash'¡r, Elegy 241.

world, which cannot be reached unless through existential expansion of "ego". This is the same intuition, which is possessed not only by mystics ('uraf₁) but also by great scholars. **Fifthly**, is man an afflicted and wretched being, and can only religion remove this affliction and wretchedness? Is there another formula that can play the role of religion? Discussing the cause and need for religion, we have pointed out the answer to this question. We shall now examine it in more specific and telling terms.

As to the first part of the question, it must be stated that man is not afflicted rather s/he has a lost one s/he must find. Definitely, this truth, whatever is its name, must have the answer to his basic questions, and failure to offer the answers will end up in no less than a nihilist impasse, which many people today suffer from.

A positive answer to these fundamental questions is vital. Modern man, in view of his disregard for these questions, is not willing to accept any principle. As such, he lives in 'today' and has neither 'yesterday' nor 'tomorrow'. To put it otherwise, if a person lives in comfort, ease and pleasure today, he has everything including the past and the future. For this reason, it can be asserted that contemporary man is haunted by *present*. The source of all principles and laws that determine human duty in relation to the quadruple relationships is lost, i.e. religion. That which is lost is not something imaginary. It confirms all realities and without it, nothing can be considered good or bad.

Yet, the factor which prompts a person to find himself first and then his lost item is to pay attention to the fact that man is a meaningful part of a logo-centric world, and in order to bring to fruition his potential, he must practically observe certain principles. From the religious perspective, people can perceive themselves as well as the philosophy behind man's creation from the Origin of creation. It is by means of understanding this reality that a person can find himself first and then his lost item (religion).

But as to the second part of the question, it must be noted that first of all, some people have turned away from religion and replaced it with notions like universal ethics, universal rights, global culture, and finally 'humanism' the fascinating of all modern terms. And, neither theoretically nor practically, these terms could show what has essentially been lost.

On the other hand, even if man can take these concepts out of academia and put them into practice, their supposed claims can only ensure a wholesome life in the realm of natural and social relations. While the real lost one that has to address the sextuple questions will remain unknown as one can easily infer from the status quo of eastern and western societies. To hide the true nature of the lost item from their people, the egotist authorities of these communities has discovered a strong drug, i.e. living in every possible condition.

Sixthly, it has become clear so far that the need for religion is a real need whose essence does not change with the change of man's perception about himself, the world and religion. The essence of the need for religion—as an extra-human reality—is something fixed and it does not change with the changes in man's perceptions about himself and the world he lives in. Religion is indeed related both to man and his life. This relation is inalterable whether it emanates from superficial elements or genuine factors because man's essence and its basic elements are inalterable.

Religion is related to man and his life just as intellection, feelings, self-love or self-preservation are related to man. Thus, even if human perceptions of the quadruple relationships change, the essence of intellection, feelings and self-preservation will never change.

If it is assumed that a time will come when man will lose his essential reality as well as his feelings, willpower, intellect, and desire for self- preservation, there will be no human beings then, let alone their essential features,like inclination to religion and its need.

Chapter 2
Scope of Jurisprudence

If jurisprudence (*fiqh*) refers to the laws prescribed by God, in the individual and social dimension of human life in the shape of obligations and prohibitions, then it does not encompass religion as a whole. The scope of religion is much larger than that of jurisprudence. But if one takes jurisprudence in its general sense which includes the higher and the lesser jurisprudence, religion will be coextensive with it.

If one sees jurisprudence as a part of religion, then s/he has to distinguish between the ideal of religion and that of jurisprudence. The ideal of religion consists of addressing every issue regarding the quadruple relationships in two realms of "is-ness" and "ought-ness". It is clear that these issues include beliefs, laws, duties, all types of divine and human rights, and discerning one's place in the world. The ideal of jurisprudence lies in the declaration of all laws pertaining individual and collective duties and rights in the realm of obligations and prohibitions. In fact, human life in the world is meant to bring to fruition his personality while moving toward eternal life. Without laws this very important enterprise with turn impossible. That is why God has conveyed these laws to His servants. The ideal of jurisprudence is that the jurisprudential laws encompass all aspects of activities and self-restrictions that are significant in bringing human personality to fruition.

The ideal of religion lies in giving answers to the questions of a person in dealing with the quadruple relationships, and human ideal lies in mobilizing every possibility in individual and social spheres to bring to fruition his personality while moving toward eternal life. The quadruple relationships are pursued in two domains, i.e. domains of "isness" and "oughtness". It is needless to say that these relationships must be organized according to all natural, rational, and moral sciences that guide along the path of human perfection.

Human Relationship with Himself

The two basic elements of the ideal of religion in this domain are: self-knowledge and self-building.

Self-Knowledge

The basic proofs of religion—consisting of Qur'ịnic verses, traditions (a'ịdīth), rational proofs, and consensus (ijmị')—regarding the need for self-knowledge are so many that there is no need for further elaboration. We shall mention some of them here:

Qur'ịnic Verses underlining the necessity of self-knowledge:

> *Soon We shall show them Our signs in the horizons and in their own souls.*[1]

> *In the earth are signs for those who have conviction, and in your own souls [as well]. Will you not then perceive?*[2]

> *And do not be like those who forget Allah, so He makes them forget their own souls.*[3]

> *Does not man remember that We created him before when he was nothing?*[4]

It goes without saying that man can realize his past state of nothingness if he has already advanced and touched perfection. Therefore, the requisite of understanding the past and its nature is to understand the present state.

> *Rather man is a witness to himself, though he should offer his excuses.*[5]

---

1. Sịrat Fuẓẓilat 41:53.
2. Sịrat al-Dhịriyịt 51:20.
3. Sịrat al-°ashr 59:19.
4. Sịrat Maryam 19:67.
5. Sịrat al-Qiyịmah 75:14-15.

It is for sure that reflecting on this great feature can either be through the primordial nature (*fitrah*) and common sense, or through in-depth study and research. In both cases, knowing oneself indicates growth [in a person].

> *We certainly created man in the best of forms.*[1]

> *And in your creation [too], and whatever animals that He scatters abroad, there are signs for a people who have certainty.*[2]

There are numerous Qur'ānic verses stating the superb order of the physical constitution and the greatness of human soul as well as her amazing faculties. There is no doubt that it is not only a reality but also encourages and urges man to know himself. A person who does not know himself is not different from animals. In fact, in terms of guidance, his condition is worse than animals. In this regard, God says:

> *They are like cattle; rather they are more astray.*3

> *Traditions highlighting the emergency of self-knowledge*
> *He who knows himself knows his Lord.*[4]

This tradition has been widely quoted by religious authorities and scholars. We all know that no knowledge is greater and more essential than the knowledge of God. Therefore, self-knowledge as the prerequisite of such a highly respected knowledge proves to be most essential and indispensible of all human knowledge .

> *The true gnostic is he who knows his worth.*[5]

> *To recognize one as ignorant suffices it to know that he does not know his worth.*[6]

---

1. Sūrat al-Tīn 95:4.
2. Sūrat al-Jāthiyah 45:4.
3. Sūrat al-A'rāf 7:179.
4. Āmadī, Ghurar al-ḥikam wa Durar al-Kalam, vol. 5, p. 194.
5. Nahj al-Balāghah, Sermon 103.
6. Ibid.

He who is ignorant of his worth transgresses his due limit.[1]

He who knows himself touches the perfection.[2]

The following traditions prove the necessity of self-building in the realm of "ought-ness".

He who manages himself knows management [and executes it, be it for himself or for others].[3]

Is it not so that an individual with all his talents and existential dimensions represents humanity as a whole?

Examine yourself in terms of individual perfections you've acquired.[4]

The best of Allah's servants in His sight is he, who helps Allah in regards to himself (his self-building).[5]

Whoever keeps himself with other than it, shall remain overwhelmed in darkness.[6]

"The worst of dealings is, for you to evaluate the world with yourself."

That is, to take the world in exchange with yourself in a barter trade.

That is, in this world, every person must utilize his potential for the sake of self-building.

Self-building

Quranic Verses underlining Self-building

Indeed the noblest of you in the sight of Allah is the most God-wary among you.[7]

There are numerous Qur'¡nic verses enjoining God-wariness (*taqw¡*). *Taqw¡* means complete protection of the self from

---

1. Ghurar al-°ikam wa Durar al-Kalim, vol. 5, p. 197.
2. Ibid., p. 208.
3. Ibid.
4. Nahj al-Bal¡ghah, Sermon 222.
5. Ibid., Sermon 87.
6. Ibid., Sermon 157.
7. S£rat al-°ujur¡t 49:13.

pollution and impurity as well as self-refinement, to deserve eternal bliss.

O, you who have faith! Take care of your own souls. He who strays cannot hurt you if you are guided.[1]

The importance of self-building is such that if all people are misguided, every person must reform himself.

If you do good, you will do good to your [own] souls, and if you do evil, it will be [evil] for them.[2]

But as for him who is awed to stand before his Lord and forbids the soul from [following] desire, his refuge will indeed be paradise.[3]

O, you who have faith! Save yourselves and your families from the Fire.[4]

The verses in the Noble Qur'ın enjoin self-building in various ways. For example:

1. Verses which state that every person shall see his soul on the Day of Judgment the way he moulds it:

And every soul shall be recompensed fully for what it has earned.[5]

2. Verses which indicate that real loss belongs to those who let themselves incur a loss:

Say, 'Shall we inform you about the biggest losers in regard to actions? Those, whose endeavors go awry in the life of the world, while they suppose they are doing good'.[6]

Indeed the losers are those who have ruined themselves and their families on the Day of

---

1. S£rat al-Mı'idah 5:105.
2. S£rat al-Isrı' (or Banç Isrı'çl) 17:7.
3. S£rat an-Nızi'ıt 79:40-41.
4. S£rat al-Tahrçm 66:6.
5. S£rat ıl 'Imrın 3:25.
6. S£rat al-Kahf 18:103-105.

Resurrection.[1]

According to Islam, every type of knowledge or learning which can be acquired in a course of time must be utilized in both realms of isness and oughtness. Of course, this epistemic openness does not contradict the existence of some universal principles in intelligible life as conceived in Islam. Islam uses this universal principles to address the constant needs both in unchanging and changing realms.

The ideality of Islam and Islamic jurisprudence in this domain lies in the fact that Islam sets some primordial beliefs and rules that address human permanent and changing needs pertaining his relationship with himself.

We shall quote some examples of these beliefs and rules hereunder:

Beliefs in the Realm of Self-Knowledge as It Is

I. Man possesses a body and soul.

II. According to Divine Wisdom, man has been created for a lofty goal, which he must strive hard to achieve.

III. The goal of human life is to bring his personality to fruition for eternity through exposing himself to divine radiations.

IV. The basic factors that help human advancement toward perfection along the path of supreme telos are his transcendent feelings, intellection and pure conscience (*fitrah*).

V. If by making use of the above factors, man does not attain any spiritual growth the ground is paved for him to become a beast.

VI. Man has lofty positive faculties as well as lowly negative traits.

VII. Man has an essential dignity, which can pave the ground for ideal (acquired) dignity through God-wariness (*taqwị*).

VIII. Man's basic talent after perceiving the origin and goal of life is his capacity for social life.

---

1. S£rat al-Sh£rị 42:45.

IX. Man seals a contract for social life.

X. Man has an infinite potential for perfection in the physical domain as well as in the stages of spiritual growth, through teaching, learning, intuition, mystical unveiling (*iktishᵢfᵢt*), and practical inquiry.

XI. Among human positive gifts is his committed freedom. The scope of his responsibilities is stated in jurisprudence and ethics. The sources of these beliefs are the Qur'ᵢn, *Sunnah*, reason (*'aql*), and the consensus (consensus) of all learned men in every period and society, whose members possess a high level of culture.

Rules in the Realm of Self-Knowledge as It Ought to be

I. Man must know himself as much as he can, and he must strive hard to reform and enhance his personality. Then one should keep oneself away from "self-alienation".[1]

II. It is necessary to provide amenities for a decent life. Negligence in providing the amenities for a decent life is forbidden.

III. It is necessary to change an environment that fosters moral and religious corruption. It is unlawful to lead a life in such an environment.

IV. It is essential to have self-esteem. It is unlawful to tolerate meanness, contempt and anything that undermines nobility.

V. It is necessary to learn as much as possible whatever is essential for intelligible life. It is unlawful to refrain from learning it.

VI. It is necessary to be concerned as much as possible with what is good and evil for society. It is unlawful to be indifferent

---

1. The proofs of the prohibition of abandoning the prescribed have been debated by some authorities, but in view of the definite evil of abandoning fundamental obligatory acts, the prohibition of abandoning them is indisputable whether this is based upon verbal or rational proofs. Nevertheless, we deem it necessary to prove this prohibition categorically for the sake of emphasis.

and apathetic to the welfare or corruption of society.

VII. It is necessary to strive hard for the enhancement of constructive abilities and discovery of what is essential for individual and social life.

VIII. It is necessary to stage a serious campaign against anything that can corrupt the soul. It is forbidden to excuse the self from facing the agents of corruption and be indifferent to them.

IX. It is necessary to seek to have committed freedom. It is unlawful to prevent the self from facing the factors that could possibly achieve comitted freedom in the realm of values.

X. It is necessary to establish free connection with the amenities of the world so that they become man's possession. Man's possession of any amenity of the world is prohibited which leads to his expected downfall.

Since these beliefs and rules lie in the domain of rational, primordial and moral self-building, one can understand their basis without resorting to sophisticated reasoning. By obtaining the basis and cause of each of them, the necessary rules (obligatory) and meritorious rules (recommendatory) can also be understood. For example, it is essential to know, reform, and advance, to rescue the self from ignorance and self-alienation. In order to achieve this goal, it is obligatory to undertake a bit of mental or rational activities. In the parlance of jurisprudence, these are called *mustahabbįt* (recommendatory acts). In the above example, it is obligatory for one to increase his knowledge about himself to the extent necessary and to deal with terms above that necessary.

HumanRelationship with God

The ideal of religion in this relationship has two elements: beliefs in the realm of human relationship with God and, rules in the realm of man's relationship with God.

Beliefs in the Realm of Human Relationship with God

Beliefs in the realm of human relationship with God are as follows:

I. God is the One and Only Being. He has no partner and equal. He is the All-knowing, the All-mighty, the Most Just, and the Most Wise.

II. God is the Creator of the entire universe who created it with His absolute will and perfect wisdom.

III. God is above everything. He encompasses everything and is needless of all things.

IV. God possesses all the Perfect Attributes of Beauty and Glory. Although the concepts of His Attributes are generally understandable to human beings, their ultimate essence or nature is beyond human comprehension.

V. God is beyond the universe, time, and any determinate or indeterminate space. He is eternal, everlasting and infinite.

VI. Of all the creatures in the universe, He bestows special grace and favor to man so that he can expose himself to divine radiation by acquiring knowledge and making sincere practical efforts.

VII. God reflects rays of His Lights into the hearts of those who succeed in observing the rules of Allah (¡d¡b All¡h) and emulating the manners of Allah (akhl¡q All¡h).

VIII. Man is a being created according to the divine wisdom and perfect will of God.

IX. The perpetuity of human existence, as in the case of all other creatures, lies in the perpetuity of God's favor.

X. The power, means and laws which govern volitional acts of man—what he says, does and thinks as well as any other activity within him—come from God while the intention, decision and choice lies within man. For this reason, man is responsible for his volitional act.

XI. Man has the potential to achieve nearness (qurb) to God. This is the noblest of all power existing in man in relation to God and activated by knowledge and God-wariness.

XII. The quantity and quality of man's proximity to God are beyond every measure and description because there is no specific end for this state.

XIII. The love and mercy of God towards His servants is

vaster than anything else and His wrath or anger has something to do with the offense committed by the sinful person, and not as revenge in its common sense, which emanates from the defective and unpleasant feeling of the avenger.

XIV. Human self-oblivion and self-alienation leads to being forsaken by God, which in turn leads to his self-centeredness and self-interest.

Rules in the Realm of HumanRelationship with God

Since man can touch the truth in this life that all his actions (speeches, deeds, thoughts, intentions, and avoidances) are under the supervision of God, then as the noble verse states,

> Say, 'Indeed my prayer and my worship, my life and my death are all for the sake of Allah, the Lord of all the worlds'.[1]

One can choose his actions in such a way that they can be referred to God.

Referring those actions to God whose being obligatory (wᵢjib), recommendatory (mustahabb), unlawful (harᵢm), and abominable (makrūh) have been clarified by legislation and reason is perfectly clear and it needs no special proof. Regarding the permissible acts (mubᵢhᵢt), however, a certain mubᵢh action can be referred to God with the intention that with it one wants to break the monotony of life and be reinvigorated for actions that can be directly referred to God. In a nutshell, with the knowledge of the fact that the universe is [in] the presence of God and with the intention of being worthy to be in His presence, all actions and avoidances can be referred to God. The ideality of religion and its respective jurisprudence depends on the fact that it states the wisdom, nature and proofs of these rules in a rational and convincing fashion.

Human Relationship with the Universe

This relationship has two forms: human relationship with the universe as it is and as it ought to be:

---

1. Sₑrat al-An'ᵢm 6:162.

Human Relationship with the Universe as It is

Although man is apparently part of the universe, in view of great gifts s/he has been conferred, s/he can be a 'universe' vis-à-vis the universe. In fact, due to constructive search along the path of perfection, this being can reach a loftier station and his "ego" can encompass the entire universe. Nevertheless, the nature of this vast universe is like a very vast farm. Through the favor of the Gardener of the entire universe, the seeds of human talents and gifts germinate. This gift is immense [volume 1 of *Tarjumeh wa Shar*ı*-e Nahj al-Bal*ı*ghah*] Moreover, the power of personification, ingenuity and its varieties are still unknown to man. This is an evaluation of the human being "as s/he is".

Meanwhile, let us proceed to the universe "as it is". It is true that in the course of history, man has tried to know himself and the universe and has also achieved remarkable success. By knowing the general principles which describe that fundamental system of man and the universe and state human duties in it, he has been able to direct himself along the path of a purposeful life and this can guarantee his prosperity in the eternal life.

Since man *as s/he is to be* was discussed above under self-knowledge and we shall now deal with the general principles of the universe *as it is*. Some of these principles are:

I. The universe is real and it is not a product of the human mind.

II. The coming into existence of the universe is true in the sense that it is created by Divine Will and Wisdom, and not by accident which goes against the law.[1]

III. The universe can be known in two ways:

- The human mind develops a relationship with the universe like a mirror, only showing physical appearances. This is a superficial connection, which does not refer to anything beyond the object of

---

1. That the universe is true means that in addition to being real, the universe is worthy of coming into existence and subsisting.

experience.

- In addition to sensible observations and objective empirical experiments, the human mind can perceive the Divine signs as expressed in the astounding order and splendor of the universe. The Noble Qur'ın has strongly emphasized on acquisition of such vital knowledge about oneself and the universe. Philosophically speaking, one should say that without the universe's direct connection with God, which exhibits the existence of law, order, motion and other components dependent upon Him, man and the universe can not be interpreted and justified in a convincing fashion. It is in view of this aspect of the universe that we say that for the conscious person, this world is a vast place of worship.

IV. Like our knowledge of man, our knowledge of the universe is a product of two basic elements:

- The reality of man and the universe apart from the perceiving subjects.
- The connection of the perceiving subjects with their special features, as eye establishes connection with shapes and colors according to its particular constitution, and provides its special product of knowledge. By the same token, laboratories and any means of extending or increasing our knowledge, with all the special features they have, clarify our knowledge.[1]

V. Without referring to God, the universe is beyond understanding and interpretation, a plaything in which no moral virtue or value has any meaning.

Since the cosmic order is beyond our control and with utmost order and splendor, one cannot destroy the universe,

---

1. In a treatise I have written about the two basic elements of knowledge (reality for the self and reality for us), the fact is mentioned that our knowledge is influenced by nine factors.

create another universe as replacement and then say that we must create the entire universe in the way it is supposed to be.[1] This is because the world "as it is" is the same world in which we live as part of it.

Since our physical life and spiritual life is not possible without change, the components of the universe could not have come into existence without activity and effecting of change in the course of history. In fact, it can be said that without effecting change, mankind cannot survive for even a day.

Human Relationship with the Universe as It Ought to be

I. It is essential to know the universe as much as possible because knowing part of the world implies knowing a divine sign. This not only increases the knowledge of a person, but, affects his intelligible life, and contributes to his spiritual growth and perfection.

II. Changing parts of the world and conducting a pertinent research to secure an ideal life should not lead to the destruction of the environment. Regrettably, however, with utmost heedlessness the environment (land, air and sea) has been treated ruthlessly and is on the verge of total destruction.

III. Since nature has been provided by God for all, it should not be used in such a way that it is beneficial to some but detrimental to others. In this regard, the Holy Quran says:

> *It is He who created for you all that is in the earth then He turned to the heaven, and fashioned it into*

---

1. There are two reasons for our inability to create the universe as it is supposed to be. One is that our knowledge about the universe is so limited and even it cannot help us to know a particular unknown issue let alone the unknown of all unknown. In the words of Ni'¡m¢,

If someone knows how this universe came to existence/ thus he can bring it again into existence

The other reason is what we have mentioned earlier and whose implication is that the universe, in terms of the potentiality and actuality of its components and laws, has come into being and subsists in its optimum possible form. And overall change in it necessitates its destruction and bringing into existence another universe.

seven heavens, and He has knowledge of all things.[1]

Human Relationship with His Fellow Human Beings

This relationship also has two faces: as it is versus as it ought to be

Human Relationship with His Fellow Human Beings as It is

I. Man is an animal that lives collectively. Is the cause of this phenomenon, like the collective life of ants and termites, his intrinsic need, or is it because of his many needs and gifts, which cannot be addressed by individual life? The latter is the current view upon which man is conceived as a social being.

II. There are various natural (through blood), conventional (through marriage), internal, and external connections that man has with his fellow human beings, and each of these rapports is the source of specific rights and duties.

III. If there was no training, education, laws and penalties or, they didn't work well, there would be chaos due to human natural trend toward egotism and selfishness.

IV. There are two types of competitions among human individuals:

- Constructive competition that ends up in progress. It means accepting the equality and unity of all people along the path of intelligible life. It is obvious that this acceptance requires training and education as well as rational collective management. By realizing it human beings understand the life-giving Qur'ịnic verse which states that all are equal to one and one is equal to all:

  Whoever kills a soul, without [its being guilty of] manslaughter or corruption on the earth, is as though he had killed all mankind, and whoever saves a life is as though he had saved all mankind.[2]

- Fatal competition which ends up in destruction. In

---

1. Sịrat al-Baqarah 2:29.
2. Sịrat al-Mị'idah 5:27.

every society whenever divine religion or morality is unable to control rivalries, fatal rivalry prevails over constructive competitions. This is a specific manifestation of human selfishness and egoism, which only divine religion or morality can deal with. The compulsive psychological element of vengeance, retribution and stringent legalism stands in the way of the fatal rivalry in the physical sense, not uprooting it from human nature. The best witness to this are the wars, revolutions and uncommon conditions of social life in which retribution and laws fail to function and the people emancipate themselves from the inner chain of fatalism and revolt, and sometimes they are more savage than the predators in grappling with each other.

Human Relationship with His Fellow Human Beings as It Ought to be

I. Legal relations that have their origin in various human relationships with his fellow human individuals. We have mentioned the gist of these relationships under the heading "human relationship with his fellow human beings".

II. Just division of labor among all members of society

III. Harmonizing society and using its collective wisdom and conscience

IV. Dynamic and purposeful management of society

V. The most successful manager is one who regards all parts or members of the facility under his management as part of himself and himself as the collective "I" (personality).

VI. Everyone has to regard other members of society as members of the caravan that moves toward God along the path of "intelligible life".

VII. The members of any establishment must have the highest degree of expertise and commitment possible and assume responsibilities according to their disposition, but this disposition should not stand in the way of sublime perception and feelings for humanity.[1] For example, a judge with judicial expertise and commitment must never forget that he is a human being dealing with fellow human beings. An artist must acknowledge that he must always cultivate his artistic disposition with sublime feelings and perceptions.

VIII. Every human individual should struggle after fulfillment of the decent life. To put it otherwise, it is not merely up to the state to better the life condition rather all human individuals and groups should play their role as best as they can.

IX. Defending dignity, committed freedom and other fundamental human rights is necessary for every individual as we mentioned before.

X. Moral education of the people in society is essential. From the Islamic point of view, moral corruption of society is tantamount to its degeneration. The basic reason for the mission of the prophets, according to the saying of the Messenger of Allah (¥), is the fulfillment and perfection of the virtuous morality.

XI. In social relations, the primary principle is social welfare, justice and benevolence for all. In this regard, the Holy Qur'¡n says:

> *Allah does not forbid you in regard to those who did not make war against you on account of religion and did not expel you from you homes, that you deal with them with kindness and justice.[2]*

And in another verse, it states:

> *Certainly We sent Our apostles with manifest*

---

1. If a person is really committed, in principle his disposition must not stand in the way of his sublime feelings and perceptions about humanity. But, sometimes, since a particular person, as in the case of a judge, is bound to discharge prescribed duties, he may possibly commit a mistake due to various reasons. Since he is a human being, his being a judge must not make him forget his feelings and perceptions about human beings.
2. S£rat al-Mumtahanah 60:8.

proofs, and We sent down with them the Book and the Balance, so that mankind may maintain justice.[1]

It needs to be noted that the primary rule of human relationship with his fellow human individuals is justice. In his order to Malik al-Ashtar,[2] Imam Ali said:

> *O Malik! You must teach your heart the kindness, compassion and love for your subjects. Do not behave towards them as if you are a voracious and ravenous beast and your success lies in devouring them. Remember that among your subjects there are two kinds of people: those who have the same religion as you have; they are brothers to you, and those who have religions other than that of yours, they are human beings like you.*[3]

After these discussions on human quadruple relationships we now state in detail the conclusions, which we have earlier stated in brief.

As a whole, the ideality of a religion lies in the perfectness of the set of primordial and rational beliefs substantiated by clear proofs of material and spiritual guidance, as well as a whole jurisprudence, which can address all individual and social problems of man in both the physical and spiritual realms.

As it is suggested by Islamic philosophy and theology, the totality of fundamental beliefs such as the necessity for religion and the existence of the One and Only God who possesses all Attributes of Perfection like knowledge, power, wisdom, and justice, along with the 'internal proof' '(reason, pure human nature), and the 'external proof', i.e. prophets, mankind is guided towards the Supreme Telos of life. Human need for proof (ḥujjah) is a perennial one. Accordingly, Shī'ah believes

---

1. Sūrat al-ʿadīd 57:25.
2. Mālik al-Ashtar: more fully, Mālik ibn ʿᵢrith from Nakha' and better known as al-Ashtar, was among the prominent commanders of Imām 'Alī's army and the governor appointed to Egypt by the Imām, but on his way to Egypt, he was killed through the conspiracy of Mu'āwiyah. For the text of the Imām's famous order to him before heading to Egypt, see Nahj al-Balāghah, Letter 53. [Trans.]
3. Nahj al-Balāghah, Letter 53. [Trans.]

that after the Holy Prophet of Islam (¥), the pure Imjms ('a) are the proofs of God on earth. Like the Prophets ('a), the Imjms are infallible (ma'¥ūm) and are immune from sin and error. After Imjms come the accomplished scholars ('ulamj') and jurists (fuqahj) who are impervious to carnal urges and possess extraordinary justice. Their justice and knowledge of the totality of the roots and branches of religion are below that of the Infallibles (ma'¥ūmīn) ('a). The basis of this claim is the famous tradition which reads:

"And of the fuqahj, whoever is wary of himself, opposes his carnal desires and obeys the command of His Master, it is incumbent upon the people to follow him."

It can be inferred from the term ¥j'inan (wary) that justice ('adjlah), which is one of the conditions set for the marja' al-taqlīd,[1] is above the term 'adjlah in jurisprudence (fiqh), deducible from the ¥ahīhah (authentic narration) of 'Abd Alljh ibn Abī Ya'fūr.[2]

This is what is meant by 'adjlah of the marja'al-taqlīd in the Shī'ah world, that he is not even supposed to entertain in his mind the wish or inclination to go against religion and morality. This is the very meaning of "wariness" [moral integrity] and "opposing carnal desire". It has been the observance of this condition of purity throughout the history of Shī'ism that the Shī'ah have unconditionally followed the marjji'al-taqlīd in self-sacrifice and struggled along the correct path.

It can be concluded from the previous discussions that the ideality of Islamic jurisprudence includes the perfectness of

---

1. Marja' al-taql¢d (literally means 'source of emulation') : a scholar of proven learning and piety whose authoritative rulings one follows in matters of religious practice. [Trans.]

2. The description of 'adjlah in the ¥a!¢!ah of 'Abd Alljh ibn Ab¢ Ya'f£r on the authority of Imjm Ja'far al-¯jdiq ('a) is as follows: "I asked the Imjm ('a): 'How to know the justice of a Muslim may his testimony in favor or against them be accepted?' The Imjm ('a) said: 'Whoever is known in modesty, purity and wariness in food and sexual desire, whose hands and tongue are free from error and shuns away from major sins, God gives good news to him.'" Shaykh al-An¥jr¢, Al-Makjsib al-Mu!arramah, p. 325.

laws, which help plan a social life that addresses human relationship with fellow human beings.

Salient Features of Islamic Jurisprudence

We shall now embark on examining the salient features of Islamic jurisprudence.

First Feature

Fiqh means "knowledge of religious laws based on their circumstantial proofs".[1] The subject of jurisprudence covers all human actions — inward or outward, spoken or unspoken. From this definition, we can realize that jurisprudence is different from its sources. Juristic views are within the context of Islamic sources; that is, the Qur'¡n, the *Sunnah*, consensus of scholars (*ijm¡'*), and reason (*'aql*). This does not mean, however, that Islamic jurisprudence is identical with the juristic views of the jurists. This is also true in the case of Islamic philosophy vis-à-vis the views of Muslim philosophers in the sense that all Muslim philosophers have moulded their philosophies within the framework of the Islamic outlook so as to keep their ideas in tune with Islamic *weltanschauung*. This does not imply, however, that Islamic philosophy is identical with the views of those philosophers. The existing facts in Islamic sources are one thing and the fuqah¡'s understanding of them as 'jurisprudence' is something else. This is the connotation of classifying *fuqah¡* as *mu¥īb* (well-chosen) and *mukhtī'* (mistaken).

Therefore, the basic source of the ideality of jurisprudence, legal system and judiciary program must be sought from the Book of Allah, the *Sunnah*, *ijm¡'*, and *'aql*, although the interpretation of the *fuqah¡* from the primary sources also gives additional knowledge of the various aspects of juristic rules. This is particularly true if we consider the fact that [even]

---

1. Of course, by 'knowledge' we mean the means of discovering the realities, whether its basis is intrinsic such as knowledge of rationally independent laws and knowledge of the essential decrees in jurisprudence, or its basis can be proven through rational prepositions and other primary sources of jurisprudence.

fuqah¡'s occasional juristic slips in the course of deducing laws (*istimb¡t¡t*) has a juristic significance.

Second Feature

Intelligible life lies at the heart of Islam, according to all Islamic sources, and through it man is supposed to bring his personality to fruition and embark on the path of eternity. This is why the right to a decent life has been declared the most fundamental decree in all juristic sources and any obstruction in this path is seriously banned. There are numerous textual and verbal evidences that substantiate this thoughtful approach to life:

I. According to the divine value system, every human being is equivalent to all human beings:

> *That is why We decreed for the Children of Israel that whoever takes a life, without [its being guilty of] manslaughter or corruption on the earth, is as though he had killed all mankind, and whoever saves a life is as though he had saved all mankind.*[1]

The human value equation according to this verse and other Islamic sources is as follows: 1 = all and all = 1

We must also bear in mind that "Children of Israel" [in this context] does not refer to a specific race or nation; rather, it refers to those people who have truly followed the religion of Prophet Ibr¡hīm (Abraham) ('a), and any community or nation that follows the religion of Abraham must regard the above mentioned equation as a definite principle. For this reason, one needs to say that Islam, Christianity or any other religion whose Abrahamic origin has been proved must subscribe to the abovementioned principle.

II. No law or duty in Islam is suspended except when it harms human life, nor applicable to a person who is to be harmed; for example, the non-compulsoriness of ablution (*wu¤ū*) to a person for whom the use of water is harmful, and

---

1. S£rat al-M¡'idah 5:32.

the non-compulsoriness of °ajj pilgrimage for a person who is incapable of travelling.

III. Any person who is downtrodden and abject in life and can emancipate himself from this state, yet he does not strive for it shall earn Divine wrath:

> *Indeed those whom the angels take away while they are wronging themselves, they ask, 'What state were you in?' They reply, 'We were abased in the land.' They say, 'Was not Allah's earth vast enough so that you might migrate in it?' The refuge of such shall be hell, and it is an evil destination.*[1]

IV. Islamic jurisprudential sources have 32 legal provisions regarding the animal rights.[2] It is indeed needless to say that a divine religion which has prescribed some rights for animals must have provided a perfect legal system for human rights.

In view of these two points, it can be established that the basis of Islamic jurisprudence is man. Therefore, the scope of Islamic jurisprudence is equivalent to human dimensions of 'intelligible life'.

Third Feature

Islamic jurisprudence (*fiqh*) or the legal system responds to all problems in life by opening the door of *ijtihᵢd*[3] in all periods.[4]

---

1. S£rat al-Nisᵢ' 4:97.
2. See M. T. Jafari, Tarjumeh wa Tafsₑr-e Nahj al-Balᵢghah, vol. 12, pp. 165-185.
3. Ijtihᵢd: juristic derivation of laws applicable to new conditions on the basis of the general principles laid down in the Qur'an and the Sunnah. [Trans.]
4. If we regard jurisprudence (fiqh) as "knowledge of religious laws based on their circumstantial proofs," then it must be noted that it is a set of laws—pertaining to different subjects which man encounters in life. The function of fiqh is to state the ruling for every subject. In other words, the role of fiqh is to specify the ruling for every issue. In fact, if fiqh is perfect, its ideality is due to the universality and comprehensiveness of its laws as well as to the quality and nature of rulings it states. Those who have imagined that if we subscribe to the correct proposition that "there is a ruling for every subject or issue," in reality we have also believed in the wrong conclusion that "All our problems are jurisprudential in nature and jurisprudence has the solution to all our problems." Such fellows have actually confused two things, without knowing

that the proposition "There is a ruling for every subject or issue" does not necessarily follow that "All our problems are jurisprudential in nature and jurisprudence has the solution to all our problems." It is wrong to say that "All our problems are jurisprudential in nature and jurisprudence has the solution to all our problems." Yes, fiqh which has a ruling for every problem does not claim that by stating their rulings, all issues and problems can be solved. For example, if fiqh rules that burying nuclear wastes in any region is ¡ar¡m (unlawful) as it causes environmental pollution and endangers the lives of people and animals, the same fiqh does not claim that by stating this ruling, it has also presented the solution and way of preventing the burying of nuclear wastes. Of course, it is necessary, for the jurists (fuqah¡) must constantly supervise the presentation of all solutions pertaining different subjects in order to avoid any contradiction between scientific methods and solutions, on one hand, and religious laws and guidelines, on the other hand.

To state the matter otherwise, firstly, fiqh must have supervision over all programs and methods experimental sciences offer so that these programs and methods do not contradict or encroach upon religious laws and guidelines. Secondly, if we say the role or function of fiqh is not to present a method or program, but to state the rulings on subjects. This statement is only correct in some instances. It means that in most cases, fiqh states the rulings on issues and subjects but there are also cases in which it also presents the program or method of solving a problem. For example, in a case that the husband and wife can no longer live together harmoniously, fiqh has specifically prescribed divorce (§alaq). But at the same time, the sources of jurisprudence (for example, in the Holy Qur'an) have offered a method or program which is suitable to solve husband and wife differences, and that is, to appoint a wise person from the wife's family and his counterpart from the husband's family to investigate and solve the couple's problem in this way. It is to be noted that in such a case, jurisprudence has not only stated a ruling but also presented a method or program for solving the couple's dispute. Moreover, even here, granted that jurisprudence does not offer a plan for solving the couple's problem, is not the stipulation of divorce, in itself, a sort of plan for solving the lack of understanding and harmony between husband and wife?

Here, it is noteworthy that sometimes a certain ruling in itself is only a matter of stating a ruling for a certain subject or problem, but for another subject or problem, it is a kind of program or method. For example, the stipulation of divorce is a legal and logical method or plan of solving the issue or problem of dispute between husband and wife that can no longer live together. Yet, the same stipulation of divorce for a disputing couple (but not to the extent that they can no longer live together in harmony) is a mere ruling, and not a method or plan for solving dispute.

Thirdly, until the accurate definition of the plan and the nature and conditions of its connection to other things are not clarified, one cannot easily state the correct meaning of the proposition, "Jurisprudence gives a ruling but does not

A few years ago, the Faculty of Law of the University of Paris, held a conference with the aim of discussing Islamic jurisprudence. The theme was "Islamic Jurisprudence Week", and a group of orientalists and law professors from European and Muslim countries were invited. During the conference sessions, legal experts of France and other countries, as well as well-known orientalists, acknowledged the comprehensiveness of Islamic jurisprudence, confirming its competence for human societies in all periods. During the conference, the head of lawyers in Paris said: "I do not know how to reconcile these two things. On the one hand, through various propaganda campaigns, it is known everywhere that Islamic jurisprudence, notwithstanding its profundity, is not competent to serve as the legislative foundation of the needs of contemporary societies. On the other hand, in these conference sessions, in the course of presentation of scholarly studies and intellectual inquiries by experts in the field, I have learned certain points that refute those misconceptions through solid proofs and existing textual evidence and rulings." At the end of the conference, a resolution signed by the participants who were lawyers and legislators was issued, confirming the dynamism of Islamic jurisprudence and its competence to respond to all problems of human society. At the closing program, all participants

---

offer a program or method." If "plan" refers to the logical guiding mechanism of a subject to its intended purpose while taking into account the existing obstacles and possibilities, it must be said that each of the jurisprudential rulings (in most cases) on each subject is only a ruling and not a plan. Yet, the totality of the same jurisprudential rulings is a plan regarding man, in the sense that as a set of obligations and prohibitions, these rulings guide a person, while taking into account the existing obstacles and potentials in him, to a transcendent goal. Therefore, each of the laws is a ruling for a subject pertaining to a person in one way or another. Yet, as a whole, the same laws are not rulings for the subject "man" but rather a plan for the guidance of man for an intelligible and noble life. Apart from the abovementioned points, it is worth mentioning that the totality of these laws by themselves—by taking into account the fuqahī's deduction of laws and subjects which is at the disposal of an expert—can be used as plans for solving legal problems on different subjects. [Ed.]

expressed their interest in continuing the "Islamic Jurisprudence Week" but unfortunately, due to some reasons, it was not continued.[1]

Fourth Feature

A perfect religion refers to primordial and rational beliefs substantiated by clear proofs guiding man in all his dimensions — physical and spiritual — while perfect jurisprudence offers the solution to all legal problems — individual and social — as to the quadruple relationships (human relationship with himself, God, the universe, and fellow human beings). Therefore, any legal or even moral system is "Islamic" proportionate to the degree of its consistency and compatibility with Islamic beliefs, jurisprudence and laws. For instance, in societies where the people believe in the One God and His Attributes of Glory, they believe in Islam to that extent. Societies whose people avoid killing, committing adultery, using liquors, telling lies, vilification, treason, and violating human rights actually observe the Islamic laws to that extent. People who regard order, law and honesty in life as essential and act upon them observe Islam to that extent. For this reason, when one of the Islamic figures returned home from his travel to some Western countries where he studied their way of life, he was asked to comment on the state of affairs there as compared to his own country. He said that if a person from an officially Muslim country travels to some Western countries and imagines that he goes to an absolutely un-Islamic society is absolutely wrong.

Fifth Feature

The alternative legal systems have been designed to organize and better the fourth type of human relationship (human relationship with his fellow human beings) in natural social life, and get things ready for its realization, by regulating the insatiable desires of man that lead to fatal rivalry. As to

---

1. ±ịhị 'Abd al-Bịq¢, Dawlat al-Qur'ịn, pp. 187-189.

what extent they have correctly understood the stated goal is another story. However, Islamic jurisprudence regulates the insatiable desires of man through principles and laws that are compatible with all four types of relationship (human relationship with himself, God and the universe). In order to explain this point, we can compare Islamic jurisprudence to other legal systems of other societies as mentioned by a legal expert called Robert H. Jackson,[1] ex-US Attorney General. He says:

> For an American, there is a fundamental contradiction between law and religion. In the West, even in countries where there is a profound belief in the separation of church and state, the legal system is considered a secular matter in which exigency of the time plays a vital role. Of course, religious influences in the evolution of law have been very effective and strong. The Pentateuch that consists of the first five books of the Torah and the Christian teaching and church rules — each of them has contributed in our legal thought. In the past unusual or uncommon times influential statesmen would appoint judges and legislators from the clergy. Be that as it may, law has still remained a mundane matter. Legislatures for the enactment of laws, and courts for their execution, have existed. And these are considered institutions of this world that have something to do with the state and not with the church or religion. As such, our law in America does not determine religious duties. On the contrary, it cogently eliminates them. Law in America has only a limited link with the discharging of moral duties. In fact, an American might be morally obedient to the law, and at the same time, a mean and corrupt person.[2]

It can be clearly inferred from the above passage that

---

1. Robert Houghwout Jackson (1892-1954): United States Attorney General (1940–1941), an Associate Justice of the United States Supreme Court (1941–1954) and also the chief United States prosecutor at the Nuremberg Trials. [Trans.]

2. Maj¢d Khad£r¢ and Herbert J. Lybsny, with the introduction by Robert H. Jackson, Law in Islam, pp. i-iii (originally in English).

nowadays, laws in the United States and other Western societies, are codified for the management of secular life only; in the physical life of the members of society in the context of coexistence, a purely mechanical life. In such systems, no individual or group recognizes a duty above the law even if it is related to the life, honor and committed freedom of others. For example, if an individual, a group or society faces an epidemic, a bloodthirsty murderer or an exploitative system, no one has the right or duty to take steps to prevent it. In the legal systems of Western societies, man's origin, end and goal of life does not signify. His rights and duties revolve around a mechanical, purely natural dimension of life. Obviously, Islamic law cannot allow man with such nobility to be humiliated to that extent. Jackson continues:

> But, on the contrary, in Islamic laws the fountainhead of legislation is the will of God which is discovered and made explicit by His Prophet Mu!ammad. This law and this will of God consider all believers a single community although they belong to various tribes and nations and have different conditions and locations, far and near. Here, religion is a wholesome force that binds the community together, and not nationality and geographical boundaries. Here, the state itself is subservient and subject to the Qur'jn and there is no more room for another legislator, let alone giving room for any sort of criticism, skepticism and hypocrisy. For the believer, this world is a passageway to the other world, which is a better one. The Qur'jn specifies the rules, laws and manner of behaving with one another and another group so as to ensure a wholesome change from this world to the other world. It is impossible to distinguish political or judicial theories and views from the Prophet's teachings—teachings that determine the mode of behavior in relation to religious principles as well as the personal and sociopolitical way of life of all. These teachings determine more duties and responsibilities than rights for

man.[1]

Due to his insufficient knowledge of Islamic jurisprudence, Jackson was unaware that in our jurisprudence, duties are of two types:

I. Personal duties (like acts of worship), and

II. Mutual duties of individuals, societies and the state

Every duty prescribed to an individual, society or state breeds a right, and the emergence of a right requires the existence of a duty.

In interpreting the duties prescribed by Islam to the people, Jackson says:

> That is, moral commitments which an individual is required to fulfill are given more attention, and no position on earth can exempt him from fulfilling them. And if he disobeys, his future life will be endangered.[2]

Another mistake of Jackson's is as follows:

Firstly, the term "moral commitments" requiring "fulfillment" is not appropriate because the merit of morality lies in its being voluntary. Thus, moral commitments neither mean natural fatalism nor are based upon compulsory duty.

Secondly, Jackson should bear in mind that the discharge of duties of individuals, groups and the government in a society is impossible without the materialization of rights. He himself acknowledges, thus:

> The teachings related to religious or philosophical principles reject Islamic laws. The fact, however, is that the same system considered to be impractical has achieved astounding success. Approximately one century after the death of Muḥammad, his vibrant and unifying religion—although devoid of a well-established state, a permanent army and common political ideals—was able to mould his tribe and nation to reach the shores of Africa, overrun Spain and threaten France.[3]

---

1. Ibid., Jackson's "Introduction," p. iii.
2. Ibid.
3. Ibid.

It is necessary for those particularly in Muslim societies, who, in spite of having no sufficient knowledge, talk about religion and Islamic jurisprudence, to pay attention to the following points:

α. "The fact, however, is that the same system considered to be impractical has achieved astounding success."

β. "Mu ׀ammad's vibrant and unifying religion", and review their baseless remarks of religion in the light of conscience and reason. Jackson contintues in the following words:

> The main point is that we have just started knowing the fact that this religion, which is the youngest in the world, has founded a jurisprudence that gives a sense of justice to millions of people under the scorching skies of Africa, Asia and thousands of other people living in American countries.[1]

This statistical data was true approximately 30 years ago. Based on recent statistical data, the world Muslim population has reached about one billion and two hundred million. Eight million of them live in Western Europe and ten million in America and other non-Muslim countries.

Jackson [also] argues:

> Although it is possible that in relation to religious inspiration, we are doubtful of its rights, these rights give us very important lessons regarding the implementation of laws. Now, the time has come not to consider us as the only people who want justice or understand the meaning of justice. This is because in their legal systems, Muslim countries have been trying to achieve this goal and their experiences give vital lessons to us.[2]

If the Islamic laws or jurisprudence was identical or similar to others, the above passage would have been totally senseless.

The last part of Jackson's passage contains a very significant confession, which can serve as a lesson to those who talk narrow-mindedly about Islamic laws or jurisprudence. He says:

---

1. Ibid., p. x.
2. Ibid.

It usually happens that in the course of time legal terms connote a set of beliefs and ideas, especially for the freshmen [in law]. For example, our terms like "according to the due process," "courts' opinion," "based on justice," "trial before the jury," and "judicial review" have meaning for the English-speaking people which cannot be understood by other people. The same is true with many Islamic legal terms. It is possible for an Islamic legal term to have many meanings to interpret, which we may possibly interpret, but since we do not have a similar term in our laws, we cannot find a suitable legal term for it.[1]

In order to complete the earlier discussions about the salient features of Islamic jurisprudence, it is necessary to have an overview of the types of general rules based on the principal sources of jurisprudence, viz. the Qur'¡n, *Sunnah*, consensus (*ijm¡'*), and reason (*'aql*).

Types of General Rules Based on Principal Sources

I. **The stipulated rules or the prescribed rules***:* This specifies rules (*qaw¡'id*) that are stipulated in the Qur'¡n or the *Sunnah*:

- *No harm inflicted no harm done.* This rule (*q¡'idah*) can be deduced from many textual references, including the famous story of Samarah ibn Jundab. In the said story, the Prophet (¥) is reported to have said, *"No harm inflicted no harm done"*. That is, in Islam there is no law that brings harm or loss to the discharger of duty or to another person.

- *The denial of hardship and severity.* This rule says that no law which brings difficulty and adversity is imposed in Islam,. This rule is deduced from the following verses:

  Allah does not desire to put you to hardship.[2]

  Allah desires ease for you, and He does not desire

---

1. Ibid.
2. S£rat al-M¡'idah 5:6.

hardship for you.[1]

II. **The inferred rules**: Such rules are not inferred from a specific text but taken from the totality of the sections (*abwₐb*) in jurisprudence that cover the implication of the rule; for example:

- Pondering on what is more important in cases of contradiction of two laws, such as the permission to pass by an area without the owner's permission, to save someone from drowning. Since saving a life is more important than passing by an area without its owner's permission, the permission to pass by (to save life) takes precedence over what is important (the owner's right to his property).

- Every contract and promise, nay every kind of commitment, is based on intention. In other words,
  "Contracts and what follows them depend on intentions."

As it is obvious, such rules are based upon the dictates of reason.

III. **Self-evident rules of reason**: Universal propositions which are based on the dictates of reason are called 'rational rules' (*qawₐ'id 'aqliyyah*); for example:

- Rule of order: Since the social life of human beings is impossible without order and harmony between objectives and means, every action and idea that fosters it are necessary. Reason considers them obligatory.

- Rule on preventing probable harm: In every situation in which there is a reasonable probability of harm, reason would consider giving it a rule. Of course, if one regards this rule as part of *no harm inflicted no harm done*, it will be covered by that general rule.[2]

IV. **The rules agreed upon by the men of reason**: The difference between 'rational laws' (*ahkₐm-e 'aqlᵢ*) and those

---

1. Sₑrat al-Baqarah 2:185.
2. After this discourse, we shall separately examine the 'rationality' of the majority of jurisprudential rules.

agreed upon by the men of reason (*ban¡'-ye 'uqal¡'*) is that, there is no specific proof supporting the propositions agreed upon by them, but are confirmed and acted upon by men of reason for their being men of reason. Meanwhile, rational propositions or laws can be actually proven by appropriate proofs or, like self-evident truths (*badīhiyy¡t-e 'aqliyyah*), to prove them does not require any proof, or they are like substantiated propositions whose proofs are embedded within; technically, they are called "propositions followed by their syllogisms" (*qa¤¡y¡ qiy¡s¡tuh¡ ma'ah¡*).

V. **The rules the cause of which has been indicated**: concerning the reason for a juristic ruling, whenever the reason or cause is *indicated* the said ruling is called *man¥ū¥ al-'illah*. The scope of this ruling depends on the scope of the cause. For example, in the traditions related to the ruling on *zak¡t* (poor-rate),[1] the elimination of poverty in society is the cause. So, the items liable for *zak¡t* must be increased until the elimination of poverty in society.

VI. **Rules whose cause can be certainly discerned**: The term used refers to the set of rulings whose cause is not explicitly mentioned. However, in view of the truthfulness of the ruling and definite motive behind it, its cause can certainly be identified, as in the case of the prohibition of *hoarding*. Apart from its being rational, its ruling can be deduced from numerous traditions. Although the cause behind this very important ruling cannot be discerned in the text of the traditions, by considering the nature of the items which are forbidden to hoard and the span of time of doing it, it would be certain that the real cause behind the prohibition is to remove the emergency needs in human life. By citing this cause, the jurisprudent (*faqīh*) can give a ruling on the prohibition of hoarding items indispensable for people's daily life; for example, medicines, vehicles and telecommunication devices.

VII. **Rules issued upon juritic sense**: in many cases, there

---

1. Zak¡t: the tax levied on various categories of wealth and spent on the purposes specified in S£rat al-Tawbah 9:60. [Trans.]

may be no specific proof to support a ruling, or the proof is ambiguous, or there may be proofs but they contradict each other. In such a case, by taking into account the totality of principles, general rules, proofs, criteria [and wisdom] of the jurisprudential sources inculcated in his mind, the jurisprudent can discern a given ruling through intuitive jurisprudential sense. For instance, in discussing whether intention (*niyyah*) is a part (*juz'*) or condition (*shart*) of the acts of worship, some high-ranking jurisprudents maintain that "it is more akin to condition"; that is, intention is more likely to be a condition rather than being a part of the acts of worship.

The above mentioned rulings and cases can be categorized as follows:

- Rulings on duties (*ahkᵢm taklīfiyyah*);
- Rulings on positions (*ahkᵢm waᵬ'iyyah*);
- Primary actual rulings (*ahkᵢm wᵢqi'ī awwalī*);
- Secondary actual rulings (*ahkᵢm wᵢqi'ī thᵢnawī*);
- Primary outward rulings (*ahkᵢm ᵬhirī awwalī*);
- Secondary outward rulings (*ahkᵢm ᵬhirī thᵢnawī*);
- Rulings based on the jurist's guardianship (*wilᵢyat al-faqīh*);
- Legal topics (*mawᵬū'ᵢt shar'iyyah*); and
- Customary topics (*mawᵬū'ᵢt 'urfiyyah*).

The Role of Islamic Jurisprudence in Organizing Intelligible Life

Islamic jurisprudence is in charge of organizing and reforming all aspects of human intelligible life. By the same token, one can logically contend that "scientific and philosophical knowledge is in charge of organizing and correcting all human perceptions of human quadruple ontological relationships." It goes without saying that the elements of these primary sources such as sensory perceptions, observations, experiments, intellection, power of discovery, and other means utilized by man to increase and deepen his knowledge have not ceased to work in the course of past centuries.[1] Man has remained the same for the past hundreds of

---

1. Scientists believe that in the course of some forty thousand years past no

centuries and can address his alterable and inalterable, primary and essential needs and continue by using the same elements and sources.

Since the content of the sources of Islamic jurisprudence has its origin in primordial nature (fi§rah), common sense ('aql), justice and humanocentrism, and whereas no essential change has occurred in them as well as in the meaning of justice, which is the most fundamental factor in organizing individual and social human life, then Islamic jurisprudence shall continue to thrive with the same pace. The fact that the content of Islamic jurisprudence originates from human primordial nature, common sense and justice is documented to decisive proofs clearly deducible from the Qur'¡n, and authentic traditions.

1. Regarding *fitrah*, the following noble verse is cited:

> *So set your heart on the religion as a people of pure faith, the origination of Allah according to which He originated mankind. There is no altering Allah's creation.*[1]

2. Concerning reason ('aql), there are many verses which enjoin people to follow the dictates of reason; for example,

> *Will you bid others to piety and forget yourselves, while you recite the Book? Do you not apply reason?*[2]

Similarly, there are numerous authentic traditions that clearly establish reason as (¦ujjah) the 'inward proof' in contrast to the 'outward proof', which refers to the prophets. For example, regarding the motive behind the mission of the prophets, Im¡m 'Al¢ ('a) said:

> *... to unveil before them the hidden virtues of wisdom...*[3]

3. Regarding justice, Qur'¡nic verses and authentic traditions support the indispensability of justice in organizing and

---

major change has ever happened in human cognitive and physiological makeup.

1. S£rat ar-R£m 30:30.
2. S£rat al-Baqarah 2:44.
3. Nahj al-Bal¡ghah, Sermon 1.

molding human life both in individual and collective forms; for example,

> *Certainly We sent Our apostles with manifest proofs, and We sent down with them the Book and the Balance, so that mankind may maintain justice.*[1]
>
> *The word of your Lord has been fulfilled in truth and justice. Nothing can change His words, and He is the All-hearing, the All-knowing.*[2]

The Functional Scope of Islamic Jurisprudence

As previously stated, the functional scope of Islamic jurisprudence comprises delineation of laws, rights and human obligations with regards to his/her genuine needs—including the changing and fixed needs—in relation to quadruple ontological relationships and in the light of values and virtues and their respective issues (not just ingenuine needs). In order to have a concise view of this scope, it is necessary to pay attention to the meaning of need and its types.

Genuine and Ingenuine Needs

For every being—whether human being or nonhuman entities—there exists a canonically desirable and natural identity which determines its reality in the universe. Having said this, every factor involved in this identity is an essential moment of it without which that identity can never emerge as a whole. To put it otherwise, whatever that is part of the identity and sustains it is certainly required by that identity. For example, the ideal identity of human existence is health and wellbeing. As a result, wellbeing is a true human need.

Genuine needs can be divided into two:

1. Fixed needs are always there due to the constant dependence of the ideal identity of man on them; for example, wellbeing, knowledge, responsible freedom, honor, dignity, and the like.

---

1. S£rat al-°ad¢d 57:25.
2. S£rat al-An'¡m 6:115.

2. Changing needs: things, which enter the realm of 'intelligible life'; for example, means of transportation, international relations, technological varieties, spread of diverse fields of knowledge, and the like.

It goes without saying that egotist individuals and communities will never be contented with satisfying their real needs. Instead, they will introduce pressing ingenuine needs after which they will be compelled to enact laws and rules pertaining to those needs; for example, the laws and rules pertaining to usury (ribⱼ). The essence of human need for money is as follows:

1. As the means of exchange between two sets of goods, two sets of services, goods and service, and vice versa

2. As the index of monetary value which the money owner can use to acquire goods and services needed for society

3. As the means of acquiring wealth

Human need for laws and rights pertaining to the aforementioned matters regarding money is an essential need, and Islamic jurisprudence explicitly addresses those needs based on texts or rules extracted from reliable sources. Yet, hundreds of legal items related to the legality of usury have no place in Islamic jurisprudence because the need for such legal items stems from radical utilitarianism and economic domineering and is an ingenuine need. In such cases, it should not be declared that Islamic jurisprudence is insufficient as it does not consider the essence of usury legitimate, let alone legislate and enact laws and rules for it.

Similarly, it is also possible for certain societies to repel existing conditions and rules governing sexual relations and regard illegitimate relations as legal (whether with the same class (¥inf) or the opposite one)[1] and then to enact specific laws for such relations! However, since it does not recognize

---

1. It is not appropriate to apply the term 'sex' (jins) for man and woman because man and woman are two classes (¥inf) of the genus 'human being' which is one of the sexual genera (anwⱼ') called 'animal'. Thus, it is more accurate to use the term 'class' than 'sex'.

illegitimate relations, Islamic jurisprudence also regards the need for laws pertaining to them ingenuine. Like other artificial items coupled with the tricks of selfish individuals, it creates artificial demands and uninformed people will be drawn to them, thinking that the created demands are indeed natural and demanded.

Jurisprudential Rules: Their Primordial and Rational Nature

As it was promised earlier in this point we turn to the rational or primordial nature of the universal rules in Islamic jurisprudence.

I) The notion of rule and principle invariably applies to the maxims stipulated in the Book (Qur'ᵢn), *Sunnah* and those inferred from the proofs. The difference between rule (*qᵢ'idah*), principle (*a¥l*) and circumstantial evidence (*amᵢrah*) lies in the extent of revealing realities. Revealing reality by means of circumstantial evidence (such as Qur'ᵢnic verses, traditions (*aↄ idīth*) and rational rulings) precedes rule and principle, while revealing reality, by means of rule and principle, only removes doubt and confusion.

II) The fact that the forms of devotional worship (*'ibᵢdᵢt*) are not primordial or rational does not mean they oppose human primordial nature or reason; rather it signifies silence of the two (*fitrah* and *'aql*) as to the reasons behind the specific forms of worship; for example, the reason behind two *rak'ahs* of *fajr* prayer and loud recitations (*jahr*) in it, and the seven times circumambulation (*tawᵢf*) of the Ka'bah in a specific manner. However, primordial nature and reason can provide as more reasons for the quality and quantity of the devotional actions as those concerning the need of worship. As a matter of fact, after accepting the necessity of exposing oneself to the divine radiations of the Absolute Perfection (God, the Glorious and Exalted), one finds it necessary to worship his Lord with all sincerity following the maxims of his reason and primordial nature. It is obvious that if we limit ourselves only to mental vigilance (*murᵢqibah*) and do not verbally recite anything or perform specific movements, like kneeling down (*rukū'*), prostration (*sujūd*), circumambulation, with specific conditions of time and place, illogical claims will replace these acts of worship with the passage of time, and extinguish the very essence of worship. As stated in *'Ilal al-Sharᵢyi'*,[1] by leaving the quality and quantity of worship to the discretion of the people, its importance will gradually fade away. Furthermore, these qualitative and quantitative aspects have subtle signs which can clearly be discerned by a sound mind; for example, bending in *rukū'* is a gesture of humility and placing the forehead on the ground is the utmost sign of surrender and submission.

III) Jurisprudential rules refer to universal propositions applicable to particular cases. In giving a ruling on particular cases, those propositions shall be referred to; for example, the rule of "neither loss nor harm" (*lᵢ ¤arar wa lᵢ ¤arᵢr*) and the principle of the exigency of transactions. In acting upon these propositions, the *mujtahid* and the *muqallid*[2] are the same. To put the matter otherwise, they are both obliged to abide by them. Nevertheless, it is only the qualified jurist who infers the jurisprudential propositions from the principles of jurisprudence upon rational proofs and evidences.

IV) The rules cited in jurisprudence can be generally divided into two.

A) Those rules which are cited in primary sources; for example, the rules of "negation of distress and constriction" and "neither loss nor harm" as provided for in this Qur'ᵢnic verse:

Allah does not desire to put you to hardship.[3]

B) The rules inferred upon reliable proofs; for example, the preponderance of what is more important (*ahamm*) to what is important (*muhimm*) in cases of contradiction.

---

1. 'Ilal al-Sharᵢyi': an important treatise by Shaykh al-˜ad£q (died 329 AH) on the philosophy of Islamic tenets and practices. [Trans.]
2. Muqallid (literally, imitator, emulator or follower): the person who follows a certain marja' al-taqlᵢd (source of emulation or reference authority) in matters of religious jurisprudence. [Trans.]
3. S£rat al-Mᵢ'idah 5:6.

V) In jurisprudence, the ways of discovering realities differ, but all of them are supported either by the perception of primordial nature, such as *yaqīn* (certainty) and *qata'*(suspension of judgment), or by reason. For example, rational rulings that revoke the rulings' requirement, and data, whose being discovered is completed by the Legislator, such as Qur'ịnic verses, whose indication of the reality is abstract, and traditions, whose issuance (being authentic) is not definite. However, by complementing their proofs by other means, their potential of revealing legal realities is rational. Meanwhile, the principles that are cited to remove any confusion in doubtful cases, such as the principle of disavowal [of the polytheists] (*barị'at*) and the principle of preponderance of eliminating harm over gaining profit, are rational propositions, although their rationality can also be consolidated by the endorsement of the Islamic legislator.

VI) In view of their functional scope in jurisprudence, jurisprudential rules can be generally divided into two:

A) General rules that can be implemented in all sections (*abwịb*) of jurisprudence

B) Particular rules that can be cited in some sections of jurisprudence.

Examples of General Rules

1. The negation of harm and loss: "There is neither harm nor loss in Islam."

2. The negation of distress and constriction:

> *Allah does not desire to put you to hardship.*[1]

3. The negation of punishment for the action of someone whose intention is good:

> *There is no [cause for] blaming the virtuous.*[2]

4. The preponderance of what is most important over what is important in cases of contradiction between the two.

---

1. Sịrat al-Mị'idah 5:6.
2. Sịrat al-Tawbah (or Barị'ah) 9:91.

5. Universality of religious obligation:

We did not send you except as a bearer of good news and warner to all mankind.[1]

6. The lack of interference between cause and effect

7. The primacy of correctness: "Let your Muslim brother act properly."

8. The primacy of the correctness of the obliged person's (*mukallaf*) action in relation to himself; that is, according to the level of awareness and free will, every person takes his own action as correct.

9. The primacy of the correctness of things: this principle is not limited to a Muslim or believer's action but rather includes all things, states and human actions in the domain of nature's rational laws.

10. The elimination of harm takes precedence over gaining profit

11. Exigencies suspend prohibitions.

12. The suspension of prohibitions is proportionate to exigencies.

13. Evil and harm must be eliminated as much as possible.

14. Generality and majority can be an evidence for a prescription.

15. Every religious obligation that cannot be discharged in full should not be abandoned as such.

16. The impermissibility of participation in sin and impermissible actions.

17. The generality of the posited rulings in relation to different conditions; for example, warranty on squandering the property of another person irrespective of his age, level of knowledge (in managing his property) or any other condition pertaining to the attainment of maturity or age of responsibility.

18. Forcing every nation to that which is considered by it obligatory.

19. The principle of acting upon the previous religious codes

---

1. S£rat al-Saba' 34:28.

of law (*shariyi'*) provided that they do not contradict Islamic laws.

20. The principle of acting upon the views of men of reason, except in case they contradict Islam, in which case, it is obligatory to avoid contradicting Islam.

21. Whatever is needed by the legal course of individual life, the responsibility of procuring it lies upon the shoulder of the individual if he is capable, and in case he is incapable, it is a collective responsibility.

22. Whatever is needed by the system of social life, it is *wijib kifi'i*[1] (collective obligation) to procure it and in case only some individuals can procure it, it becomes *wijib 'aynī* (personal obligation).

23. The principle of the absence of superiority of one person over another except for a reason, which is proven, like the superiority of the guardian over the minor.

24. The guardian (*walī*) Imim is he who has no guardian.

25. The actions done by a person prior to his becoming Muslim has no retroactive effect: "*Islam loves what comes before it.*"

26. Acting upon legitimate conditions is obligatory: "Muslims are associated with their conditions except that which contradicts the Book (Qur'in) or the Sunnah."

27. In determining the cases of ambiguity when there is no proof of determining any of them, the principle of casting lots (*qur'ah*) can be used: "*Casting lots pertains to every problematic matter.*"

28. *Isti¥i ib* or the principle of continuance of every ruling or subject which has existed before and its present existence is doubtful.

29. The principle of permissibility of things: "everything is pure even if there is prohibition in them."

30. The principle of immunity for non-Muslims (*Ahl al-*

---

1. Wijib kifi'¢: the obligation which is on every member of the community as long as it is unfulfilled, but as soon as a person or some persons have fulfilled it, it is no longer an obligation on those who have not fulfilled it. [Trans.]

Dhimmah).[1] .

31. Ignorance suspends a ruling except in case of ignorance by shortcoming: *"My people are free from whatever they do not know."*

32. Compulsion and coercion suspend a ruling: "My community is beyond… what is imposed upon it."

33. Constraint does not annul transactions although the transaction of constrained individuals is imposed.

34. In actions whose cause totally brings about their actualization and the person that supervises their performance as the agent, the discretion is with the cause, and the actions shall be attributed to the cause:

35. If acting upon a religious ruling brings about harm on the life, property and honor of a person at the hands of followers of another belief, acting upon that ruling is suspended under the necessity of dissimulation (*taqiyyah*) and behaving contrary to it is obligatory except in case of killing somebody, because even motivated by *taqiyyah*, one is not allowed to kill someone else.

> *Whoever renounces faith in Allah after [affirming] his faith—except someone who is compelled while his heart is at rest in faith...*[2]
>
> *... except when you are wary of them out of caution.*[3]

36. The principle of the absence of imposition of a ruling and duty on others except in cases like [loud] recitation in congregational prayers done by the *imjm* on behalf of his followers (*ma'munīn*).

37. If the reason behind a ruling has many components, all those components are integral parts of the reason. So, negation of one of them leads to negation of the reason, and therefore the supposed ruling shall be negated.

---

1. Ahl al-Dhimmah: non-Muslim citizens of the Islamic state, whose rights and obligations are contractually stipulated. [Trans.]
2. S£rat al-Na¡l 16:106.
3. S£rat ¡l 'Imr¡n 3:28.

38. The rule of justice: this rule is one of the most fundamental rules of jurisprudence in all its sections.

39. A ruling's inclusion of a case which has not been a subject of the ruling but later becomes a subject of it; for example, when a person endows something for the poor and later he becomes poor, he will also be entitled to the endowed item.

40. Those who are the nearest to a person take precedence in acquiring anything good from him as well as in incurring any harm from him over those who are distant from him; for example, the issue of inheritance and blood-money. This law is the most fundamental element of human interrelationship which cures man's illness of alienation from one another as well as alienation from his own self.

41. Actions are judged upon intentions:

Every man shall have what he intended.

Indeed actions are [judged] by the intentions.

Intention is the spirit of action.

42. In the case of a particular or general ruling supported by a particular reason, this ruling is repelled by the absence of the reason behind it.

43. Writing a will (*wa¥iyyah*) is the right of every Muslim:

Prescribed for you, when death approaches any of you and he leaves behind any property, is that he make a bequest for his parents and relatives, in an honorable manner—an obligation on the God-wary.[1]

44. He who is more meritorious is more deserving than others to acquire a thing.

45. The statement of a person which has no way of proving except himself is a proof, unless he is accused of lying: *"The saying of one who is unknown before, except as an accused, must be heard."*

46. If the suspension of the impermissibility of a ruling

---

1. S£rat al-Baqarah 2:180.

depends on the existence of a condition or cause, it is necessary to present the condition or cause to give a ruling on its permissibility.

47. If the suspension of an obligatory ruling depends on a condition or cause, one must present the said condition or cause in order to give ruling on the permissibility of its suspension.

48. A useful work is valuable and its value must not be taken away from it.

49. The real value of a work must always be taken into account:

> *And do not deprive people of their goods.*[1]

50. The child for a legal wife serves as the stone of penalty for the adulterer: *"The child is for the bed while the adulterer is for the stone."*

51. It is unlawful (har¡m) to consume property wrongfully:

> *Do not eat up your wealth among yourselves wrongfully.*[2]

52. Maturity, reason and physical strength are among the general conditions for the assumption of responsibility and commitment:

> *Allah does not desire to put you to hardship.*[3]

"The pen is lifted for the immature and the crazy."

"Engagement is for the obliged person (mukallaf)."

53. The impermissibility of imitation (taqlīd) in matters of the principles of beliefs and all rational cases on which reason rules: *"The principles of belief are by discernment and inference and not by imitation."*

54. The principle of the sufficiency of a solitary report (khabar w¡hid) as proof (¡ujjah) on certain subjects as substantiated by proofs such as the meaning of the Quranic verse, *"O you who have faith! If a profligate [person] should bring you some news, verify it, lest you should visit [harm] on some people out of*

---

1. S£rat al-A'r¡f 7:85.
2. S£rat al-Baqarah 2:188.
3. S£rat al-M¡'idah 5:6.

ignorance, and then become regretful for what you have done,"[1] and the views of men of reason.

55. Determining the ways of discharging responsibilities and proving the posited rulings depend on reason and the men of reason.

56. Application of general concepts and propositions to their concrete extensions is rational.

57. Anyone who benefits from something shall also incur the harm it may bring.

58. Anything which is permissible to be loaned shall also be permissible to be rented.

59. That which is religiously impossible is also most likely rationally impossible.

60. That which may possibly be ignored in secondary matters cannot be ignored in matters of principles. For instance, it is invalid to give as endowment that which does not exist but it is valid to give as endowment what is nonexistent but comes into existence later.

61. The categorical is engaged in the common extension provided that the engagement is not primary.

62. An opinion cannot be attributed to someone silent although he can speak for himself, unless there are pieces of evidence proving or disproving it: *"A saying cannot be attributed to the silent."*

63. It is no longer allowed to suspend the expression in the time of emergency.

64. What is left outside the scope of will upon a premise of will is not in contradiction with the will and responsibility.

65. That which is established in the past as righteous practice and there is no proof to the contrary, shall remain as such:
"And do not refute certainty upon doubt."

66. Confession in the position of composition shall be deemed composition.

67. A principle serves as the proof as long as there is no [contrary] proof: *"The principle is a proof where there is no proof."*

---

1. S£rat al-°ujur¡t 49:6.

68. Relying and acting upon a statement is better than overlooking and neglecting it.

69. Permitting something implies permitting its axiomatic properties.

70. As there is no more obstruction, prohibition takes effect.

71. Reconciliation is the mother of all transactions.

72. Where two proofs or rulings are contradictory, both of them are suspended.

73. Reconciliation of two contradictories to the extent possible is better than neglecting them.

74. When a probability arises ratiocination becomes annulled.

75. The owner's possession of a property which is transferred from him to another person through a transaction or any other way is annulled, and possession of a property which is transferred to him is the effect of and permitted by the transaction.

76. Commitment to something means commitment to its requisites.

77. Suspension of a ruling on a quality (wa¥f) proves the causality of the quality for the ruling.

78. In case of contradiction between quality (wa¥f) and allusion (ishjrah), the latter shall prevail provided that the alluded peculiarities and qualities are clear.

79. Incapability to perform religious duties leads to suspension [of the obligation to perform them.

Examples of Particular Rules

I. Some Applications of Judicial Principles and Rules

1. Clear evidence concerns the plaintiff while taking oath concerns the accused.

2. Confession of the people of reason against themselves is permissible.

3. Everyone has the authority to confess about anything he owns. From one perspective, this rule is one of the forms of the above rule.

4. Confession after denial is not valid.

5. Giving testimony is obligatory and its concealment is forbidden.

6. When there are doubts as to accusing one as a convict or exonerating him the latter has the preponderance.

7. One is permitted to punish the religious offenders and criminals when the punishment is just and based on the goals of 'intelligible life'.

II. Exetensions of the Principles and Rules of Retaliation, Penal Law and Fines

1. No blood of any Muslim (according to Qur'¡nic verses, traditions and dictate of reason) and noble person shall be shed:

"The blood of a Muslim shall not be overlooked."

"And whoever kills a believer intentionally, his punishment is hell; he shall abide in it."

> *That is why We decreed for the Children of Israel that whoever takes a life, without [its being guilty of] manslaughter or corruption on the earth, is as though he had killed all mankind, and whoever saves a life is as though he had saved all mankind.*[1]

2. °ud≤d[2] shall be annulled by mere doubt.

3. In case of unintended murder, the reasonable man has to pay blood-money:

الدية في القتل الخطأ على العاقلة.

4. In case of premeditated murder, the penalty is one of the three, viz. qi¥¡¥,[3] [giving] blood-money (*diyah*), or pardon

---

1. S£rat al-M¡'idah 5:32.

2. °ud£d (literally means boundaries or limits) in the Islamic law is generally applied to penal law for punishments prescribed for particular crimes whose extent is determined by law. [Trans.]

3. Qi¥¡¥ (literally means retribution or retaliation) in the Islamic jurisprudence is to be executed against a criminal, according to the legal decree, who has committed crimes such as murder, amputation of a body limb, or laceration and beating in case the victim or his guardians are seeking retribution in lieu of receiving fine or blood money. [Trans.]

(*'afw*):[1]

5. If the repayment or fine, or its value is not stated in the religious texts, the judge has to determine it.

6. The burden of punishment is to be shouldered individually. This does not contradict giving blood money by someone with a sound mind in case of unintended murder.

7. In case of ambiguity (*lawth*), swearing has been prescribed. *Lawth* means the existence of a prior indication or indications that there is a proof that the murdered person has been killed by the defendant or defendants.

Qasimah refers to oaths taken by the plaintiffs—50 oaths in case of premeditated murder and 25 oaths in case of unintentional murder; otherwise, it is the case of *lawth* according to the primary principle, *"Clear evidence lies on the plaintiff while taking oath lies on the accused."* *Qasimah* is done in this manner: initially, the accused will be requested to bring evidence and if he fails, it is the turn of the victim's relatives to undergo *qasimah*.

III. Extensions of Legal Principles and Rules

1. Contracts and what serves as a covenant is built upon the intention of the parties involved.

2. Dissolution of contracts to the components of their subjects if the dissolution is possible.

---

1. It can be said that one of the most formidable rational cases in Islamic jurisprudence is the penalty for premeditated murder and one of its three forms is qi¥¡¥. Just as God has mentioned a noble way, "There is life for you in retribution, O you who possess intellects! Maybe you will be God-wary!" (S£rat al-Baqarah 2:179), if the members of society clearly know that in case of committing murder, the murderer shall also be executed, by endangering his life as well the murderer will understand better the value and greatness of human life. That some narrow-minded individuals today consider the penalty of retaliation improper, and imitating the views of some Westerners, say that as one person is killed there is no point of killing another person, shows that they do not understand the important deterrent effect of qi¥¡¥ in preventing mass murder or suicide. When people think that killing an innocent person is also one of those crimes beyond reparation by society, the value of life is underrated to that extent. Is one's soul like a commodity that can be compensated by some money and few days of imprisonment?

3. To act upon every legitimate condition is obligatory:

O you who have faith! Keep your agreements.[1]

"The Muslims are attached to their terms except whatever goes against the Book (Qur'¡n) or the Sunnah."

4. A condition which goes against the intent of the contract renders this contract invalid.

5. A crooked condition does not invalidate the whole contract.

6. If it is impossible to abide by the meaning of any contract it is invalid.

7. The provision in contracts is necessary.

8. Like his life, man's property is respected.

9. Reconciliation is permissible and predominant.

And settle your differences.[2]

Reconciliation between Muslims is permissible except in making lawful unlawful and unlawful lawful.[3]

Reconciliation between people is permissible.[4]

10. The one who is deceived by someone should refer to the one who has deceived him.

11. Guarantee transfers the liability for the amount due from the debtor to the guarantor:

"The guarantor is a carrier of burden."

12. Loss of trust of the guarantor through his infringement or falling below the conditions set for a guarantor.

13. Whoever spends another person's property becomes its guarantor.

14. In loan there is no guarantor except loan of gold and silver, or through his infringement or falling below the conditions set for a guarantor.

15. In a wholesome Islamic society, possession of a property by means of control over it is a sign of ownership.

---

1. S£rat al-M¡'idah 5:1.
2. S£rat al-Anf¡l 8:1.
3. Was¡'il al-Sh¢'ah, "Kit¡b al-̄ul¦," section (b¡b) 3.
4. Ibid.

16. Anyone who takes something from another person (not through any dealing or as a trust or loan) is the guarantor of it until he returns it to the owner.

17. The Muslims' market is proof (*ujjah*) (in every society in which Islamic laws are acted upon or at least most people follow Islamic laws, the rule in that society is the primacy of sayings, acts and intentions).

18. Every debt (*dayn*) is instantaneous (and must be given without any delay) except in particular cases discussed in jurisprudence.

19. Debt must absolutely be paid back.

20. The necessity of giving due respite in paying debt.

21. The guarantor must be able to do his or her function.

22. Just as every item which is a subject of transaction and must be guaranteed in case of its validity, that which invalidates the transaction must also have a guarantor.

23. Any item which has an equivalent can be guaranteed by its equivalent and any item which has no equivalent, its price must be paid.

24. In case of death or extinction of the subject of guarantee, the basis of payment is the current value.

25. The free can neither be bought nor sold.

26. Anyone who possesses a property through negotiations becomes its owner..

27. Anyone who cultivates a barren land becomes its owner.

28. The people are absolutely free to spend their properties.

29. Waiving of rights in relation to a property forfeits one's ownership of it.

30. The private property is customarily at the disposal of the owner.

31. The principle is that a person cannot own anything by force except by inheritance and testament (*wa¥iyyah*).

32. The lack of any objective or expedient transaction except on the part of the owner or anyone who is his equivalent.

33. Any sold item which perished before being possessed by the buyer is considered still owned by the seller.

34. In any case selling and buying is valid, mortgage is also valid..

35. Mortgaging is conditioned by receipt.

36. The usurper must be punished severely except in times of famine and emergency.

37. Apostasy (*kufr*) and committing murder deprives one of inheritance.

38. The need for observing envy in obsolete things.

39. Anyone who can directly interfere in a matter can take a proxy in relation to it.

40. Any endowment (*waqf*) must be done according to the intention and objective of the endower.

41. Anyone who owns an item also owns the benefits to be taken from it.

42. If one of two or some business partners wants to sell his share from a shared property, any partner or partners take priority in buying it.

43. In writing contracts, the weaker party is supposed to write and have a copy of the contract because there is a stronger possibility of ambiguity and bullying on the part of the stronger party. (Obviously, this is not a general principle or rule, but only applicable in case of removing any possible injustice to be done against the weak.)

44. Guarantee can be canceled by permission.

45. In cases of the possibility of rejection when the one who has the right to do so does not reject it, it shall be regarded as approval.

46. Deprivation of a gain which a person may acquire naturally or legally shall be regarded as a loss.

By a close examination of these jurisprudential principles and rules, the following two very important conclusions can be drawn:

First conclusion: Islamic jurisprudence has not enacted artificial, unrealistic and irrational limits and frameworks for the management of human life in the course of realization of human evolutionary charcter. In other words, Islamic jurisprudence is an open system because every principle or rule it has prescribed for individual and social life is in harmony with the dynamic nature of human life. Moreover, whereas man treads the path of intelligible life, i.e. pure life, a life which is based on clear evidence and guidance, these very principles and rules serve as the driving forces toward the abovementioned life.

Second conclusion: By setting human life under the spotlight of perfection, the said jurisprudential principles and rules, backed by sublime human morality, make Islamic jurisprudence possess both merits of being a 'forerunner' and an 'adherent'. It is a 'forerunner' in the sense that it guarantees unchanging physical and spiritual needs of human life. It is an 'adherent' in the sense that it totally acknowledges the openness of human existential dimensions toward the emergence of new subjects and phenomena in nature as well as the technology. It does not stand in the way of its expansion and diversity, except in cases that threaten dynamic and purposeful human life; for example, producing narcotic drugs, providing the means to incite carnal passions and setting the scene for the moral corruption of society that leads to nothing but the feeling of futility in life.

Here, we have no option but to mention a very important point and that is, purely 'adherent' laws that have nothing to do with the constructive morality of intelligible life only regulate the human inclinations for the benefit of collective life (i.e. a peaceful life with one's fellow human beings). This form of life is indeed to introduce the alienated individuals to the purposeful life. In order to clarify these two conclusions, we have no option but to examine the qualitative nature of Islamic legal and jurisprudential system in terms of its openness or rigidity.

Openness or Rigidity of the Islamic Legal and Jurisprudential System

While being axiomatic,[1] the Islamic jurisprudential system is totally open—not rigid—in the realm of purely human dimensions and needs.

Since the early twentieth century, some Muslim scholars unfamiliar with the reality of Islamic law followed the footsteps of a group of western writers in giving rise to the illusion that the scope of Islamic laws and jurisprudence is limited and thus, it cannot be responsive to all human predicaments.

Now we shall try to demonstrate the scientific and philosophical baselessness of this illusion. It goes without saying that the intrinsic power of life has set this phenomenon (life) in motion, and expanded it in the vast realm of matter and motion with such a systematic rule of law, that it never became stagnant or paused along the way. It is also clear that human life, like those of animals, has also passed through the same regulated stages and reached the present state.

Scientifically and philosophically speaking, one cannot find even a single instant in which the phenomenon of life—whether in human, animal or vegetative domain—has ever gone against the laws of nature. In other words, given their legal constraints, the components of nature and the laws governing them are currently in motion in a 'systematic' manner, in modern scientific parlance. Meanwhile, in this arena of quest of the living and lifeless worlds, the most powerful source of life is that of the human being. By means of the wonderful brain, it is always moving from one state to another. There is no doubt at all that like the phenomenon of life, man, in whatever natural and social state (political, religious, moral, legal, cultural, and historical) he may be, is subject to innumerable laws.

From this observable state of affairs, we arrive at the definite conclusion that by having intrinsic active power and unlimited potential, man always moves through the highly systematic force that transforms the natural and conventional systems (in which he lives). Yes, had it not been for this sublime and

---

1. Axiomatic in the sense of having principles and bases.

transformative force, he would certainly have been extinguished within the complex systems hundreds, nay thousands, of centuries ago.

While passing through the obstacles of the closed systems of nature and aspects of life, man preserves the basic principles of his identity.His inalterable needs in the domain of human quadruple ontological relationships (with himself, with God, with the Universe and with his fellowmen) do not undergo any fundamental change. That which changes is the emergence of secondary and less important needs, or the ingenuine needs that are imposed by elements outside the 'human intelligible life' into the realm of collective human life.

Chapter 3
Interview on the Scope of Jurisprudence

Interviewer: Can one claim that it is modern science and technology and not Islamic jurisprudence that provides us with a model of living?

M.T.J: If by 'model' you imply that jurisprudence provides a pattern for "a justifiable life along the path of a lofty goal," then it is obvious that the answer is positive. We read in the Qur'ın, thus:

> *Thus We have made you a middle nation that you may be witnesses to the people, and that the Apostle may be a witness to you.*[1]

> *And wage jihıd for the sake of Allah, a jihıd which is worthy of Him. He has chosen you and has not placed for you any obstacle in the religion, the faith of your father, Abraham. He named you 'Muslims' before, and in this, so that the Apostle may be a witness to you, and that you may be witnesses to mankind.*[2]

Having the realities on the ground in sight, however, no one would cast any doubt of the fact that it was with this very jurisprudential and legal system that Islam has introduced so many outstanding pious figures in the history of Islamic world every one of whom can serve alone as the archetype of intelligible life.

When the notorious materialist Shibli Shamil, says,

> *The leader, 'Alī ibn Abī ±ılib, the greatest of all great figures, is*

---

1. Sırat al-Baqarah 2:143.
2. Sırat al-°ajj 22:78.

a unique exemplar. Neither has the East nor the West,
yesterday or today, ever seen a copy of this original.[1]

Can any sensible person ever think that a time or situation
would come in human history in which 'Alī ibn Abī ±ılib ('a)
would not be the best model for the people's intelligible life at
that time and condition?

Granted that sublime human principles and excellent
morality will remain the same, in which period or situation
would such characters as Salmın al-Fırsī, Abū Dharr al-Ghiffırī,
Mılik al-Ashtar, 'Ammır ibn Yısīr, Miqdıd ibn Aswad, Uways
al-Qarnī, Ibn al-Tayhın, Kumayl ibn Ziyıd al-Nakha'ī, and
hundreds of others, not be able to live?

When sublime human principles are removed from the
scene, and human society turns into a factory of unconscious,
helpless screws, nuts and bolts, there will be no room for
Abraham, the Friend, Muıammad ibn 'Abd Allıh, Mūsı ibn
'Imrın, 'Īsı ibn Maryam, 'Alī ibn Abī ±ılib ('a), and those
enlightened men and women who have succeeded to expose
themselves to the divine radiations of perfection.

It is needless to say that technologies and human sciences
can contribute to intelligible life both materially and spiritually
when they serve human identity to flourish through his
quadruple ontological relationships and not promoting
narcissism, hedonism and hegemony. This cooperation has its
philosophy in a jurisprudential rule reading:

> *Cooperating to provide whatever is needed in the system of a*
> *wholesome social life is a collective responsibility (wıjib kifı'ī);*
> *when its realization requires some individual efforts, it is a*
> *personal obligation (wıjib 'aynī) for each one of them.*

Having said this, two extremely important factors are
required for the encouragement of innovation and acquiring
disciplines that further human knowledge about the universe:

First factor: Qur'ınic verses, authentic traditions and the
maxims of reason dictating the pursuit of disciplines that

---

1 George Jurdac (1956), The Voice of Human Justice, p. 17 (originally in Arabic)

further our knowledge of the cosmos. This is particularly the case with the authentic traditions which highlight the necessity of reflecting on our experience to unravel new realities. According to the Commander of the Faithful Imam Ali:

> *Through experiences (experiments), [new horizons of] knowledge shall be acquired.*[1]

Second factor: A close examination of scientific methods and incessant discoveries by Muslims, from the late second century up to the mid fifth century AH, at the time of the Dark Ages in the West.

Q1: Do all religious values originate from jurisprudence, or does ethics play a role as well? Can jurisprudence and religion assume the responsibility of managing society, or should human knowledge take control of this management?

Jafari: Since the two questions above deal with a single issue, we shall address them together. The most fundamental factor giving rise to such questions is the lack of understanding of Islam and Islamic jurisprudence. Thus, although the meaning of jurisprudence has been clarified in our previous discourses, we shall briefly define jurisprudence again in its general sense. Jurisprudence means knowledge of the laws pertaining to all human actions and avoidances in both the physical and spiritual realms, in connection with God, as basically substantiated by the Qur'ịn, the Sunnah, consensus and reason. These proofs bespeak of what is good and evil for the 'intelligible life' without which it is impossible to achieve otherworldly success. So all knowledge —be it physical or mental, natural or covenantal, or ideological is encompassed by Divine Universal Law. Rūmī used the term "jurisprudence of the Sublime God" (fiqh Allịh al-akbar) in the first book of Mathnawi indicating the vastness of the scope of jurisprudence, for he expressed therein his ideas while seriously keeping in view the exegeses of Qur'ịnic verses. The late Sabziwịrī says

---

1. The injunction to conduct experiment in discovering realities can be seen in more than 10 authentic traditions.

that the Mathnawi embarks on giving a commentary of the content of the Qur'¡n and around 600 moral, mystical and psychological traditions, as well as the basic principles of knowledge and learning in the realms of "is-ness" and "ought-ness".

By closely examining the dimensions of Islamic laws, it can be proved that, all actions and aspects of human intelligible life in the individual and social domains which contribute to his worldly and otherworldly felicity are encompassed by jurisprudence in its true sense, and not only limited to dealing with human personal engagement with God, i.e. acts of worship ('ib¡d¡t).

Therefore, Islamic jurisprudence consists of the following sections:

1. Jurisprudence on the acts of worship;
2. Jurisprudence on personal conditions;
3. Jurisprudence on business transactions, contracts and obligations;
4. Moral jurisprudence;
5. Mystical jurisprudence;
6. Political jurisprudence;
7. Technological jurisprudence;
8. Jurisprudence on international relations;
9. Cultural jurisprudence;
10. Jurisprudence on management;
11. Jurisprudence of jih¡d and defense;
12. Jurisprudence on sciences;
13. Jurisprudence on discoveries;
14. Jurisprudence on rights;
15. Judicial jurisprudence;
16. Jurisprudence on resistance against oppression and corruption;
17. Jurisprudence on resistance against inappropriate practices;
18. Jurisprudence on encouraging and enjoining what is appropriate;

19. Jurisprudence on prospective trends; and

20. Jurisprudence on the information received about whatever transpires in the world.

In order to prove the justifiability of this categorization, it is essential to consider the following proofs:

First proof: *"I was not sent but to perfect the moral virtues."* This tradition has been narrated in numerous instances from the Holy Prophet (¥). This tradition presents the purpose behind the mission of the Holy Prophet (¥) as perfection and completion of morality and self-refinement of the people. Therefore, morality is a very important segment of the prophets' mission, which is within the scope of jurisprudence in its general sense.

Second proof: In numerous verses, the Noble Qur'¡n regarded *"teaching the Book and wisdom"* as the purpose of the mission of the Holy Prophet:

> *It is He who sent to the unlettered [people] an apostle from among themselves, to recite to them His signs, to purify them, and to teach them the Book and wisdom.*[1]

It is obvious that the contents of the Divine Book and wisdom undertake organizing the welfare of human intelligible life, and not merely some acts of worship and their quantitative and qualitative features.

Third proof: In the first sermon of *Nahj al-Bal¡ghah*, the Commander of the Faithful (Imam Ali) thus says about the prophets' mission:

> *Then Allah sent His Messengers toward them to make them fulfill the pledges of His creation, to recall His bounties, to exhort them by preaching, to unveil before them the hidden virtues of wisdom, and show them the signs of His Omnipotence; namely, the sky, which is raised over them, the earth, that is placed beneath them,*

---

1. S£rat al-Jumu'ah 62:2.

and the means of living, that sustains them.[1]

These proofs reveal the validity of the aforementioned divisions of Islamic jurisprudence. Of course, to identify the subjects, relations and ways of application of subjects to particular cases in various sections of jurisprudence is the responsibility of pious authorities and experts. After the authorities this responsibility is assigned to the jurists who engage in deducing laws and rulings from the sources of jurisprudence.

Q2: Can one say that religion and jurisprudence are perfect and it is people's understanding of them that is flawed?

Jafari: This question is as if to ask that is it not so that the universe is a well ordered system and it is merely our understanding of it that proves imperfect?

Yes, just as the universe is not identical with our perception of it, it is clear that religion and jurisprudence as such are not identical with our perception or understanding of them. But there is one thing that should not be forgotten and that is, since perfection is laden with positive value and imperfection (defect) with negative value, academically it seems more appropriate and correct to use the word 'limitation' or 'relativity' with respect to our perceptions of religion and jurisprudence. This is due to the short span of human life as compared to innumerable issues regarding human intelligible life and his quadruple ontological relationships, and the limitations of scientific means at the disposal of man. On the other hand, our understanding is historical and temporally grounded and this makes it relative and limited; and this limitation and relativity does not impede the regulation of intelligible life. This limitation and relativity has been accepted in all branches of knowledge, including philosophy and even mysticism (*'irfịn*). A slogan has been written at the façade of the magnificent palace of human knowledge that: "Everything is known to everyone while everyone is yet to be born." (That is, so much knowledge

---

1. Nahj al-Balịghah, Sermon 1.

and learning has been entrusted by the past generation to the future generation.) Mawlᵢnᵢ (Rūmī) says,

> You say that the orator is digging a channel may water reach the next generation
>
> Although [in] every generation there is one who brings the word [of God], yet the sayings of them that have gone before are helpful.[1]

The Divine Revelation, through the great prophets, has presented to mankind an overview of the principles of the universe and the bases of jurisprudence, while scientific discoveries make clear the levels, dimensions and aspects of the insignificant corner of the universe we are located in. As acknowledged by scientists, compared with what is unknown to us, what we know of the universe is insignificant. Yet, all the scientists and philosophers still undertake activities, knowing well that the universe is not identical with what is known about it, and that they will never succeed in knowing all about it. They are still so busy working in their respective fields that it is as if they can see the entire universe within the confines of their respective fields!

The factors that stand in the way of knowing all dimensions of all components of the entire universe are as follows:

1. The use of sensory perceptions while taking into account their structural limitations, such as eyes and ears;

2. Interference of intrinsic features of the means and tools for expanding knowledge; for example, telescopes, microscopes and other equipments and tools;

3. Specific aim in knowing things limits man's perspective on the universe;

4. Premeditated general principles, which consciously or unconsciously foster and justify acquired pieces of knowledge;

5. Premeditated personal principles that influence human quadruple relationships in choosing goals and means of knowledge.

Revelation as a source of knowledge of the universe differs

---

1. Nicholson, The Rumi's *Masnavi*, Book 3, lines 2537-2538, p. 281. [Trans.]

from science in that the former offers an exceptional tranquility that no one can ever find in any other epistemic source. In usual scientific understanding of the universe, human beings acquire two things: (1) some components of the universe for the needs of physical life, and (2) delight or stupefaction with such limited recognition with some levels and components of the universe, which can never reach the tranquility-giving absolute degree.

Q3: Is it jurisprudence that 'seizes' (*qab¤*), 'expands' (*bas§*) and gives form to life, or is it the form of life that 'seizes' and 'expands' jurisprudence (and schools of law)?

Jafari: In view of discussions propounded in some contemporary essays, it means presenting changes in the general sense, and not *qab¤* and *bast* in the special sense of the terms. The terms *qab¤* and *bast* were found for the first time in a tradition by Im¡m al-⁻¡diq ('*a*). The tradition is as follows: Yūnus ibn 'Abd al-Rahm¡n narrates on the authority of °amzah ibn Mu¡ammad al-±ayy¡r that Im¡m al-⁻¡diq ('*a*) said:

> *There is no qab¤ or bast except in what God, the Exalted, has willed, predestined and inflicted.*[1]

In another tradition, Fa¤¡lah ibn Ayyūb narrates on the authority of °amzah ibn Mu¡ammad al-±ayy¡r that Im¡m al-⁻¡diq ('*a*) said: "There is nothing in the commandments and prohibitions of God in which there is *qab¤* and *bast* except in which God, the Exalted and Glorious inflicts a decree (as a trial)."[2]

The first tradition has not determined a specific subject for *qab¤* and *bast*. Then, it can be said that it includes anything in which *qab¤* and *bast* is possible. In the second tradition, the subject of *qab¤* and *bast* has been specified and that is, the commandments and prohibitions (laws and duties) of God.

This tradition can be interpreted in two ways: divine matters that somehow pertain to human existence—whether ontological

---

1. U¥£l al-K¡f¢, vol. 1, p. 152.
2. Ibid.

matters (*umūr-e takwīnī*) such as, specific course of human creation and his relationship with the universe; or, legislative matters (*umūr-e tashrī'ī*), such as, the laws and duties prescribed by God. These matters both in *qab¤* and *bast* states are based upon Divine decree and will, as well as, a trial for His servants.

There are three possibilities about *qab¤* and *bas§*:

1. Brevity and elaboration;
2. Union and dissension;
3. Obstruction and adversity, and opening and welfare

The second way of interpreting this tradition is that there is no Divine commandment and prohibition in which there is brevity and elaboration, or obstruction and opening, except that, which God, the Blessed and Exalted, has set as a trial or test for His servants. Generally speaking, considering that the Divine commandments and prohibitions are also related to human life for perfection in whose substance and purport God has set a trial or decree for His servants. This reading of the tradition has nothing to do with what can be seen in some contemporary essays in this regard.

Now let's turn to the question. The pioneer jurisprudence prepares human individuals for benefitting from their positive talents and gifts even if technological developments and science have not brought any major change into human life. This can be easily discerned, for example, in the profound acquaintance of luminaries and enlightened figures of Divine Word which is never possible to be acquired by the laity. The way that such men as F¡r¡bī, Ibn Sīn¡, Khw¡jah Na¥īr al-Dīn al-±usī, Ibn Rushd,[1] Jal¡l al-Din Rūmī, ¯adr al-Mu'allihīn (Mull¡ ¯adr¡), and Mīr D¡m¡d have benefitted from Qur'¡nic verses can never be compared with the laity's notion of them. Although there was

---

1. Ab£ 'l-Wal¢d Mu!ammad ibn A!mad ibn Rushd better known as Ibn Rushd, and in European literature as Averroes (1126-98): an Andalusian Muslim polymath; a master of Aristotelian philosophy, Islamic philosophy, Islamic theology, M¡lik¢ law and jurisprudence, logic, psychology, politics, Arabic music theory, and the sciences of medicine, astronomy, geography, mathematics, physics, and celestial mechanics. [Trans.]

no major technological breakthrough even in two centuries ago these great men have played a vital role in founding useful knowledge in the present world. At the time when the informed scholars and jurisprudents of the past centuries were concerned with the rights of animals in jurisprudence, categorically mentioning them in books of jurisprudence like *Jawₗhir al-Kalₗm*,[1] there had been no news about the advancement of science, technology and communications.[2] During the third, fourth and part of the fifth centuries AH, following the strong encouragement given by Islamic sources as to the promotion of knowledge Muslims travelled through the East and the West to acquire knowledge, such that Oriental and Western historians—even those who did not believe in any religion—acknowledged that Muslim societies had been the forerunners in research, innovation and intellectual pursuits in the world. As *Adventures of Ideas* (1967) suggests, this Muslim enterprise was indeed an original intiative; since although they drew on Greek philosophy, in empirical sciences, they acquired great advancements without imitating and following other nations and societies. Their experiments served as the foundations of important scientific and technological discoveries and exerted a far-reaching influence on the West. The 'pioneer' jurisprudence, then, played a vital role in the advancement of sciences, worldview, technology, and other principles of an advanced culture.

Meanwhile, the emergence of new issues and events can also contribute to the comparative development of jurisprudence and laws. Numerous books which are published today about newly emerged issues and include principles, rules, ratiocinations and certain deductions, bear witness to this claim. No authority has yet cast any doubt over this current.

---

1. Jawₗhir al-Kalₗm: a treatise on various subjects of fiqh (jurisprudence) written by Shaykh Muḥammad °asan ibn Bₗqir al-Najafₑ (d. Sha'bₗn 1266 AH), a great faqₑh (jurisprudent) as well as a prominent marja' al-taqlₑd. [Trans.]
2. In Tarjumeh wa Tafsₑr-e Nahj al-Balₗghah, vol. 12, pp. 158-164, the rights of animals have been thoroughly discussed in 34 articles.

In view of what has been said, it can be concluded that one should distinguish between 'adherent' and 'pioneer' jurisprudence and law as well as the jurisprudence and law that have both aspects:

1. In the 'adherent' jurisprudence and law which are allegedly functions of the desires, way of thinking and attitudes of the people, the answer is positive. The changes and modifications have their origin in the changes in social relations and emergence of new phenomena and activities, provided that this claim [about changes] is exactly correct.

2. Meanwhile, the 'pioneer' jurisprudence and law maintain that the criterion for organizing social relations is the discretion of legal and juristic authorities because the desires, way of thinking and attitudes of the laity not supported by rational principles, can neither identify nor organize human material and spiritual felicity. For this very reason, as long as changes in social relations do not duly affect the system of jurisprudence and law as far as the views of authorities are concerned, they cannot have any effect in the transformation of the said system.

A close examination and survey of the jurisprudential and legal systems throughout history reveal that none of the two models ('adherent' and 'pioneer') has ever existed in the absolute sense. No one doubts that after the Renaissance in the West, philosophers and social scientists in general have influenced laws and legislations a lot, by exercising freedom of expression. As preeminent thinkers of the time, their statements impelled the people, consciously or unconsciously, to accept such notions as usury (*ribi*), libertarian sexual relationship, legally incorporating them on the basis of people's consent and approval! On the other hand, it is impossible for a legal system to portray itself as totally pioneer and still disregard the primordial desires of people and the emergence of new relations. In line with this, you can observe changes in some socialist laws such as those of the family.

3. The hybrid model of jurisprudence and law has the claim of both adherence and pioneering. In view of the needs of

mankind that remain inalterable with the passage of time amidst changes in science, social relations and others, this model is 'pioneer' and in view of the emergence of changes in subjects and applications of phenomena and aspects of life as well as the appearance of new relations, it is 'adherent'.

Islam has a hybrid jurisprudential and legal system. To state the matter differently, in view of the Islamic jurisprudence or law's adherence to the subjects and manifestations of life as well as the set of rational principles approved by Islam, its system is 'adherent'. And, because of the rulings and laws related to the inalterable material and spiritual needs of people, it is 'pioneer'. These rulings and laws encompass all issues pertaining to the quadruple relationships, which are primordial and permanent.

Q4: How does a juristic and legal system become defected?

Jafari: If the identity of a juristic and legal system has come into being on the basis of divine revelation, common sense and primordial nature, no element can tarnish it and no defect or damage can find its way into it in the same way that no defect or damage can ever reach the true results of science. Of course, the change in the results due to the change in circumstances is not a defect. This is because the necessity for change and reconsideration of opinion on issues, principles and rules due to the emergence of [new] events, subjects and applications is not a defect or shortcoming. It rather affirms the capability of a juristic and legal system and is considered a proof of the system's resilience and greatness.

The ways through which defects and shortcoming can permeate into juristic and legal systems are related to things outside the essence of the system, such as:

1. The quality of their implementation;

2. Radical trend towards archaisms in the sense that the jurist is more pleased by whatever idea or theory which proves by him to be archaic!

3. Radical belief in the value of one's personal views and inference, and negligence of the emerging changes in subjects,

relations and the like;

4. The spirit of extreme submission (not a feeling of rational respect) to prominent figures in law and jurisprudence;

5. Movement through an exclusive professional channel (understanding in jurisprudence and law) that jurisprudents and legalists rely more on jurisprudential and legal disposition, without paying attention to the causes, motives and inclinations of the two (jurisprudential and legal). Of course, since veracity ('adilah), God-wariness (taqwi) and prominence in knowledge are conditions of being a jurisprudent and legalist in Islam, one in charge of the said two fields can volitionally be the factor for the penetration of this defect or shortcoming.

Q5: Whether people's form of life is the product of a legal (jurisprudential) system alone or there are other factors than law and jurisprudence that are involved in the formation of human life?

Jafari: If "form of life" in this context refers to the physical appearances of life which human beings have shown throughout history in different societies, it is clear that by removing conflicts and contradictions among human inclinations, legal systems have been considerably effective in shaping human life. In other aspects, however, the influence of legal system upon human life is not to that extent. And the reasons for this can be sought in the following factors:[1]

1. Human personal attitudes driven by the strong element of selfishness;

2. For the selfish holders of power law and other obligatory arrangements are mere 'cobwebs' that catch only the weakest of animals, but not Hobbesian Leviathans,[2] or Nietzschean/Machiavelian 'expediencies'.

---

1. Since the functional scope of jurisprudence (fiqh) is wider than that of law (huq£q), encompassing acts of worship and laws pertaining to man's relationship with himself as well, in reply to question 7, jurisprudence must be distinguished from law, and each of them must be examined separately in relation to this question.

2. Leviathan: a sea monster or any big animal that preys on other animals

And if "form of life" refers to the general course of human life in the course of history, we must say that there are different factors—both immediate and mediated—involved along this process. Discourses on the philosophy of history, particularly what pertains to the 'moving factor of history', undertake the explanation and interpretation of these different factors. Common (non-Islamic) legal systems function like filters for the preservation of the system and form of life. As such, throughout history, due to the emergence of revolutions, which topple down previous systems and give way to new systems, old filters go and give way to new ones. Other matters come into being in history, transforming legal sytems, and thus, changing the form and course of human life in turn.

Now, we shall deal with the effects of Islamic jurisprudence in shaping human life while keeping its definition in view. There is no doubt that every Muslim—both in the individual and collective sense—benefits from jurisprudential laws in shaping life as much as possible. It is explicitly recorded in history that Muslims in different societies have been committed to act upon their beliefs and jurisprudential laws, which the ruling elite in those societies do not believe in and regard them as hostile to their political systems, and in many cases, they deprive the people of different aspects of social life. This thing happens in some neighboring countries and also happened in our society before.

Q6: Are legal (and jurisprudential) systems capable of clashing with natural realities and laws, or should these systems be consistent with these realities and laws?

Jafari: If legal and jurisprudential systems, in general, go against natural laws and realities, they will definitely go in abeyance and cease to function. In the parlance of logic, this major premise is axiomatic but the main question of the minor premise is the above proof and that is, can legal (and jurisprudential) systems in general endure while clashing with natural realities and laws? The answer is undoubtedly negative. The crux of the matter is that we must have some explanation about natural realities and laws to know the source of the prohibition or order while harmonizing legal (and jurisprudential) systems with natural realities and laws.

Natural realities and laws encompass all events, phenomena and laws. At the time of their emergence, they can destroy natural human life; for example, earthquakes, floods, pandemics, etc. It is needless to say that in order to save himself, mankind is compelled to struggle against the realities and laws that push him to the verge of destruction. If there is somebody who urges the people to submit and not struggle against natural realities and laws, some sensible person must deal with him.

Now, this question comes to the fore: Isnt the power of humanoid beasts something natural? Yes, the penetrating eyes of Napoleon Bonaparte[1] whose glances could make a brave soldier forget his words were something natural. The ingenuity of savage Asian conquerors like Genghis Khan,[2] Hulagu Khan,[3] Tamerlane[4] and bloodthirsty European butchers like Nero,[5] Caligula[6] and Cesare Borgia,[1] were also natural phenomena.

---

1. Napoleon Bonaparte (1769-1821): a military and political leader of France and Emperor of the French as Napoleon I, whose actions shaped European politics in the early 19th century. [Trans.]

2. Genghis Khan (1162–1227): the founder, Khan (ruler) and Khagan (emperor) of the Mongol Empire, which became the largest contiguous empire in history after his death. [Trans.]

3. Hulagu Khan (c. 1217-65): a grandson of Genghis Khan and Mongol ruler who conquered much of Southwest Asia. [Trans.]

4. Timur, normally known as Tamerlane in English (1336-1405): a fourteenth-century conqueror of Western, South and Central Asia, founder of the Timurid Empire and Timurid dynasty (1370–1405) in Central Asia, and great great grandfather of Babur, the founder of the Mughal Dynasty, which survived until 1857 as the Mughal Empire in India. [Trans.]

5. Nero Claudius Caesar Augustus Germanicus, commonly known as Nero (37-68 CE): the Roman Emperor from 54 to 68 CE and the last emperor of the Julio-Claudian dynasty, whose rule is often associated with extravagance and tyranny, including the execution of his mother and stepbrother. [Trans.]

6. Gaius Julius Caesar Augustus Germanicus, commonly known as Caligula and sometimes Gaius (12-41 CE): Roman Emperor from 37 to 41 CE. After two years of his reign, surviving sources focus upon his cruelty, extravagance, and

This does not mean that they had freely developed the essence of ingenuity, or found it and inculcated it in their minds.[2]

Anyway, in a bid to destroy all original cultures and advanced civilizations, it is enough for you to say, "O builders of advanced cultures and civilizations! Sit idly and do not resist natural realities and laws and let these destructive forces run their courses."

Meanwhile, all social scientists who are familiar with all dimensions—physical and spiritual—of human existence, know that just as nature or, in general, the universe—in which human being is included—has realities and laws of its own, the human soul also has its own realities and laws. It is clear that the most fundamental condition for logical understanding of natural realities and laws is [correct] understanding of the realities and laws pertaining to the human soul. Now, if the selfish nature of a person says, "I am the goal while others are means," will moral, legal and religious laws not take any action against this by relying on the vicious notion: "The scorpion's sting, through optional grudge, is with human beings. But, it is not the dictate of its nature to sting and endanger human lives! Set aside the nature, and let it follow its own course." It was the same baseless statement, which was once the slogan of French Physiocrats[3]: "Take your seat and graciously place your life at the disposal of the factors of death!" It is never so; the truth is as follows:

The scorpion's sting is not through spite.
Its nature dictates it to bite.

---

sexual perversity, presenting him as an insane tyrant. [Trans.]

1. Cesare Borgia (1475/6-1507): Duke of Valentinois, a Valencian condottiero, politician, cardinal, and son of Pope Alexander VI of Spain and his long-term mistress Vannozza dei Cattanei. He is known for his cruelty and treachery. [Trans.]

2. Of course, the naturalness of the forms of power and ingenuities has no contradiction with justification and benefiting from those that are devoid of freewill and responsibility.

3. Physiocrats: a group of economists who believed that the wealth of nations was derived solely from the value of "land agriculture" or "land development". [Trans.]

No one can deny the fact that just as nature has its own laws, the human soul also has its own laws. Now, we shall point out some of these laws:[1]

1. Human soul by her nature requires immortality and subsistence not deterioration and extinction. To prepare the human soul for a felicitous subsistence, one must overcome selfishness, extreme profiteering, hedonism, and egotism first. Any event, phenomenon or natural law, which opposes this vital law that guarantees eternal life, must be checked in favor of the law of "the soul in its general sense".

2. Human soul yearns for reaching the Supreme Telos of life.

3. Human soul ardently desires to understand her relationship with herself so as to discipline and refine it for sublimation of its pure natural life, shared by other animals, to the "intelligible life", whose end is to expose oneself to the radiations of Divine Perfection.

4. If human soul wishes to attain the station of harmony and solidarity with her fellow human beings, who are also parts of the caravan heading to felicity, it must achieve the degree of "one equals all and all equal one".

Disregarding these primordial laws of human soul vis-à-vis the realities and laws of nature is tantamount to a fatal campaign against the self. Now, we shall explicitly state the gist of the reply to the question, thus:

If the jurisprudential systems show any sign of contradiction with natural realities and laws; if those natural things confront the established realities and facts of human principles, naturally those natural things (natural events and laws) must be checked in favor of the human principles. And, if the jurisprudential systems become so static that they lack the necessary measure to deal with natural events, realities and laws, there is a need

---

1. Let us be reminded of this immortal saying which is the divine logic of the prophets and pious sages including Plato:

"Die willingly so as to live naturally."

That is to say, kill (i.e. suppress) your selfish inclinations to attain eternal life with the original nature of the soul.

for their reform. Even in this case, however, generalization does not solve anything or stimulate any progress. In fact, they must be dealt with on a case-to-case basis and be affirmed as clear manifestations of the contradiction of a certain legal and jurisprudential system with natural realities and laws. [Thereafter,] you must strive for the solution.

The task of both jurisprudents and natural scientists is to engage in their respective fields with a fresh perception, understanding and research. It is not that only jurisprudence and law are not supposed to grapple with natural realities and laws, but rather natural and social sciences are also not supposed to consider themselves authoritative—in the name of scientism—to express an opinion on jurisprudence, law and other social sciences by means of a probability, supposition, hypothesis, or theory.

We say "in the name of scientism" because in the past two centuries, hundreds of theories, hypotheses and presumptions have been propounded by thinkers in the arena of human knowledge, and the narrowminded and ignoramuses have regarded them as "science". In the end, however, with the discovery of their refutations, they have been thrown out of the domain of definitive sciences. With this distinction, it can be proved that so far there has been no jurisprudential and legal principle or law that goes against any established scientific *fact* (not theory, hypothesis or presumption).

Q7: Does Islamic legal system allow any type of legal system to emerge?

Jafari: Islamic legal system is like the Islamic philosophical system. By keeping its own worldview and essential presumptions in relation to the quadruple ontological relationships, this philosophical system has the capacity to offer tens, and perhaps in some cases, hundreds of philosophical and epistemological doctrines, and to tolerate all types of idea, principle or rule expressed on the basis of reason and pure primordial conceptions. This is because as demonstrated through these discourses, Islamic legal system revolves around the axis of "human intelligible life". For instance, since the emergence of machine and hundreds of other amenities on the scene of human life, which have given rise to tens of principles and rules, Islam has never adopted an opposite stance against these principles and rules. However, that Islam could accommodate tens, and perhaps in some cases, hundreds of philosophical tendencies as its depth and vastness are more than enough to require a detailed reasoning.

Q8: Is it possible for the outside world to go to the extent of rendering the Islamic legal system totally inefficient and replace it with a totally different legal-jurisprudential system?

Jafari: If the physiological and psychological makeup of man is so transformed that man with his immense potential ceases to exist, it is clear that in such a time Islamic legal system will cease to function absolutely, because there will be no human being whose legal-jurisprudential system it is supposed to regulate.

The Judge said [to the Sufi], "Make the roof firm, O son,

So that I may decorate it with good and evil [1]

You are not supposed to discuss the ineffectivity of the Islamic law and jurisprudence as merely the result of natural and technological transformation and change in human relations, and the like. You can also observe the ineffectivity of the Islamic law and jurisprudence prior to those changes, when the devastating storm of utilitarianism, lust, hedonism, and greed for power crushed the arch of human life in the ocean of history with the rocks of the said proclivities, shattering them and leaving no trace of humanity. Just like bolts and nuts of a lifeless machine in the hands of selfish power-worshippers, tens of millions of people plunged into luxury and pleasure, like unconscious and unthinking dolls leaping on their hands. It was because of the possible coming of such a day that Einstein,[2]

---

1. Nicholson, The Rumi's *Masnavi*, Book 6, Part 47, line 1534, p. 175. That is, first prove your case, then I will give judgment. [Trans.]
2. Albert Einstein (1879-1955): German, Swiss and American mathematician and atomic physicist who stimulated a revolution in physics by discovering the

one of the famous contemporary figures, had warned of a third world war, saying that if this war occurs, the world and its inhabitants will be annihilated. With utmost clarity, he also said, "Will you feel bad about the extinction of the human race?" The story is as follows:

> In 1949, Einstein thus wrote about his meeting with an American leader: 'I was recently discussing with a smart American figure who was apparently a good man. I reminded him that the menace of a new war threatens humanity and if such a war occurs, the human race will likely be wiped out and only a transnational organization can prevent such a menace. But, with utmost surprise, I heard his reply, 'For what reason do you oppose the extinction of the human race to such an extent?''[1]

If we examine the succeeding words of Einstein in interpreting his interlocutor's reply, we will find out that one of the main reasons that induced him to give such a shocking reply was the same depreciation of human life and mental activities that emanate from the misuse of the bounties God has bestowed to His servants in this world. People have totally crushed spiritual mirth from human life and only live on the basis of fatalism, hedonism or libertarianism. Einstein continues in following words:

> Such a harsh and categorical reply indicates inward suffering and outward affliction which is a product of the modern world. In my opinion, this reply is that of a person who has strived hard to excel but failed and has lost even the hope to succeed. This reply bespeaks of a painful seclusion from which all human beings suffer.[2]

Q9: In your opinion, to what extent can religion interfere in

---

theory of general relativity and for which he received the Nobel Prize in physics in 1921 and is often regarded as the father of modern physics. [Trans.]
1. Philipp Frank, Einstein: His Time and Life, trans. ᵒasan ⁻affᵢr¢, p. 541 (originally in English).
2. Ibid., p. 542.

worldly affairs? Can one say that religion has drawn the overall lines of material prosperity, leaving man to himself with respect to the minute details?

Jafari: It goes without saying that the schools—both religious and non-religious—that set the limits of human obligations and virtues in both realms of corporeal and eternal life are concerned with the general matters and not with particular facts and issues. But, the burden of identifying this general guideline and applying it to particulars cases lies on the people. It is for this reason that we say that Islam has both aspects of 'pioneering' and 'adherence'. This religion pays attention to all beliefs, laws and duties related to the permanent material and spiritual needs of man. Given its aspect of 'pioneering' and the regulation of permanent material and spiritual needs, it brings human beings to perfection, but as to the details, subjects and choice on the ways of living (provided that they are not against reason and the established Islamic rules), it has approved the intelligible choices of people. In modern parlance, it is adherent and this is why Islam is essentially innovative and constructive and this helps it to remain intact in the course of time.

Islam's guidance is at utmost perfection in view of human potentialities in his intelligible life both in the domain of his worldly and otherworldly life. And, if there is a person or a society who lack such potential, for whatever reason, no defect whatsoever can be attributed to the perfect guidance of Islam.

Q10: Ibn Khaldūn once said that in order to have an average or moderate society, there is no need for prophets, and as a result, for religion, and history shows that people who had no prophets were not incapable or inept in leading their lives. Thus, anyone who insists that it is only under the aegis of religious thought that mundane prosperity could be ensured only expresses his own religious conviction. But, if one approaches religion as an outsider, he will find it inconsistent with historical facts, rather, discover the opposite. That is, there were nonreligious nations that were able to manage themselves well and if ever they had problems, these were common human problems, which were not caused by irreligiosity and the lack of religious supervision. What is your idea of this theory of Ibn Khaldūn?

Jafari: First of all, we must examine Ibn Khaldūn's statements in this regard. In his seminal *Al-Muqaddimah*, he says:

> *The weapons [naturally] made for the defence of human beings against the aggressiveness of dumb animals do not suffice... Thus, something else is needed for defence against the aggressiveness of human beings toward each other... The person who exercises a restraining influence, therefore, must be one of them. He must dominate them and have power and authority over them, so that no one of them will be able to attack another. This is the meaning of royal authority. It has thus become clear that royal authority is a natural quality of man, which is absolutely necessary for mankind. The philosophers mention that it also exists among certain dumb animals, such as the bees and the locusts. One discerns among them the existence of authority and obedience to a leader. They follow one who is distinguished as their leader by his natural characteristics and body. However, outside of human beings, these things exist as the result of natural disposition and divine guidance, and not as the result of an ability to think or to administrate. The philosophers go further. They attempt to give logical proof of the existence of prophethood and to show that prophethood is a natural quality of man. In this connection, they carry the argument to its ultimate consequences and say that human beings absolutely require some authority to exercise a restraining influence. They go on to say that such restraining influence exists through the religious law ordained by God and revealed to mankind by a human being. He is distinguished from the rest of mankind by special qualities of divine guidance that God gave him, in order that he might find the others submissive to him and ready to accept what he says. Eventually, the existence of an authority among them and over*

*them becomes a fact that is accepted without the slightest
disapproval or dissent. This proposition of the philosophers is
not logical, as one can see. Existence and human life can
materialize without [the existence of prophethood and religious
law] through injunctions, which a person in authority may
devise on his own or with the help of a group, that enables him
to force the others to follow him wherever he wants to go.
People who have a [divinely revealed] book and who follow the
prophets are few in number in comparison with the
Zoroastrians who have none. The latter constitute the majority
of the world's inhabitants. Still, they have possessed dynasties
and monuments, not to mention life itself. They still possess
these things at this time in the intemperate zones in the north
and the south. This is in contrast with human life in the state
of anarchy, with no one to exercise a restraining influence.
That would be impossible. This shows that the philosophers are
wrong when they assume that prophethood exists by necessity.
The existence of prophethood is not required by logic. Its
[necessary character] is indicated by the religious law, as was
the belief of the early Muslims. God gives success and
guidance.[1]*

There are some points of weakness in Ibn Khaldūn's
comments the most important of which are the following:

1. Ibn Khaldūn regarded divine guidance as essential for the
animals rather than human beings, who enjoy innumerable
gifts. He considered human beings needless of divine guidance,
or he regarded the guidance endowed to other creatures as
sufficient also for human beings. However, because of his
extremely diverse potential and faculties, human need for
special guidance is more pressing.

2. "This proposition of the philosophers is not logical, as one
can see. Existence and human life can materialize without [the

---

1. Ibn Khald£n, Al-'Ibar wa D¢w¡n al-Mubtada' wa'l-Khabar f¢ Ayy¡m al-'Arab
wa 'l-'Ajam wa l-Barbar, better known as Al-Muqaddimah, vol. 1, pp. 43-44.
The translation is adapted from Ibn Khaldun, The Muqaddimah: An
Introduction to History, trans. Rosenthal, pp. 47-48. [Trans.]

existence of prophethood and religious law]", Ibn Khaldūn claims. He must indeed be reminded that the goal of human life cannot be summed up in a few days of eating and drinking, sleeping, anger, and lust. If man is left to himself, he would not give up carnal desires and sensual life in order to reach the supreme telos of life, which is exposing oneself to the radiations of Divine Perfection. Human movement towards "intelligible life," (*tayyibah*), life grounded on clear evidence or linked with God (*My life and my death are all for the sake of Allah, the Lord of all the worlds*[1]) is not possible without intellection and divine law.

3. Ibn Khaldūn has committed a mind-boggling historical mistake which is beyond explanation. He says that "people who have a [divinely revealed] book and who follow the prophets are few in number in comparison with the Zoroastrians who have none. The latter constitute the majority of the world's inhabitants."

Firstly, to have fire-temples in Persia, China and India does not make the Zoroastrians the majority of the world's inhabitants. **Secondly**, as we read in books on comparative religion, the established theory about the Zoroastrians is that they have a religion and their prophet is Zoroaster (Zartusht) and their sacred scripture is called the Avesta. Of course, the complete details of this religion and the history of emergence of Zoroaster are considerably unclear. What is certain is that the Zoroasterians believe in two sources that regulate the universe, viz. Yazdịn (representing good and light) and Ahriman (representing evil and darkness). They also acknowledge the existence of angels with whom they seek closeness. They regard simple elements, particularly fire, as sacred, linking all creatures to the Supreme Being. They have a scripture and perform a specific ritual of worship. In sum, Zoroastrianism is a religion and for this reason, it is officially recognized in Muslim countries. One speculation regarding Ibn Khaldūn's statements

---

1. S£rat al-An'ịm 6:162.

would be that what he meant was the notion of divine grace whose manifestation, among many others, according to the theologians (*mutakallimīn*), is the sending down of the prophets, and not justice necessitated by rational necessity.

4. In Chapter 51, Ibn Khaldūn said something contradicting this theory. He argues:

> *We have mentioned before in more than one place that human social organization is something necessary. It is what is meant by "civilization" which we have been discussing. (People) in any social organization must have someone who exercises a restraining influence and rules them and to whom recourse may be had. His rule over them is sometimes based upon a divinely revealed religious law. They are obliged to submit to it in view of their belief in reward and punishment in the other world, (things that were indicated) by the person who brought them (their religious law). Sometimes, (his rule is based) upon rational politics. People are obliged to submit to it in view of the reward they expect from the ruler after he has become acquainted with what is good for them. The first (type of rule) is useful for this world and for the other world, because the lawgiver knows the ultimate interest of the people... The second (type of rule) is useful only for this world... Now, the afore-mentioned rational politics may be of two types. The first type of rational politics may concern itself with the (public) interest in general, and with the ruler's interest in connection with the administration of his realm, in particular. This was the politics of the Persians. It is something related to philosophy. God made this type of politics superfluous for us in Islam at the time of the caliphate. The religious laws take its place in connection with both general and special interests, for they also include the maxims (of the philosophers) and the rules of royal authority... Muslim rulers, however, practice this type of politics in accordance with the requirements of the Muslim religious law, as much as they are able to. Therefore, the political norms here are a mixture of religious laws and ethical rules, norms that are natural in social organization together*

with a certain necessary concern for strength and group feeling. Examples to be followed in (the practice of) this (kind of politics) are, in the first place, the religious law, and then, the maxims of the philosophers and the way of life of rulers (of the past).[1]

In our opinion, these words of Ibn Khaldūn echo a totally correct belief. It is clear that life anchored in religion is more comprehensive than living according to pure intellection (if it is possible at all).

Q11: It seems that the religious framework is indeed universal and perfect in the sense that it ensures both prosperity in the world and felicity in the Hereafter. But, life anchored in nonreligious policy largely manages mundane life. Even then, it is not clear whether this management is identical with worldly prosperity or not. Moreover, there is no guarantee if the otherworldly felicity is ensured or not for a person.

Human life is an integrated reality consisting of two stages; viz. this world and the Hereafter, and to be more precise, two domains, viz. prior to death and after death. These two stages are not of the same width but of the same length; human life in the Hereafter is the crystallization and inward dimension of his life in this world, and by considering the inward effects, religion manages and guides human individual and social life, which the human intellect is incapable of doing without the guidance of religion. Therefore, one cannot rely on mere schemes of the human intellect, in ensuring the individual and social prosperity in this world with the otherworldly felicity of human beings, without reliance on religious guidance, except in cases in which the religion itself has allowed us to follow rational guidance.

I would like to ask another question. Some empiricist philosophers of religion in the West believe that if religion is

---

1. Ibn Khald£n, Al-'Ibar wa D¢w¡n al-Mubtada' wa'l-Khabar f¢ Ayy¡m al-'Arab wa 'l-'Ajam wa l-Barbar, better known as Al-Muqaddimah.
The translation is adapted from Ibn Khaldun, The Muqaddimah, pp. 256-257. [Trans.]

really meant for mundane prosperity, this claim can be tested in this world, but if it is also meant for otherworldly felicity, this claim of religion cannot be verified in this world because no one has seen the Hereafter. What is your idea on this issue?

Jafari: The laboratory for testing religion's claim as to bringing felicity in the Hereafter consists of human reason, conscience and primordial nature (*fitrah*) that can distinguish baseless things linked with fleeting animal desires from facts that are compatible with the perfect and progress-seeking essence of man. Felicity in the eternal world belongs to those who earn the merit in this world to *dwell in* the Divine Threshold in the eternal world. It belongs to those who spend their lives in this world craving for perfection by means of organizing and rectifying the quadruple ontological relationships. Thus, any religion or set of beliefs that explains to the people the various channels of this feeling and ardent desire has ensured their felicity in the Hereafter.

Q12: I would like to ask you to give us a short account of Islamic notion of art and that what does ensure the religiosity and Islamic essnece of an art?

Jafari: To begin with, we must give a general account of art. A complete *definition* of art, like the definition of other categories particularly the mysterious truths inside man—such as mind and soul—is either impossible or at least very difficult to reach. Hence, we shall content ourselves here with a *description* of art.

We must regard art as having three poles or phases:

First pole: It is a special feeling caused by a specific genius or enthusiasm. Art is one of the innermost realities of human nature and does not pertain to imagination, illusions and nominal things. It is like genius, discovering and craving for them. Apart from the essential value of this reality it has the potential to possess actual value.

Second pole: It is the mental framework, the identity of a person. When an artistic feeling is under way like a limpid fountain, it accommodates special features of the mental framework, and is ready to appear in society. In terms of special features, quality and values, the fate of art in this phase is determined. Like a limpid fountain, which flows from a pure source, it follows its course before reaching the bases of trees, flowers and plants or being mixed with other things, detrimental or beneficial to the roots of plants. As such, one must scrutinize the main root of decency or indecency of the various arts. It must be seen which mind provides the life-giving water of artistic feelings and which human identity justifies it. The morally corrupted arts, which unfortunately go against and undermine the pristine values of human"intelligible life" in the name of arts and culture, belong to the first category. The expressed sense of genius in the second phase can either be contaminated by harmful substances, or presented as excellent elements of man's "intelligible life" in this phase.

Third pole: It is the actual piece of art in the outside world. It is in this phase that art is connected with the members of society. If the purpose behind making an artistic work is to relieve the pain and suffering of people, and to rectify, organize and improve their lives in the context of "intelligible life". (*My life and my death are all for the sake of Allah, the Lord of all the worlds*[1]), then this art is not only religious or Islamic but it is also highly desirable, and regarded as obligatory (*w¡jib¡t*). This is the general law governing art from the viewpoint of religion. Of course, there are ample discussions on how to identify the actual manifestations of decent and indecent arts contained in pertinent treatises and books.

If the goal of art is solely to present artistic talent and show sublime feeling which the artistic talent generates—provided that it does not bring about any arbitrary effect on the people's morality and does not deprive them of religion—there is no problem at all, except when the artist does it out of selfishness. Like an oil lamp, he sets himself on fire and temporarily gives

---

1. S£rat al-An'¡m 6:162.

light so that his work draws interest. Like law ('pioneer' law and 'adherent' law) there is, 'pioneer' art and 'adherent' art. The value of 'pioneer' art lies in the fact that with pure mind and soul, the artists activate their artistic talent by benefiting from lofty human principles, justifying them by the discovery of a wholesome life toward the Sublime Threshold of Perfection and benefiting from it.

Q13: What is your conception of "religious technology"?

Jafari: No technogical instrument, device or stuff is 'religious' or 'nonreligious'. In fact, when human basic needs push him to pursue a technological innovation or invention so as to meet those needs, this is something indicated in the Qur'¡n:

> *Prepare against them whatever you can of [military] power.*[1]

That is, "You amass and prepare whatever you can of power for the sake of defending your life, prestige and honor against the enemy. Such a device is motivated by religion. In the past, some simpletons tried to extract the principles of all the technological inventions and advancements ever achieved by mankind, from the Qur'¡n and traditions (*ahadīth*). This was a futile attempt because the main function of heavenly books and religious sources is not to teach mankind the necessity of mathematics, physics, chemistry, botany, and geology. The main function of the prophets and the heavenly books is to teach mankind the basic needs in the realm of "intelligible life" and to campaign for meeting those needs. But the quantity, quality and nature of the devise or instrument supposed to perform the aforementioned function depends on the dictates of reason, types of understanding, acumen for discovery and invention, and kinds of skills God has given to His servants.

It is needless to say that just as the reason behind the necessity for and the manner of preparing the shovel for farming, a specific equipment for constructing a building, and

---

1. S£rat al-Anf¡l 8:60.

formulating different types of medicines for curing diseases is not a function of the prophets and heavenly books. By the same token, it is not the function of the prophets and the heavenly books to state the ways of producing technological devices, manufacturing computers, analyzing atomic particles, and the like. Sometimes, there are general indications about basic principles governing the universe so that supernatural leaders (the prophets, Im¡ms and *awliy¡'*), the heedful, the wise and the authorities (*ūlū 'l-alb¡b*) know and prove to other people that the knowledge contained in the heavenly books are based upon knowledge of the general principles and fundamentals.

Q14: As you know, economics has two facets, i.e. value and knowledge, can one say that since economics is a science and deals with the external world, it is not specified if it is Islamic or not, and since it is value-laden and is of mentally posited (*i'tib¡rī*) categories, it can be Islamic or non-Islamic?

Jafari: We need to take it into earnest attention from the very outset that the term *i'tib¡rī* is not accurate in value-laden cases of obligations and virtues because *i'tib¡r* (validity) does not only signify *ja'l* (forge), *wa¤'* (standing), or *insh¡'* (composition) which is *i'tib¡r* in a sense. In fact, when an *i'tib¡r* or an *insh¡'* appears, there are realities such as self-preservation, instinct, primary or secondary needs in prior phases, and there are also realities that will appear after appearance of *i'tib¡r* (composition, standing, or convention) and all of them have actual reality. Let's now turn to the question. We must first take into account the [main] principles and then deal with the secondary principles and rules. Islamic economics is based upon a number of general principles and fundamentals some of which we shall mention below:

1. In Islam, ownership is not a goal but rather a means. It addresses some human instincts and regulates his relationships with his fellow human beings.

2. Economics in Islam has both individual and social dimensions.

3. Based on the above principle, ownership in Islam is not

limited, and as long as it does not obstruct the livelihood and rights of other people in society, it is free.

4. Ownership is allowed as far as it does no damage to other citizens' properties. For this very reason, some types of ownership are prohibited. For example:

- Hoarding of essential items for society
- Hoarding that leads to inflation and disruption of economic activities
- Production and distribution of harmful products
- Production and distribution of means of debauchery
- Usury (*rib*ᵢ)
- Production and distribution of narcotic drugs
- Selling of weapons to hostile states and nations at the time of war, except defensive devices
- Production and distribution of the articles of excessive luxury
- Extravagance in whatever form
- The necessity for preparing the means of livelihood from the most basic animals' fodder to the highest means of livelihood, whether they are basic agricultural products or produced by the most advanced technology ever available
- In the production and distribution of economic commodities, priority is given to those which are more essential for human life

5. The value of work, both mental and physical, in accordance with the Qur'ᵢnic verse, *"And do not cheat the people of their goods,"*[1] must be real not artificial. The outcome of this vital economic principle is that if a worker is not aware of the real value (amount of wage) of his work, or due to an emergency situation, he is satisfied with a wage lesser than the real value of his work, he does not get the real value of, or wage for, his work and the ruler is supposed to prepare the grounds for the worker to get the real value of his work.

---

1. S£rat al-Shu'arᵢ' 26:183.

In case of free competition, the supervision and guidance of the state is indispensable as this prevents people motivated by self-interest to violate the rights of others

6. Economic relations with other people and nations are free, provided that they do not go against the Islamic laws.

It is clear that the execution of these general principles requires specific cases, means and tools, as well as establishing relations with nature and people, and acquiring sciences and crafts which are needed to provide for and organize those affairs. As such, they pertain to the channel of religious obligations, whether these sciences and crafts can be learned within Muslim societies or in foreign communities provided that, this does not lead to foreign domination and spread of corruption in Muslim societies.

These remarks make it clear that any reality that is related with Islamic concerns, in one way or other, such as the relationship between subject and judgement, premise and conclusion, means and end, and the like, ceases to be neutral and acquires a religious color. If providing the means of livelihood for people requires the learning of related sciences and acquiring a specific technology, anyone (state, society, or individual) who does not take the necessary steps shall be regarded as accountable and offender.

[**Comment**: what is worthy of note following Jafari's remarks is that since man is a free being and this freedom diversifies his economic life too, a stable economic condition cannot be discerned for man. It is also for this reason that Islam has not introduced a rigid science of economics for all stages of human life, although certain morals and legal decrees in the form of real cases are taken into account for all periods, and whose difference with economics shall be scrutinized elsewhere. This point is not a defect in the religion of Islam but one of its merits. Moreover, no school of thought or science can offer a fixed science of economics. The essence of science, including economics, changes or evolves according to the conditions and exigency of time, and a fixed science of economics is something impossible. Nonetheless, Islam supervises and guides economics in two aspects, i.e. in terms of jurisprudence (legality) and morality. Economic moral orders, and economic decrees, and jurisprudential rules of Islam, do not establish a distinct science of economics but, at the same time, they cannot allow just any science of economics to emerge and operate. Thus, the science of economics allowed to emerge and flourish in Islamic society is that which harmonizes itself with the moral and jurisprudential rules as well as the moral and legal decrees of Islamic economics. Similar is the relationship of Islam with other new branches of social sciences such as sociology, psychology and political science. In other words, Islam does not offer a distinct sociology, psychology, political science, and economics. Yet, it has stated certain principles in those fields and by relying on them, any field is allowed to emerge and flourish. Therefore, if we ever talk about "Islamic sociology," "Islamic psychology," "Islamic political science," or "Islamic economics," this means that they are organized in corcordance and harmony with the Islamic views and fundamentals in those fields. This does not imply that Islam has brought down a complete and comprehensive "science" in economics, political science, psychology, sociology, and the like, thus making us needless of human research in those fields. Keeping this in view, in economics, too, any economic system that succeeds in harmonizing itself with the legal foundations, requirements and rules as well as economic values of Islam is religious and Islamic. And any economic system that fails to conform and reconcile with them is neither religious nor Islamic, and Islam and Islamic society must not allow it to emerge and operate.]

Q15: We discussed "religious art" and "religious technology". Now I want to propound a more general question: does labeling everything as "religious" suggest that everything can be a means or vehicle for understanding and realizing religious thought? Can all things have such a function?

Jafari: Some thinkers do not have a correct notion of

religion. Many Western thinkers, in particular, belong to this group. They have accepted the notion that religion is a personal matter between man and God and, severed religion from all matters and aspects of material and spiritual life. By making this *heroic* step, they have actually separated the essence of religion from human existence, practically reducing man—in the words of the conscious and wise men of the West—to the level of unconscious dents of a machine, and talking about Epicurus and Epicureanism[1] in order to amuse him. They have entertained him with debauchery, a drinking spree and addiction, so much so, that in the words of Mawlįnį (Rūmī), they have undermined his thinking and mental power.

> *Nihil est religio et precatio ejus nisi penis:[2]*
>
> *His thought has borne him down to the lowest depth.[3]*

This intellectual degradation in the past centuries, as in the time of Mawlįnį (Rūmī), was upheld by a minority and advocated behind closed doors, but, in contemporary time, thanks to such figures as Freud—the Genghis Khans plundering human souls with a dim light labeled "science" in their hands and with "scientific masks" on their faces—have drawn the people to futility. During this period, by taking pleasure in the life discipline of bees and "libertarianism," they have ceased to think and talk about the essence of life, and some have even gone to the extent of impudently saying, "Thinking is an illness as such."

This destructive weapon against the essence of man can also be detected in the minds of figures like Sartre who said, "Man has history but has no essence"; that is, [only] man and his

---

1. Epicureanism: a school of philosophy founded around 307 BC on the basis of the teachings of Epicurus, an ancient Greek atomic materialist philosopher, who believed that the greatest good was to seek modest pleasures in order to attain a state of tranquility (ataraxia) and freedom from fear, as well as absence of bodily pain (aponia) through knowledge of the workings of the world and the limits of one's desires. [Trans.]

2. That is, "There is nothing from his religion and prayer except the penalties." [Trans.]

3. Nicholson, The Rumi's *Masnavi*, Book 2, Part 89, line 3151, p. 331. [Trans.]

behavior exists!

To elaborate this answer in discursive terms, it is suggested to refer first to the general definition of religion we have presented earlier. If the first level of consciousness, which is vigilance (*yaq̈ah*), is given to a person, and remains in him, all moments of his life shall be directed according to the Qur'¡nic verse, *My life and my death are all for the sake of Allah, the Lord of all the worlds'*.[1] After that—from his most trivial action to his greatest exploits and thoughts; from a simple notion to the most elaborate and intricate scientific-technological ideas; also, from the initial chant of *All¡hu akbar* (Allah is the greatest) to the acts of worship performed at all times —all moments of his life shall be irrigated by the water of religion.[2] Now, this question arises: What is this vigilance, which if possessed by a person, his entire life acquires religious color?

Vigilance refers to that consciousness which makes a person consider himself a purposeful part of a grand totality that operates according to the direction and command of Divine Law, and moves towards eternity moment by moment. This vigilance breeds another vigilance, which a person will experience with utmost clarity:

> As God created the world/ He sealed a different destiny for man/ we were delegated to search for secrets/ so as to discover the clues to creation.

It is with this realization that a person understands that if all knowledge and learning in the world are inculcated in the mind, yet they do not contribute at all into the process of his perfection, he will acquire no benefit from them except their natural existence.

Considering the fact that we know primordially that all moments and minutest details of human life are under the supervision and dominance of God and life is an indispensible part of a purposeful totality which is moving toward the

---

1. S£rat al-An'¡m 6:162. [Trans.]
2. S£rat al-An'¡m 6:162. [Trans.]

Presence of the Lord, human enthusiasm for reaching the Lordly Presence flows from his inner nature, and thereafter, even the drawing he makes is in a state of searching, and this as a whole is an act of worship.

> *Every one who is left far from his source,*
>
> *Looks back for the time when he was united with it.*[1]

In conclusion, you can ask, which action, saying, thinking, moments, and even breathing of such a person is not religious?

In the words of Mawl¡n¡ (Rūmī),

And our souls, like this breath (of ours) steals away,
Little by little, from the prisons of the world
The perfumes of our (good) words ascend even unto Him,
Ascending from us whither God knoweth.
Our breaths soar up with the choice (words),
As a gift from us, to the abode of everlastingness;
Then comes to us the recompense of our speech,
A double (recompense) thereof, as a mercy from (God) the Glorious;

> *Then He causes us to utter good words like those (already uttered),*
>
> *That His servant may obtain (something more) of what he has obtained*[2]

Q16: Can one say that in the call of the prophets and revealed religions, in general, and Islam, in particular, although benefiting from the world and nature is not prohibited, no emphasis can also be seen on stimulating and encouraging the people to maximize benefiting from the world and the bounties of nature?

Jafari: The overall context of the divine religion conveyed by Prophet Ibr¡hīm (Abraham) (*'a*) and perfected in the mission of the Prophet of Islam (¥) has given so much importance to the lives of people in the world that blindness in this world is deemed tantamount to blindness in the Hereafter. In this regard, the Holy Qur'¡n states, thus:

---

1. Nicholson, The Rumi's *Masnavi*, Book 1, Part 1, line 4, p. 7. [Trans.]
2. Ibid., Part 41, lines 881-885, p. 95. [Trans.]

But whoever has been blind in this [world] will be blind in the Hereafter.[1]

The Qur'ᵢnic verses that invite the believers to delve into the universe as divine signs, do not mean that we have to obtain some academic degrees and be delighted with having them. Instead, in this world the personality of a person must come to fruition, and this coming to fruition is the synthesis or product of science, knowledge and expansion of the "human ego" in the objective world, without which it is impossible to benefit from the world for the intelligible life. In reply to the current question, we shall point to some Qur'ᵢnic verses and traditions pertaining to exertion of efforts for life in this world. In another verse of the Holy Qur'ᵢn, it is thus stated:

By the means of what Allah has given you, seek the abode of the Hereafter, while not forgetting your share of this world.[2]

In this noble verse, organizing life in this world is not considered unlawful. In fact, it has an extremely subtle point on the merit of life in this world and the means of livelihood as a launch pad for the eternal life. Keeping this in view, the reproached and blameworthy kind of life in this world is that which plunges man into materialism, thus depriving him of the life worthy of the connection with God—*My life and my death are all for the sake of Allah, the Lord of all the worlds.*[3] Another point regarding this verse is that even this worldly life does not bar one from enjoying its pleasures and benefits as long as they do not turn his "intelligible life" into an animalistic one.

Say, 'Who has forbidden the adornment of Allah which He has brought forth for His servants, and the good things of [His] provision?'[4]

---

1. S£rat al-Isrᵢ' (or Ban¢ Isrᵢ'¢l) 17:72. [Trans.]
2. S£rat al-Qasas 28:77.
3. S£rat al-An'ᵢm 6:162. [Trans.]
4. S£rat al-A'rᵢf 7:32.

One of the reasons behind the mission of the prophets ('a) is the regulation of the people's material aspects of life.[1]

Abū'l-Bakhtarī quotes the Holy Prophet (¥) to have said in his supplication:

O Allah! Bless our bread. (That is to say, economically organize our life in this world.) For without bread, neither can we say our prayers, observe fasting nor act upon the commands of our Lord.[2]

Imam al-¯ṣdiq ('a) is reported to have said:

He is not from us, whoever abandons his world for the Hereafter and his Hereafter for this world.[3]

It is narrated that Imām al-Bāqir ('a) once said:

I see myself an enemy of the person for whom it is difficult to strive in life, and he lies on his back and says, 'O Allah! Give me provision and let it be spread on the ground to seek the grace of Allah,' while the ant comes out of its hole to look for provision.[4]

Imam al-Baqir ('a) has also said:

Indeed I hate the person who is indisposed in his worldly affairs, and whoever is indisposed in the worldly affairs is [more] indisposed in the otherworldly affairs.[5]

[The following traditions are also recorded in the corpus of *hadīth*:]

The Apostle of Allah (¥) said: 'Indeed Allah does not like the one who is idle both in the worldly and otherworldly matters.'[6]

The Apostle of Allah is reported to have said: 'If the Day

---

1. See Nahj al-Balīghah, Sermon 1.
2. Al-Furū` Min al-Kāfī, vol. 5, p. 73.
3. Shaykh al-¯adūq, Man Lā Yaḥḍuruh al-Faqīh, p. 353.
4. Ibid., p. 363.
5. Furū' Min al-Kāfī, vol. 5, p. 85.
6. Al-Barakah fī Faḍl al-Saḥī wa 'l-°arakah – Al-Wā¥ibū al-°abashī, p. 3.

of Judgment is to come and there is a date-palm sapling in the hand of one of you, if he could be able not to rise up unless he plants it, he must do so.' [1]

As a result, the definite requisite of the Qur'jnic verses and traditions that show the need to preserve the dignity and honor of the Muslims is to strive hard for the mundane affairs. This is because with the startling utilization of the tools for domination, exploitation and slavery, the abjectness and humiliation of the societies that neglect organizing their worldly affairs are certain. The same God who defends such life in this world says:

Prepare against them whatever you can of [military] power. [2]

The same criterion for the defense of dignity and honor has given the order for the strongest physical defense.

What is more explicit than the said criterion is the following verse:

Indeed those whom the angels take away while they are wronging themselves, they ask, 'What state were you in?' They reply, 'We were abased in the land.' They say, 'Was not Allah's earth vast enough so that you might migrate in it?' The refuge of such shall be hell, and it is an evil destination. [3]

If you scrutinize the contents of the blessed order of the Commander of the Faithful (*'a*) to Mjlik al-Ashtar[4] and his instructions to other government officials, we will definitely see that there has been no exact, necessary and sufficient program for accurately organizing the "intelligible life" of human societies, similar to those orders and instructions.

What is to be borne in mind is that worldly life is a very meaningful passageway for the eternal life in the presence of

1. Ibid., p. 16.
2. S£rat al-Anfjl 8:60.
3. S£rat al-Nisj' 4:97.
4. See Nahj al-Baljghah, Letter 53. [Trans.]

the Absolute Perfection, Almighty Allah. For this reason, all positive human gifts through sincere efforts and struggle in human relationship with himself are ordered in what is called 'utmost efforts' (described as *sa'ī*, *kabad*, *kadah*, and competition to do good deeds):

> These demands (cravings) for action were appointed in order that
>
> Your inward consciousness should come clearly into (outward) view.[1]

All the emphasis and orders to know the universe, and to know oneself, are generally not meant to make the human mind a mirror reflecting all the components of the universe and man, or to perceive the Divine Attributes of Beauty and Glory. Instead, they mean benefiting from the universe and knowing man in general as well as in relation with God, which will definitely be impossible without self-edification, honoring of man and humanity, acquisition of skills and knowledge of the world of nature. In general, we must accept that the perfection of man can only be attained by means of knowing and purifying the self through sublime human values, knowing the universe and benefiting from its various dimensions, levels and realities, to harmonize the inner world with the outer world along the path of stimulating one's total existence and potential asset.

Q17: Would you please brief us of the universal and common notions and points of Islam shared by other religions, along with the exclusive viewspoints of Islam.

Jafari: In order to identify the general and common concepts of Islam and other religions, we must first consider the types of religion:

1. The religions prior to the Abrahamic Faith;

2. The religions with unclear beliefs on the Origin (*mabda'*) and Resurrection (*ma'ịd*), such as Buddhism;

3. The Abrahamic religions presently constituted by Judaism, Christianity and Islam. Of course, it is possible that

---

1. Nicholson, The Rumi's *Masnavi*, Book 2, Part 23, line 997, p. 107. [Trans.]

the Sabians and Zoroastrians are also among the followers of Prophet Ibrₗhīm ('a);

4. Sects and denominations such as Protestantism (from Catholic Christianity) and similar groups;

5. Regional religions such as Shintoism in Japan and Confucianism in China);

6. Sectarian schools which do not have real religious roots but have been given religious color from the beginning or later on.

7. Nonreligious schools with various labels, one of which claims to be championing humanity, called "humanism", asserting that given the human principles it upholds, it can respond to all the needs and concerns of humankind. Other forms also exist and focus more on the political, legal and economic dimension of people.

Alongside these schools of thought, there are diverse views on the different elements of human life and to distinguish them from one another is worthwhile. Some of these views and perspectives are as follows:

1. The school of "adherent" (customary, conventional) law and "pioneer" law

2. Economic individualism and collectivism

3. Political systems such as democracy and republicanism in various shades, oligarchy, constitutional monarchy, totalitarianism, and the like

Now, we shall embark on stating the general and common viewpoints and concepts of Islam and other religions and schools of thought. As the Islamic school of thought is a religious school, its belief in the Origin (*mabda'*) and the Resurrection (*ma'ₗd*), i.e. God and eternity, and management of the "intelligible life" through the guidance revealed by God, the Glorious, which has been conveyed by the prophets to His servants, is naturally common to every religious school. Historically speaking, we only come to know of the beliefs of the religions prior to the Abrahamic Faith through the Islamic sacred scripture (the Qur'¡n) because apart from the Qur'¡n, there is no access to a reliable source about the basic tenets and beliefs of religions. The Noble Qur'¡n states:

> *He has prescribed for you the religion which He had enjoined upon Noah and which We have [also] revealed to you, and which We had enjoined upon Abraham, Moses and Jesus, declaring, 'Maintain the religion, and do not be divided in it.' Hard on the polytheists is that to which you summon them.*[1]

Upon this Qur'¡nic verse and other similar verses of the Holy Book, it is clear that there have been general and common beliefs and concepts in the divine religion in all periods and places although there might have been differences in details and secondary issues according to temporal and spatial factors:

> *For every nation We have appointed a rite.*[2]

The Abrahamic Faith which is the origin of all subsequent religions is the same natural religion (*religio naturalis*). In some verses of the Qur'¡n, God, the Glorious, has referred to the same faith or way of Abraham ('a). In one Qur'¡nic verse, God, the Exalted, says:

> *Abraham was neither a Jew nor a Christian. Rather he was a hanīf (monotheist), a muslim.*[3]

That is, Prophet Ibr¡hīm ('a) was the conveyor of the universal message of the divine religion, which is the same Islam. We brought the different sects into being later. All the prophets that came afterward, such as Prophet Mūs¡ (Moses), Prophet 'Īs¡ (Jesus) and the Seal of the Prophets ('a) propagated the same Abrahamic Faith with slight temporal variations. It is stated in another verse, thus:

> *Indeed the faithful, the Jews, the Sabaeans, and the Christians—those who have faith in Allah and the*

---

1. S£rat al-Sh£r¡ 42:13.
2. S£rat al-°ajj 22:34. [Trans.]
3. S£rat ¡l 'Imr¡n 3:67.

*Last Day and act righteously—they will have no fear,
nor will they grieve.*[1]

From this and similar verses, it becomes very clear that the
original substance of the religion of Prophet Abraham ('a) has
universal views and concepts which are common to all religions
with divine origin, both prior and after him.

The reliable source that can prove and explain those
universal views and common concepts in the Abrahamic
Faith—as we have mentioned above—is the Noble Qur'ın.
There are many Qur'ınic verses about the Great Prophet's (¥)
possession of traits, which show his possession of those
universal views and common concepts.

The traits possessed by Prophet Abraham ('a) of having faith
and belief in the eternal principles of the universal religion and
acting upon the rights and duties promulgated by the his
religion can be indicative of the principles and secondary tenets
of this eternal school of thought. In our view, these traits are as
follows:

1. Truthful and righteous (*Sūrat Maryam* 19:41);

2. The Imımat (*Sūrat al-Baqarah* 2:124);

3. Successful in passing a difficult trial (*Sūrat al-Baqarah*
2:124);

4. Purifier of the House of God (*Sūrat al-Baqarah* 2:125);

5. Faithful to Islam (*Sūrat al-Baqarah* 2:131);

6. One who returns to God (*Sūrat al-Baqarah* 2:128);

7. Teaches the Book and Wisdom (*Sūrat al-Baqarah* 2:129);

8. Undergoes refinement and purification of the soul (*Sūrat
al-Baqarah* 2:129);

9. Chosen one and one of the righteous (*Sūrat al-Baqarah*
2:130);

10. Endowed with rectitude (*rushd*) (*Sūrat al-Anbiyı'* 21:51)
and upholder of the creed of rectitude and perfection (*Sūrat al-
Baqarah* 2:130). This quality can be inferred from this line: *"And
who will [ever] renounce Abraham's creed except one who fools*

---

1. S£rat al-Mı'idah 5:69.

himself?";

11. Real monotheist;

12. A ¡*anīf*, i.e. someone who possesses a moderate and natural religion free from any exaggeration or deficiency (*Sūrat al-Baqarah* 2:135);

13. Friend of Allah (*khalīl Allᵢh*) (*Sūrat al-Nisᵢ'* 4:125);

14. Struggler in the way of *tawhīd* even against his nearest of kin (*Sūrat al-An'ᵢm* 6:74);

15. Possessor of insight into the dominions of the heavens and the earth (*Sūrat al-An'ᵢm* 6:75);

16. Attained a high level of certitude (*yaqīn*) (*Sūrat al-An'ᵢm* 6:75);

17. Upholder of sound rational argument (*Sūrat al-An'ᵢm* 6:76-79);

18. Seeker of his own basis for [the existence of] God, the Creator of the heavens and the earth (*Sūrat al-An'ᵢm* 6:76-79);

19. Monotheist and shunned polytheism (*Sūrat al-An'ᵢm* 6:76-79);

20. Guided by Allah *Sūrat al-An'ᵢm* 6:8-83);

21. Wayfarer and presenter of the path of safety (*Sūrat al-An'ᵢm* 6:8-83);

22. Attained the highest level of rectitude in God and along the path of His Axis (*Sūrat al-An'ᵢm* 6:162);

23. Guided to the Straight Path (*Sūrat al-An'ᵢm* 6:161);

24. Possessor and propagator of the same religion conveyed to other prophets such as Nūh (Noah), Mūsᵢ (Moses), 'Īsᵢ (Jesus) and Mu¡ammad ('a) (*Sūrat al-Shūrᵢ* 42:13; *Sūrat al-⁻ᵢffᵢt* 37:83);

25. Patient;

26. Supplicant;

27. Penitent before Allah (*Sūrat Hūd* 11:75);

28. Affectionate, sympathetic and concerned with the servants of God (*Sūrat Ibrᵢhīm* 14:36);

29. Worshipper;

30. Thankful to Allah (*Sūrat al-Nahl* 16:120-121);

31. Professed an easy and moderate religion (*Sūrat al-°ajj* 22:78);

32. Leader;

33. Exponent of the Truth;

34. One of the inheritors of the Heaven (*Sūrat al-Shu'arᵢ'* 26:78-89);

35. Reliant on God; and

36. Shunned and disavowed the corrupt people (*Sūrat al-Mumtahanah* 60:4);

Taking into account the realities and requisites of the abovementioned qualities, we arrive at this very important conclusion that the framework of the divine religion that made Prophet Abraham (*'a*) attain those qualities is perfectly rational and natural, consistent with and stimulant of positive human potential.

Nowadays, an essential and sufficient study or research on the universal views and concepts common to all Abrahamic religions can lead us, all followers of Patriarch Abraham, to a very essential and completely beneficial sense of harmony, although, unfortunately, some existing factors stand in the way of this harmony and coexistence. The first harbinger of this unity and harmony in universal views and common concepts is Islam as expressed in this Qur'ᵢnic verse:

> *Say, 'O People of the Book! Come to a word common between us and you: that we will worship no one but Allah, and that we will not ascribe any partner to Him, and that we will not take each other as lords besides Allah.' But if they turn away, say, 'Be witnesses that we are muslims.'*[1]

This word *sawᵢ'* (common) which is the greatest factor for unity of the fundamental principles is the best proof that Islam does not stand in the way of the unity and harmony among the Abrahamic religions; in fact, it is its harbinger and standardbearer. Indeed, this noble verse clearly proves that the Abrahamic Faith can justify or eliminate the differences resulting from peculiarities of each of the Abrahamic religions

---

1. S£rat ᵢl 'Imrᵢn 3:64.

believed in and practiced by their followers.

Q18: As you know one's interpretation of Islam's state of being the seal of all revealed religions varies according to his notion of this religion as such. Having this in sight, would you please tell us your mind of Islam's status as the last religion revealed to mankind?

Jafari: The teachings of Islam are based upon human infinite potential for perfection. Islam has set forth the factors of man's prosperity in this world and his felicity in the Hereafter. The clearest proof of this claim is that the ideological principles, laws, and jurisprudential, legal, moral, political, economic, and cultural duties of this religion have been laid down in such a way that up to now, thousands of people have reached the height of perfection. The exception will be when human nature is extinguished and all man's mundane and spiritual principles cease to exist. Of course, in this case, Islam cannot give any answer to the problems of man, not because it is deficient, but because of the extinction of man and humanity from the page of existence.

Now, in explaining and proving this fact, we must take into account the Holy Prophet (¥), Imɩm 'Alī ibn Abī ±ɩlib and other Imɩms, and thousands of personages that attained rectitude such as Salmɩn al-Fɩrsī, Abū Dharr al-Ghiffɩrī, Mɩlik al-Ashtar, Uways al-Qarnī, 'Ammɩr ibn Yɩsīr, Miqdɩd ibn Aswad al-Kindī, 'Amr ibn Khazɩ'ī, °ujr ibn 'Udayy, and the like. Would there be any chance for these men of rectitude not to have the Islamic principles and rules for knowing how to organize the four basic types of relationship? Islam has presented in human history the likes of Fɩrɩbī, Ibn Sīnɩ, Ibn Rushd, Abū Rayhɩn al-Bīrūnī, °asan ibn °aytham, 'Attɩr, Jalɩl al-Dīn Muɩammad Mawlawī (Rūmī), Mīr Dɩmɩd, ¯adr al-Muta'allihīn, Kulaynī,[1] ¯adūq,[1] 'Allɩmah °illī,[2]

---

1. Shaykh Abɛ Ja'far Muɩammad ibn Ya'qɛb al-Kulaynɛ (d. 329 AH/941 CE): the compiler of Al-Kɩfɛ or more fully, Al-Kɩfɛ fɛ'l-°adɛth, one of the most important Shɛ'ah collections of ɩadɛth, divided into three sections: U¥£l al-Kɩfɛ, Furɛ' al-Kɩfɛ and Rawɴah al-Kɩfɛ consisting of 34 books, 326 sections, and over 16,000 aɩɩdɛth that can be traced back to the Prophet and his family by an unbroken

and thousands of similar personalities. Obviously, it cannot be imagined that the nature of man be totally changed individually or collectively. And such men of rectitude would be incapable of living with such conditions. Human society is formed by individuals whose potential can be activated from within themselves. Today, a sublime system of universal human rights is being presented to human society on the basis of the texts and rules taken from Divine scriptures and revelations. If man abandons his selfishness and animalistic tendencies and keeps away from hedonism and profiteering, he will advance with these universal rights competing in goodness and perfection. The advancement of humanity along the path of perfection does not hinge on the astounding technological progress, but on lofty human morality. Thus man, by acquiring the "morality of Allah" (akhl¡q All¡h) and the "etiquettes of Allah" (¡d¡b All¡h), will acquire the quality of "advancement" and make purposeful intelligible life attainable.

This is the very divine religion, whose basic principles were conveyed by the great prophets in the past conforming with the primary levels of culture of those periods, came into being and Islam fostered the ability of preserving its ideological principles and all the individual and social laws pertaining to man. Given these conditions, God, the Glorious, has revealed in toto the scripture of the eternal religion on His chosen beloved, Mu¡ammad al-Mu¥taf¡ (¥).

---

chain of transmission. [Trans.]
1. Shaykh al-¯ad£q: also known as Ibn Bab£yah, one of the most important of the early Sh¢'ah scholars who died in 381 AH/991 CE. For his short biography and works, see the introduction of Shaykh a¥-¯ad£q, I'tiq¡d¡tu 'l-Im¡miyyah: A Sh¢'ite Creed, 3rd Ed., trans. Asaf A. A. Fyzee (Tehran: World Organization for Islamic Services, 1999), pp. 6-23. [Trans.]
2. 'All¡mah °ill¢, more fully 'All¡mah ibn al-Mu§ahhar al-°ill¢ (1250-1325): one of the prominent Sh¢'ah scholars who lived in the period of Mongol domination of Iran. [Trans.]

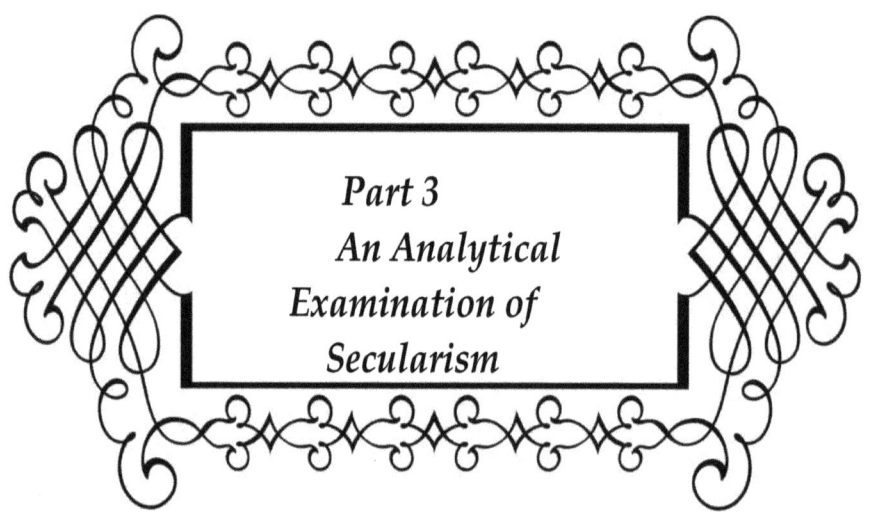

*Part 3
An Analytical
Examination of
Secularism*

Chapter 1

Secularism: Its Definition and the Reasons of Tendency towards It

Definitions of Secularism, Atheism and Laicism[1]

Secularism means opposition to religious laws and subjects; the spirit of worldliness; advocacy of mundane and customary principles. The root-word "secular" is related to the world, non-spiritual, nonreligious, laic, illiterate, outside the monastery, against religious laws, and making affairs worldly. Secularization means to make something worldly or nonreligious; to be free from the constraint of clergy and priesthood; universalization of ownership; prioritization of non-spiritual matters; to be outside the ecclesiastical domain; worldliness; materialism; giving worldly dimension to clerical beliefs or position.[2]

There are two other terms which we shall deal here so as to complete the discussion:

1. *Laicism* is derived from *laic*. It means being affiliated to a worldly and nonreligious figure; outside the clerical class; materialist; someone who is outside the clerical class; mundane; someone who is not a member of the clergy; separation of church and state.[3]

According to the definition given by *Encyclopedia Britannica*,

---

1. See ¡ry¡np£r K¡sh¡n¢, Farhang-e K¡mil-e Ingl¢s¢-F¡rs¢, root-word of "secu," p. 378; Encyclopedia Britannica, root-word of "ath".

2. ¡ry¡np£r K¡sh¡n¢, Farhang-e K¡mil-e Ingl¢s¢-F¡rs¢, root-word of "ath".

3. Ibid., root-word of "lai," p. 2795; Encyclopedia Brittanica, root-word of "lai".

laicism is a case or manifestation of secularism because separation of church and state is specific to secularism which, in turn, includes laicism. These two ways of thinking totally negate religion; in fact, they separate it from the affairs and facets of worldly life, politics in particular.

2. *Atheism* implies the belief that God does not exist. Atheist means heretic.[1] Since this way of thinking does not recognize [the existence of] God, it totally denies religion, considering it something unrealistic. Of course, it may possibly utilize it as a tool or means to advance its goals; it is the same Machiavelian principle that strips politics of morality.

Secularism entered the arena of political thoughts in the 14th and 15th centuries as a result of the contradiction between the Church's socio-political ways and methods in the West. Such a contradiction between religion and politics is impossible in Islam because religious beliefs, politics, science, economics, jurisprudence, law, culture, arts, morality, and the like are integral parts of the truth in Islam.

Is Secularism Embedded in Aristotle's Political Philosophy?

Some historians of political philosophy have traced secularism back to Aristotle.[2] But this is not true at all. It is said:

> *Another point neglected and not given attention to, by the two philosophers (Dante[3] and Thomas Aquinas[4]), is that they*

---

1. Ibid.
2. Aristotle (384-322 BCE): a Greek philosopher, a student of Plato and teacher of Alexander the Great. He wrote on many subjects, including physics, metaphysics, poetry, theater, music, logic, rhetoric, politics, government, ethics, biology, and zoology. Together with Plato and Socrates (Plato's teacher), Aristotle is one of the most important founding figures in Western philosophy. [Trans.]
3. Durante degli Alighieri (circa 1265-1321), commonly known as Dante: a major Italian poet of the Middle Ages, whose Divine Comedy, originally called Commedia and later called Divina by Boccaccio, is considered the greatest literary work composed in the Italian language and a masterpiece of world literature. [Trans.]
4. Thomas Aquinas, also Thomas of Aquin or Aquino (1225-74): an Italian Dominican priest of the Catholic Church, and an immensely influential

downplayed the gravity of the menace of secularism, i.e. worldliness and materialism, which is contained in the political book of Aristotle, especially the issues that emanate from the hypothesis he advanced: 'Civil society is in its perfect and independent form by itself, and it does not need any purification and permit from any supernatural element.' [1]

Firstly, this theme and its related issues cannot be inferred from Aristotle.

Secondly, Aristotle's original theory is as follows:

He who proposes to make that inquiry which is necessary concerning what government is best, ought first to determine what manner of living is most eligible... What is good, relative to man, may be divided into three sorts, what is external, what appertains to the body, and what to the soul. It is evident that all these must conspire to make a man happy: for no one would say that a man was happy who had no fortitude, no temperance, no justice, no prudence; but was afraid of the flies that flew round him: nor would abstain from the meanest theft if he was either hungry or dry, or would murder his dearest friend for a farthing; and also was, in every particular, as wanting in his understanding as an infant or an idiot. These truths are so evident that all must agree to them; though some may dispute about the quantity and the degree: for they may think, that a very little virtue is sufficient for happiness. (Not only he thinks that the least virtue is sufficient for him but he also sometimes believes that his virtue is more than those of others.) [2]

---

philosopher and theologian in the tradition of scholasticism, known as Doctor Angelicus, Doctor Communis, or Doctor Universalis. [Trans.]

1. Bahį'ud-D¢n Pįz¢rgįn, Tįr¢kh-e Falsafeh-ye Siyįs¢, vol. 1, p. 360 (originally in Persian). As we will see, the words of Aristotle are as follows: "Nature draws man to the political community through his instincts." Aristotle, Politics (or A Treatise on Government), translated from Greek into French by Bartolome Santhiler and into Arabic by A!mad Lu§f¢ Sayyid, Book 1, chap. 13.

2. Aristotle, A Treatise on Government, trans. William Elis (London and Toronto: JM Dent & Sons, Ltd., 1912) Book 7, chap. 1, http://www.gutenberg.org/files/6762/6762-h/6762-h.htm#2HCH0080. [Trans.]

After proving that happiness encompasses the three types of
goodness Aristotle embarked on proving that the good
pertaining to the human soul is superior and more important
than the other two, and it is this good that can materialize
human happiness. Aristotle thus said:

> If the soul is more noble than any outward possession, as the
> body, both in itself and with respect to us, it must be admitted
> of course that the best accidents of each must follow the same
> analogy. Besides, it is for the sake of the soul that these things
> are desirable; and it is on this account that wise men should
> desire them, not the soul for them. Let us therefore be well
> assured, that every one enjoys as much happiness as he
> possesses virtue and wisdom, and acts according to their
> dictates; since for this we have the example of God Himself,
> who is completely happy,[1] not from any external good; but in
> Himself, and because such is His nature… every good which
> depends not on the mind is owing to chance or fortune; but it is
> not from fortune that any one is wise and just: hence it follows,
> that that city is happiest which is the best and acts best: for no
> one can do well who acts not well; nor can the deeds either of
> man or city be praiseworthy without virtue and wisdom; for
> whatsoever is just, or wise, or prudent in a man, the same
> things are just, wise, and prudent in a city.[2]

It goes without saying that virtue, wisdom and justice—
especially in view of Aristotle's reference to God (as these
attributes are in the Essence of God)—cannot be of natural
earthly matters which exist based upon instincts and nature. As
such, the state, government or political system cannot eliminate
religion from the mundane life. Aristotle continued, thus:

> It is possible that this noble life with virtue and wisdom (i.e.
> happy) is beyond what can man endure, or at least the human
> being that leads such a life is not due to his common nature but

---

1. Happiness in relation to God refers to His majesty.
2. A Treatise on Government, Book 7, chap. 1,
http://www.gutenberg.org/files/6762/6762-h/6762-h.htm#2HCH0080. [Trans.]

because he exists in a sacred truth and this sacred principle is so great that the activity of this principle of happiness increases. Now, if perception is something sacred, it follows that the happiest life is the life of perception.

Definitely, what Aristotle meant, keeping in view of his other points, is not mere perception (understanding) but wisdom as well, whose salient feature, among others, is the possession of virtue. Particularly, by considering this explicit line, "Sacred happiness is not possible except through perpetual perception,"[1] it is clear that mere conception of eternity in its abstract form is not real happiness. Instead, real happiness is the perception and realization of eternity by being in the Threshold of Absolute Eternal Perfection beyond eternity. Aristotle said, thus:

Happiness is not a product of accident; rather, happiness is something given by God and the fruit of sweat and toil. This point is also a subject of discussion: is happiness real, or is it materialized through learning and training? Is it attained through certain habits? Or, is it possible to achieve through other similar ways? Is it true that happiness is something given by God, or something accidental? In reality, if there is something given by God[2] to the human beings in this world, we may dogmatically believe that happiness is a divine blessing. And man would easily accept this belief because for him there is nothing greater than happiness.[3]

Having these passages in sight, secularism cannot be feasibly attributed to Aristotle as it has no factual basis at all.

---

1. Aristotle, Politics, trans. Bartolome Santhiler (?), "Translator's Introduction," p. 96.

2. Here, "gods" is the exact word of Aristotle and by comparing similar passages, it become clear that by "gods" Aristotle and his likes meant beings with divine sanctity such as the angels, prophets and even righteous rulers. It is the same word used by Jean-Jacques Rousseau in The Social Contract, page 81: "Based on what has been said, only the gods can bring an ideal law for the people."

3. Aristotle, Nicomachean Ethics, Book 1, chap. 7, p. 204.

What he stated in *Politics*, "Nature draws man toward the sociopolitical life through his instincts", (Book 1, chap. 1, para. 13) does not contradict man's necessity to acquire happiness and excellence individually and collectively through the instrumentality of the state and politics. The above expression attributes man's political tendency to his nature, while identity, management and political goal, which he considers pertaining to the subsequent expression "happiness", are not mentioned in the above expression.

Meanwhile, the necessity of the search for happiness and excellence has been pointed out by Aristotle in his *Politics* as well as *Nicomachean Ethics*. In the political history of human society, instead of taking out religion from governance, theocratic rule has been discussed. In dictionaries and encyclopedia, theocracy means "divine rule; God-centeredness; religious state-government in which God is the Sovereign; belief in the necessity of divine rule; administration of a country according to religious laws, etc."[1]

In order to understand the narrative and conflict between the Church and the State as well as political phenomena such as theocracy (divine rule) and secularism (removal of religion from the temporal and political life), we need to make a brief survey of this conflict.

The Church vs. State Conflict in a Snapshot

Regarding the Church and the State, *Encyclopedia Britannica* reads:

"The bone of contention is that each of the two legal institutions (the Church and the State) commanded loyalty and obedience of the people in the same society among the same individuals. Theoretically, the precept of "Give unto Ceasar what is Ceasar's and unto God what is God's" (Matthew 21:22) was supposed to have been followed, but in practice, the respective scopes of sovereignty of the temporal and ecclesiastical powers

---

1. Dr. 'Abbjs ¡ry¡np£r K¡sh¢n¢, Farhang-e K¡mil-e Ingl¢s¢-F¡rs¢, vol. 5, p. 5723.

clashed.

"In primitive societies, this distinction between the religious and temporal aspects of social life, as is prevalent nowadays, had been practically impossible. In early civilizations everywhere, the king or the ruler had been regarded as the representative of the divine (divine-heavenly powers). Until the time of the acceptance of Christianity by the Roman Emperor, the person of the emperor had also the highest religious authority, controlling religion and the state. In fact, the emperor also used to be the object of worship as "the god on the surface of the earth".

"At any rate, the concepts of "the State" and "the Church" as two separate entities can be discussed when the line of distinction between the secular society and the religious society or societies within the same political sphere can be drawn. It is not correct for us to say that the distinction between the government and religion was brought into being by Christianity, although the main responsibility is shouldered by the said religion. It started with Judaism, for with the destruction of Jerusalem in 586 CE, the Jews no longer possessed an independent political society. From then on, they lived as a Jewish religious minority in the heart of a non-Jewish state. As such, they were forced to think about their membership in religious community and their secular citizenship as two separate matters. When Christianity was founded, for sometime the early Christians were under such conditions and circumstances that they had to live under non-Christian rulers.

"Thus, since the end of Christian persecution, maltreatment and discrimination and the beginning of the period of tolerance initiated by Emperor Constantine the Great in the fourth century, the Christians were confronted with this fundamental question: What must be the nature of relationship (between the Church and the political rule of the emperor whose subjects were the Christians themselves)? There is no doubt that the Christian emperors considered themselves holders of the same station; that is, the station held by the emperor in the ancient polytheistic Roman thinking, and they were not only protectors of the Church but also its sovereigns...

From the time of Theodosius I the Great, at the end of the fourth century, Christianity was transformed into the religion of the Roman Empire and polytheism or innovations within Christianity were rejected. Also, the period of fusion of the Church and the State as two faces of a single Christian society ushered in. During this time, the Church enjoyed a sort of religious supervision and political power on all citizens including the political leaders and rulers of society. [1]

It continues in the following words:

The Eastern Christian Orthodox Church refers to the Byzantium or Eastern System which can be defined as 'Caesaropapism' (absolute rule of religious scholars or 'caesar-papists'). The Byzantium emperors regarded themselves as protectors and vanguards of the Church on the authority of God, being authorized to enact laws on ecclesiastical affairs and rules, which would be declared by the Church as an integral part of the religious law. Of course, this does not suggest that the Church would always submit. In reality, this running fight would change according to the extent of power of the religious and political leaders in different periods. However, in view of the fact that some of the emperors would not observe the moral bounds and limits of the Church, gradually the Church kept them aside.

One of the famous Byzantium experts, Louis Brehier, does not define the Byzantium political system (Eastern Roman Empire, Constantinople) as Caesaropapism but as theocracy in which

---

1. Encyclopedia Britannica, vol. 4, p. 590 (originally in English) as translated into Persian by Dr. 'Abd al-Raḥīm Gawjhč.

the emperor enjoys a higher or highest position (though not an exclusive or exceptional position).[1]

The Roman Catholic Church

Up to the 11th century, in the West (western part of Christendom) the condition was not so different. Although the Pope claimed spiritual authority over all Christendom, he enjoyed a sense of power which the Patriarchs in Constantinople had not possessed.

The Clash between Kings and Popes

From the 11th century up to the 13th century, an assumption existed, explicitly or implicitly, that clerical power is naturally above temporal power, which can be restrained in the end. Christian clerics had no belief in this theory. It only had a great impact and was at the root of conflicts between the Pope and the Holy Roman Empire. The said theory was usually justified by the following assumption: If the ruler tramples upon Christian moral precepts, he—like any other Christian—must be subject to censors (in the sense of faultfinding, criticism, reproach, and the like) by the Church, and be compelled and coerced by the laymen loyal to the Church. (This is the argument used in relation to the Pope's indirect power in mundane affairs.)

A more extreme premise presented by Pope Boniface VIII[2] was that the powers delegated by Holy Christ ('a) to Saint Peter and other disciples and from them to their successors (priests and popes) include final temporal supremacy simply because spiritual power, on account of its nature or essence, is above temporal power. According to him, Prophet Jesus the Messiah ('a) has granted Saint Peter and his successors two swords (Luke 22:38) that symbolize spiritual and material powers.

---

1. Ibid., p. 591.

2. Pope Boniface VIII (c. 1235 – 1303), born Benedetto Gaetani: Pope of the Catholic Church from 1294 to 1303, who, in his Bull of 1302, Unam Sanctam, put forward some of the strongest claims to temporal, as well as spiritual, power of any Pope. [Trans.]

Accordingly, spiritual power is exercised by the popes, while temporal sword is entrusted to non-clerical individuals who are supposed to utilize it according to the instructions of the papacy.

The Separation of Church and State

Theoretically speaking, perhaps, the most radical view on the separation of religion from politics has been presented by Martin Luther,[1] who advanced a doctrine called "the Two Kingdoms".[2] His teaching in this regard can be practically summed up as follows: "The Gospel of God must be within the jurisdiction of the Church while His Law must govern society. If we administer the Church through the law, and society through the Gospel, people will be compelled to bring the law and ordinances into the realm of divine grace and bounty, and feelings and emotions into the domain of [social] justice, thereby, letting God be deprived of His Station of Sovereignty, letting Satan rule by us abiding with the civil order. This turned into a form of official religion in places where the majority was Lutheran such as Germany and the Scandinavian states.

In many places, princes practically assumed the kind of supervision and command which the Roman Catholic Bishops assumed. John Calvin[3] had made lesser theoretical efforts on the separation of the two realms, i.e. religious and civil. In his opinion, Geneva must turn into a theocracy in which the holy men would rule, and the divinely promised society must be founded on the divine law as revealed in the Sacred Scripture. No parts of social or city life must be so far, secular, or

---

1. Martin Luther (1483 – 1546): a German priest and professor of theology who initiated the Protestant Reformation. [Trans.]

2. Martin Luther's doctrine of the two kingdoms (or two reigns) of God, as set forth in 1580 Book of Concord, maintains that God is the ruler of the whole world and that he rules in two ways. He rules the earthly or left-hand kingdom through secular government, by means of law, and in the heavenly or righthand kingdom through the gospel or grace. [Trans.]

3. John Calvin (1509 – 1564): an influential French theologian and pastor during the Protestant Reformation. [Trans.]

unimportant, to be able to escape from the supervision of the Calvinists.

In the politico-religious history of the non-Islamic East and West, we can see that the meaning of secularism, i.e., the concept of omitting religion from the mundane, political and scientific life, is much clearer than that of theocracy, i.e. the rule of God in society. Basing the management and justification of individual and collective life on man himself is an unambiguous concept not difficult to understand. The concept of divine sovereignty in society is ambiguous because of possible interpretations. We shall mention here two important possibilities on the abovementioned concept:

The first possibility is that all political, scientific, cultural, economic, and legal figures of society are directly informed of the reality by Almighty God, through divine revelation or inspiration. This possibility is incorrect because, firstly, it has not been established that the prominent figures of society (with the exception of the known prophets) have ever claimed to be recipients of revelation. Secondly, if ever they were receiving revelation pertaining to the management of society, no conflict or clash would ever arise between and among them, whereas, so many conflicts and quarrels among the prominent figures of society can be observed.

The second possibility is that the political figures of society are so inwardly purified and polished that by the will of God, the Glorious, they can intuitively discern the reality and utilize it in the lives of people. It is clear that in addition to the conflicts, the prominent figures in society commit huge mistakes that cannot be Divine.

Thus, as it was mentioned earlier, secularism in a given social form gives rise to a serious conflict among ecclesiastical, political and social figures. All the conflicts and diversity of ideas in the 14th and 15th centuries became manifest and gradually evolved. This intellectual development happened in the course of three famous events, the first of which is discussed in this chapter, while the other two shall be discussed in the next chapter.

The Triple Events that Paved the Ground for the Emergence of Secularism

The *first event* refers to the dispute between the Pontifical System and the French monarchy from 1269 to 1303 A.D, as the result of which the assumption of papal imperialism, incorporated into the religious law, reached its highest point. But, at the same time, the integration of the French nations, the formation of the French monarchy, and the intensified feeling of nationalism in France dealt it a death blow, after which it could not recover. Opposition of papal imperialism gradually evolved at the end of the said event and its objective identified. This gave rise to the notion that spiritual power must be restrained. This thinking was of immense importance as it raised the question of independence of all monarchies and kingdoms as independent political communities. In fact, one can say that the seed of nationalism, which flourished in the 18th and 19th centuries, was sown at that time.

The *second event* refers to the dispute between Pope John XXII[1] and the Roman Emperor, Louis IV[2] of Bavaria, which centered on opposing papal sovereignty, lasted for about 25 years. In this quarrel, initially Guillaume Duckam, the spokesman of the orthodox spiritual Franciscans, opened the door of opposition to papal sovereignty, gathering around him and guiding all the elements opposing the Pope and Christian tradition. Secondly, Marcel Dupado propounded and developed the assumption of sufficiency of civil society, turning it into a form of secularism connected to God-wariness (*taqwī*) and close to Erastianism, following the belief of Thomas

---

1. Pope John XXII (1244 – 1334), born Jacques Dueze (or d'Euse): the pope from 1316 to 1334 and the second Pope of the Avignon Papacy (1309–1377), elected by a conclave in Lyon assembled by Philip V of France. [Trans.]

2. Louis IV (1282 – 1347), called the Bavarian of the house of Wittelsbach: the King of Germany (King of the Romans) from 1314, the King of Italy from 1327 and the Holy Roman Emperor from 1328. [Trans.]

Erastus,[1] that the state must take charge of religious affairs, and that the church must submit to the state. In the course of this quarrel, religious power was restricted, while the exclusive nature of its functions in the otherworldly affairs developed, leaving the Church as an important social institution.

The *third event* refers to the quarrel that took place for the first time within the Church among the clerics. This kind of quarrel was different from the disputes between the religious and temporal powers, and opposition to the absolute power of the Pope in this quarrel took a new form. It was the first time in the history of Christianity that, as reform measures, the subjects and followers of an absolute ruling power strived to impose constitutional limits and representative governance to their master. Of course, this quarrel did not end in favor of the Pope's adversaries, and the party called *Concilia* or "Conciliator" whose platform is conciliation, failed to act upon their platform. It gave way to a political philosophy which led to dialogue and dispute between the temporal leaders and their followers; that is, it also awakened the subjects of political leaders to think of restricting their power through constitutionalism and representative government.[2]

This was the origin of secularism in the West that presented religion as opposed to and repugnant to justice, freedom and science. Given these three events, the supposed pioneers of restricting [ecclesiastical authorities] gave an exaggerated account of religion and rendered a blow to humanity. Machiavelli[3] intensified this blow. If ever the current of religious life in the hearts of many people in the East and even

---

1. Thomas Erastus (1524 – 1583): a Swiss physician and theologian best known for a posthumously published work in which he argued that the sins of Christians should be punished by the state, and not by the church withholding the sacraments. [Trans.]

2. Bah¡'ud-D¢n P¡s¢rg¢n, T¡r¢kh-e Falsafeh-ye Siy¡s¢ (History of Political Philosophy), vol. 1, pp. 360-361 (originally in Persian).

3. One of the main founders of modern political science in the West, Niccolò di Bernardo dei Machiavelli (1469 – 1527) was an Italian philosopher, humanist, and writer based in Florence during the Renaissance. [Trans.]

in the West is cut, there will be no hope for the salvation of mankind from the pangs of death it was experiencing.

O, Almighty God, the All-powerful, the All-wise! How powerful and magnificent is the design of creation You have put to work, and how powerful and magnificent is Your wisdom and will! In spite of all the fatal blows and wounds inflicted on mankind by negating religion, promoting Machiavellianism,[1] and propagating the primacy of power, natural selection and other decisive tools, the geniuses have not been able to dry up the spring of religious life within man!

Those geniuses were so ignorant that they thought of allegedly determining the functions of future mankind, saying that mankind must always move along the way we determine for it! They failed to realize that the infants of the Children of Adam ('a) come to the world with new lives, minds and souls, without these geniuses determining the fate of these neophytes in the garden of creation. As such, if these neophytes are not indoctrinated by atheism and secularism by selfish materialists, they will benefit from all sublime human principles and values.

We wish they would raise their heads for a few moments and hear their own voice of regret for going to extremes in negating religion.

---

1. Deriving from the Italian Renaissance diplomat and writer Niccolò Machiavelli who wrote Il Principe (The Prince) and other works, Machiavellianism is "the employment of cunning and duplicity in statecraft or in general conduct." [Trans.]

Chapter 2

Critical Assessment of the Reasons of the Emergence of Secularism in the West

Here we shall mention some points for the researchers:

First point: Did the tyrants that considered themselves above law really believe that science and freedom were opposed to the true divine religion? The reply to the question is definitely in the negative. In view of the Absolute Perfection of the Bestower of religion, His lofty wisdom, and the purpose behind the bestowal of religion to man, we have no option but to believe that the essence of religion is to let all sublime talents strive to achieve God's Axis of Exalted Perfection. Therefore, the glorious mission and sublime purpose of the religion is to let all human beings possess rational thinking, freedom, and dignity, which are inconsistent with narrow-mindedness, compulsion, and dogmatism.

Thus, if any oppression, aggression, and promotion of ignorance and ambiguity have ever taken place in the name of religion in human history, it had nothing to do with religion, but originated from the dominance of the egocentrists masquerading as followers of religion. These geniuses would make use of Judaism, Christianity or Islam for their selfish interests. We also use the same argument to defend the lofty concepts of politics, law, economics, ethics, and art from the clutches of the egoists who want us to state all the truths for their own selfish interests. This is because we all know that politics means management of the social life of man along the path of sublime goals. Is it rational for us to say that since

Machiavellian politics spilled the blood of millions of innocent people and trampled upon their rights, it follows that politics must be removed from the scene of life?! Did the powerful not abuse their power? They certainly did. If ever by considering the abovementioned words (law, economics, ethics, and art) one would say that these truths can never be misused, he is either uninformed of constant realities in human history, or his spite has reached the point of opposing his inner self.

Second point: In order to prove the point that despotism, tyranny, cruelty, greed for power, and embezzlement have nothing to do with the divine religion (the pure Abrahamic Faith in which Judaism, Christianity and Islam have their origin), one has to refer to the Torah, the Evangel and the Qur'ın. The Qur'ın, in particular, categorically and unambiguously presents the Abrahamic Faith as opposed to oppression, aggression, despotism, ignorance, and narrow-mindedness.The Noble Qur'ın declares teaching, training, wisdom, and establishment of justice and equity among the people as the goal of the prophets' mission (*bi'thah*). Such a goal can never be harmonious with the [wicked] attitude exemplified by [self-styled] Muslim and Christian leaders throughout history.

Third point: Nowadays, we must meticulously study the issue of "elimination of religion from the world," which has been posed as a scientific and sociopolitical issue. Is the separation of religion from the sociopolitical aspects and the sheer worldliness of these aspects a natural reality explained by the authoritative thinkers? Or, by considering a number of tangible and intangible factors religion must be distinguished from politics, science, law, economics, art, ethics, and even mysticism?!

One of the strange things in this regard is that those writers who diligently write on the basis of "scientific proofs", are those who, on the one hand, have talked about the distinction between "what is right", and "what should be" on the basis of the Machiavellian method in science! On the other hand, they have paid no attention to all the convincing answers given to them. The same Machiavellian method obliges them to arrive at the "it must be such" (religion must be separated from politics) conclusion because "it is such" (that religion is separate from politics) which is nothing but an illusion!

Fourth point: Now, we shall set aside the past and argue that no matter what happened in the past, today we can observe that the way of thinking and method of "eliminating religion from mundane life" has become prevalent in the West and this thinking has brought about worldly results desired by the people. Can we afford to subscribe to this way of thinking?

The advancement in science and technology and the organized social life of people in the West is not caused by eliminating the pure divine religion from society but by sidelining the religion-innovators who interpret, conform and practice the divine religion according to their carnal desires in order to attain their selfish interests. When the people in the West sidelined religion on the ground of eliminating the obstacles to "intelligible life", they meant the "religion" artificially made by religious leaders, which was against science, progress, rational freedom, justice, and innate human dignity. This state of affairs is not logical as far as Islam is concerned because it has given to man one of the two most indigenous civilizations in human history, which would be impossible without science, politics, economics and law.

In coming discussions, we will examine as elaborately as possible the untenable bases of the false notion of "the elimination of religion in mundane life" in Muslim societies.

Fifth point: The factors contributing to the process of "the elimination of religion in mundane life" in the West by no means fit Islam. It has no scientific and real basis and has to be studied more closely so as to trace its roots into other pheonomena. The basic difference between Islam and the West has to be sought for in their various notions of life and politics.

I. The common notion of life in the West today is being-in-the-natural world and having the freedom to satisfy one's natural instincts in a selfish manner, which are controlled and molded for the benefit of social life, without specific beliefs which give meaning to life and justify the lofty goal, and without the need of possessing a sublime human character.

II. The common notion of religion in the West today refers to a personal spiritual relationship between man and God and other supernatural truths, without having the least role in human mundane life.

III. The common notion of politics in the West today refers to the management of the natural life of people in the social arena toward the goals apparently chosen by their majority. In this definition of religion and politics, the need for religion in politics and its activity is totally absent because from their perspective, people have no need at all for religion, whether in individual or social life. It is needless to say that all these notions lay the ground for the process of elimination of religion in the occident as neither western notion of life, its notion of religion nor its notion of politics fit an integral view of life, religion and politics. However, Islam has its own integrative perspective of these triple phenomena.

Islam has a totally different notion of all these three realities. Human life, thus conceived, refers to an evolutionary movement towards perfection, through conscious struggle for the fulfillment of supreme telos of creation. As one treads a stage of life to its end his motivation to pace towards the next stage increases. Human being is the forerunner of this search; the being who originates from eternity, whose passageway is this purposeful world, and whose ultimate telos is to be exposed to the radiations of Absolute Perfection in eternity. The Absolute Perfection's breeze of love, grandeur and glory reinvigorates the creatures in the universe and kindles the light of the tortuous path of material and spiritual perfection. The beginning, and end of this life can be traced back to God:

> *Say, 'Indeed my prayer and my worship, my life and my death are all for the sake of Allah, the Lord of all*

the worlds.' [1]

Islam's notion of politics revolves around the fulfillment of the supreme goals of human life both in corporeal and incorporeal domains. Religion and politics have as more critical role in intelligible life as fresh air has in natural life. Now it is time to turn to intelligible politics and religion that underlie intelligible life as such.

Islam's definition of religion depends on three main pillars:

First pillar is the belief in the existence of the One and Only God, His supervision and dominance over the universe, and His absolute justice, which is beyond whims and caprice. He is the embodiment of all Attributes of Perfection, and has created the universe based on His wisdom providing man with two types of original guides (sound intellect and the prophets) to move toward perfection and enter into the Station of Beatific Vision (*liqi' Allih*). Another is the belief in eternity, without which life and the entire universe will remain an enigmatic puzzle. These convictions depend on sound intellect and intrinsic perception.

Second pillar comprises the laws and practical program of activity leading man toward the sublime goal of life, which are called laws, duties and rights. It is anchored in two things:

1. Mandatory moral precepts which are prescribed for the acquisition of merits; and

2. Duties and Rights; duties include devotional decrees and personal duties in the arena of sociopolitical life, rights mean an advantage that can be utilized by a person. Meanwhile, decrees are also of two kinds: primary and secondary decrees. The primary decrees relate to the permanent needs while the secondary decrees pertain to the changing sources of welfare and corruption in life.

Third pillar is consisted of the subjects that include all the realities and phenomena that constitute life. With the exception of a very few cases, in all subjects Islam has given the choice to

---

1. S£rat al-An'¡m 6:162. [Trans.]

the people to deal with them with full attention, reflection, physical strength, desires, and legitimate demands.

Politics, as fathomed by Islam, implies management of human life both in the individual and collective spheres for the realization of the most sublime material and spiritual goals. The beliefs and practical laws intend to organize and reform humanity with respect to the four types of relationship. From the Islamic perspective, any thing or phenomenon, which can be utilized for the organization and welfare of human life, within the said four types of relationship, is regarded as an integral part of religion.

The Unity and Harmony of all Aspects of Human Life in Islam

Thus, science, politics, economics, law, ethics, culture in its pioneer sense, technology, and all things that contribute, in one way or another to the organization and welfare of mankind, are integral parts of Islam as a revealed religion. Whoever does not know this fact definitely does not know the religion. To substantiate the latter claim, it suffices here to quote Jean-Jacques Rousseau[1] who argues:

> The sacred religion (Christianity) has been always separate from the ruling establishment and its relationship with the state is not compulsory. Prophet Mu!ammad has correct views, putting well in order its political apparatus. So long as his form of government was in the hands of the caliphs, it was a religious and temporal government. The religious and temporal government, the legislative and the customary were one and the same that rule the entire state. But as the Arabs got rich, they became lax and other nations overwhelmed them. Then, the dispute between two sources of power started again.[2]

---

1. Jean-Jacques Rousseau (1712–78): a major philosopher, writer, and composer of 18th-century Romanticism, whose political philosophy heavily influenced the French Revolution, as well as the American Revolution and the overall development of modern political, sociological and educational thought. [Trans.]
2. Jean-Jacques Rousseau, Qar¡rd¡d-e Ijtim¡‘¢ (The Social Contract), trans. Ghul¡m-°usayn Z¢rakz¡deh, p. 195.

Elsewhere, Rousseau also said:

> *The Jewish laws which still exist, and the religious law of Mu ̣ammad, a descendant of Ishmael, which is binding in the world for the past ten centuries still gives account of the greatness of the prominent men who have codified it. Selfish philosophers and fanatic and obstinate devotees have brought [the value of] these great men to nowhere, but the real statesman within his rank could see a great inborn disposition which brings about enduring [foundations and] institutions.[1]*

---

1. Ibid., p. 86.

Chapter 3

The Consequences of Secularism

Two Seemingly Contradictory Theories of 'Abd al-Rahmِn ibn Khaldūn on the Necessity of Divine Prophets in Human Worldly Life

On the necessity of religion for human worldly life, 'Abd al-Rahmِn ibn Khaldūn has two seemingly contradictory views, which we have assessed, to some extent, while dealing with the scope of religion. Here, we deem it necessary to point out these two views.

Theory I:

As you see it is not yet proven enough that the emergency of prophecy is a rationally substantiated issue, since existence and human life can be well organized without [the existence of prophecy and religious law]...[1]

Theory II: In Chapter 51, under the heading "Human Civilization Requires Political Leadership for Its Organization":

We have mentioned before in more than one place that human social organization is something necessary. It is the thing meant by "civilization", which we have been discussing. (People) in any social organization must have someone who exercises a restraining influence and rules them and to whom recourse may be had. His rule over them is sometimes based upon a divinely revealed religious law. They are obliged to submit to it in view of their belief in reward and punishment in the other world, (things that were indicated) by the person who brought them (their religious law). Sometimes, (his rule is based) upon rational politics. People are obliged to submit to it

---

1. Ibn Khald£n, Al-Muqaddimah, pp. 43-44.

in view of the reward they expect from the ruler after he has become acquainted with what is good for them. The first (type of rule) is useful for this world and for the other world, because the lawgiver knows the ultimate interest of the people... The second (type of rule) is useful only for this world ...[1]

As you see this is Ibn Khaldūn's theory and as we have already discussed in the chapter on the scope of religion, a life without religion is the merely physical life concerned only with the material dimension of man and not the "intelligible life", which brings to perfection all dimensions of human life. Thus, we can say that there is no inconsistency in Ibn Khaldūn's view.

Secularism Leads to Personality Disorder in Human Management

A human being has four basic dimensions:

First Dimension

It consists of the body or physiological limbs and their natural properties like connection with the natural environment, nativity, procreation, and the like.

Second Dimension

It consists of the social mundane life related to the management of human collective life such as law, economics, politics, and culture. The exposition of this dimension has been offered in item 8 of, "An Example of the Principles and Values Undermined or Totally Eliminated after the Elimination of Religion from Human Life".

Third Dimension

It consists of the psychological or mental activities of man, such as imagination, conceptions, imagery, intellection, thinking, willpower, decision-making, choosing, expressing emotions and feelings, etc.

Fourth Dimension

It consists of man's perfection-seeking aptitudes, most of which pertain to religion, morality and ideologically sublime

---

1. Ibid., pp. 302-303. The translation is adapted from Ibn Khaldun, The Muqaddimah, pp. 256-257. [Trans.]

truths.

Managing the First Dimension (Animal Life)

Man takes charge of the activities related to his animalistic existence as long as he possesses the requisites of management; such as awareness, wellbeing and other capabilities. However, in the absence of those requisites, compelling factors take away management skills from a person. Most activities of the bodily limbs which are repeated many times to meet basic needs for subsistence are such that it seems those limbs unconsciously acquire from the person some sort of capability in managing him. Habitual activities are usually called actions rooted in habits. As such, in cases of rare activities one's perfect management is undertaken consciously. In managing ones natural existence, one performs his work by considering the motivating needs of the natural limbs.

Managing the Second Dimension (Life with Thematic Principles and Laws)

In the second dimension, a human being is managed in relation to the motive of collective mundane life, beyond his choice, believing that his life must be in harmony with those realities, such as law, economics, politics, and the like. The difference between the first and second dimensions is that his relationship with the second dimension is voluntary, because violation of social laws, such as violation of rights, is more possible than violation of the laws governing the bodily limbs that directly administer man's physical life. For example, opening the eyes while walking is an involuntary actions, whereas, following a legal provision of collective life is very consciously done. In the first dimension of life, man can live like other animals by only following the motives of individual physical life. In the second dimension, however, he takes a position superior than those of other animals.

Man can accept the realities of the second dimension only to provide for his mundane life, harmonizing his life with the pertinent principles and laws and not base any religious and moral values on those realities in following them.

Human Being in the Third Dimension

In managing this dimension, man deals with subtler dimensions, and in which distinguished personalities have a role in justifying those realities. In managing the psychological activities directly related to a person, it requires utmost meticulousness, analysis, synthesis, modification, and decisiveness.

Human psychological activities include conception, supposition, imagination, discoveries, intuitive knowledge, self-assessment, intellection, thinking, abstraction, management, deciding, exercise of willpower, and feeling. It is clear that none of these activities is accidental to fade away after coming into existence in man's being without any governing law.

These activities and reflections can be divided into two main types:

Type I covers those activities that do not need one's awareness and management skill; for example, conception of the things which we encounter for the first time. If the conceived things are not so important, they will be left alone and in the course of time, they will be gradually erased from the mind.

Type II comprises those activities which can be within the awareness, management and control of a person. Take for example, the following:

1. Embodiment (*tajsīm*): that is, to regard something as not existing and nothing as something that exists, or to regard certain things as different things. The best examples of *tajsīm* are the various shows in theaters and the like, in which the viewers tend to consider the actors, and appearances in the scene to be real and to behave accordingly. For instance, someone plays the role of the late Mīrzā Taqī Khān Amīr Kabīr[1]

---

1. Mērzā Taqē Khān Farāhānē, better known as Amēr Kabēr (1803-1848): the strong and popular prime minister of Naṣēr al-Dēn Shāh of the Qājār dynasty of Persia, who, by relying on his shrewdness, sagacity and perseverance managed

and other people play the role of his enemies and murderers while all the viewers are certain that the former is not the real Amīr Kabīr and the latter are not his real enemies and murderers. Yet, all these viewers treat what just happened to Amīr Kabīr as something undesirable. This is the power of the imagination.

2. Discovery or disclosure (*iktishįf*): it refers to any phenomenon which cannot be interpreted within the context of scientific rules. In the words of Claude Bernard[1] on the introduction to [the study of] experimental medicine,

> *No specific rule or instruction can be presented which holds that at the time of observing a certain thing by the researcher, a correct and fruitful idea which will serve as a sort of prior guide of the mind on the correct [method of] research would come into being. It is only after the existence or appearance of the idea that one can say how to set it according to the specific instructions of the stated logical rules, which no researcher is allowed to violate. But the reason behind its appearance is unclear and its nature is completely personal and something special, which is regarded as a source of creativity, invention and ingenuity of someone.*[2]

The overwhelming majority of the authorities in science have accepted the role of intuitive perceptions in the discoveries and inventions, and anyone who possesses such capabilities or, who has actually observed only an instance of them, acknowledges the role of intuition in the discoveries.

3. Knowledge by presence (*'ilm-e huɀūrī*) (self-awareness or self-consciousness): This can be experienced by anyone who is

---

to do away with many aspects of foreign colonialism and domestic autocracy to promote the welfare of the country in the face of many challenging difficulties. [Trans.]

1. Claude Bernard (1813 – 1878): a French physiologist who was the first to define the term milieu intérieur (now known as homeostasis, a term coined by Walter Bradford Cannon) and one of the first to suggest the use of blind experiments to ensure the objectivity of scientific observations. [Trans.]

2. Felicien Robert Challaye, Knowing the Scientific Methodology, p. 42 (originally in French).

self-conscious. In this extraordinary happening, the perceiver is also the perceived, which refers to the "I" or person. In the words of Shaykh Mahmūd Shabistarī, "This situation is similar to the man with eyes who must see himself without the instrumentality of his own eyes!"

> *Nothingness is the mirror, the universe is the picture, and man*
> *Is like the eye of that picture in which the individual is hidden.*
> *You are the eye of the picture, and he is the light of eye;*
> *Who has ever seen the vision of eye by the eye?*[1]

4. Intellection (*ta'aqqul*): it refers to thinking in the light of the established principles and laws for the attainment of one's goals in an intellectual activity. It utilizes abstracted generalities for harmonizing different cases and since perception of general cases necessitates perception of abstracted realities, it follows that the person in question also engages in a metaphysical activitiy in the process.

5. Willpower (*ikhtiyįr*): this is one of the most magnificent powers that man possesses to manage life. It is even above the sensible things, which one compares and contrasts. For this reason, he gives a noble form to his work, which is beyond natural outputs in the bodily dimension.

6. Self-assessment and self-examination: anyone with a sound mind can examine and assess his bodily limbs and give preference to one limb over another. Such a person can examine and assess his inward powers, abilities and activities. For example, Are my feelings sound? Is my thinking or intellection correct? Do my psychological activities follow the correct process? Do my faculties and aptitudes harmoniously work together? This examiner is the person himself.

There are people who would say that such examination may be traceable to one of our unknown mental powers and there is reason for the sole existence of the person. This possibility is only correct when a person sets all his limbs, faculties and aptitudes for qualitative and quantitative comparison with one

---

1. Shaykh Maǀm£d Shabistar¢, Golshan-e Rįz, part 8. [Trans.]

another, for the assumption is that they—inward and outward—have all been examined.

If we assume that assessment in this regard is related to an unknown mental power who or what is the assessor? Whoever or whatever he or it is, definitely is greater than all the given powers. This refers to the same "I" (human being). This is an example of the proofs that establish the solitude of the "I" (human being). According to some people, the proofs are more than sixty. If we disregard such activities by the sole "I" and say it is natural to "separate religion and politics" in human life, it follows that we have disregarded the incurable pain of self-alienation, which is the illness of the twentieth century. The conclusion of this discussion is that the elimination of religion from the mundane life leaves the human being in the hands of events, which are constantly changing, and negates the primacy and inalterability of religion, which originates from beyond nature.

7. The supervision of "ego" over the universe: there is no doubt that by acquiring sublime gnosis, the wary human beings occupy a sort of lofty station of epiphany with which they inwardly perceive the entire universe through knowledge by presence. They can even perceive their existence as part of the whole system of the universe.

The first thinker who has reminded us of the transcendent nature of human ego in this sense is N¡¥ir Khusrū al-Qub¡diy¡nī[1] who has poeticized this truth in the following words:

> How our reason could ever become the king of the universe/ if
> there was no universal reason to have her as its parts

8. Human personality, in addition to the aforementioned gifts and subtleties, has something stable and constant in the face of changes. If a person has committed suicide even a hundred years ago, he is a criminal and world criminal courts

---

1. Ab£ Mu'¢n °am¢d al-D¢n N¡¥ir ibn Khusr£ al-Qub¡diy¡n¢, also referred to as al-Hujjat (Proof) (1008-1088): a Persian poet, philosopher, Ism¡'¢l¢ scholar, and traveler. [Trans.]

shall treat him as a convict although his physical dimensions have already undergone so many changes. Perhaps the source of primordiality of the self stems from the same element (its essence's inalterability).

That the human personality relies on a stable and accepted principle throughout his life in relation to every sort of event, in doing any action and in uttering anything, is related to the same inalterable element. At the same time,

> *Every moment the world is renewed, and we are unaware of its being renewed, while it remains (the same in appearance).*
>
> *Life is ever arriving anew, like the stream, though in the body it has the semblance of continuity.*[1]

To put the matter otherwise, although human personality is exposed to so many changes, he always inclines to stability and inalterable principles.

> *Generations have passed away, and this is a new generation: the moon is the same moon, the water is not the same water.*
>
> *The justice is the same justice, and the learning is the same learning too; but those generations and peoples have been changed (supplanted by others).*
>
> *Generations on generations have gone, O sir, but these Ideas (Divine Attributes) are permanent and everlasting.*
>
> *The water in this channel has been changed many times: the reflexion of the moon and of the stars remains unaltered.*
>
> *Therefore, its foundation is not in the running water; nay, but in the regions whose breadth is that of Heaven.*[2]

Having said these, reducing human personality and his activities to the worldly changes and transformations is tantamount to his extinction.

Human Being in the Fourth Dimension (Intelligible Life)

The fourth dimension is that of intelligible life based on human *existence*. The mutuality of these two realities is a peculiarity of human "ego". They can be included in the realities related to

---

1. Rumi's *Masnavi*, Book 1, lines 1144-1145, p. 125. [Trans.]
2. Rumi's *Masnavi*, Book 6, lines 3175-3179, p. 355. [Trans.]

the third dimension, since the relationship of these two realities with the supernatural is direct and more important than all the isolated features of the individual, however, they treat the two as constituting an independent dimension. We shall mention here some *'descriptions'* of morality embodied in the thoughts of the authorities, both in the East and the West, throughout the centuries:

1. Morality is the blossoming of the truth within human being.

2. Morality is the reflection of human sound life and conscience. What is conscience? Conscience is the compass of the ark of humanity in the ocean of existence.

3. Morality is the interpreter of human "intelligible life".

4. Morality is the source of victory of the human being over his animalistic traits.

5. No amount of exhilaration and mirth can equal the exultation and rejoice experienced by a moral person.

6. There is no regret for a decision motivated by sublime human morality.

7. A sense of responsibility based upon activities related to moral virtues is the loftiest feeling that emanates from ones being.

8. Without sublime moral virtues, no community in history is worth studying by people.

9. In knowing a person, there is no sign equal to morality.

10. If we take away sublime morality from the life of the human being, we will then be dealing with a complex dangerous being that calls 'itself' 'human'.

Having said these, elimination of morality from human life is certainly tantamount to making human personality pointless or its complete destruction; the very reality that makes them distinct from animals. No doubt, elimination of religion from human life (secularism), whose edifice is based upon egotism and trespassing other people's rights, leaves no room for constructive personal morality.

Elimination of religion from human life based on secularism

leads to undermining of the unity of "intelligible life" and "personality".

Reducing high ideals of human personality to the disjointed and transitory worldly aspects and eliminating religion from them is exactly like persuading the man to witness particular tangible things, which are registered in the human mind through sensory perceptions and experiments. If human intellect did not organize and abstract the law from those tangible things, it would be impossible for human beings to discern scientific laws in the universe. With the elimination of religion, human life will lose the ability to present the fundamental laws and methods of a purposeful life.

The greatest havoc wrought by eliminating religion from human life is the division of human life and personality into the mundane and spiritual aspects!

It is impossible for "intelligible life", whose main root stems from a higher world to end in a lower world or, to be divisible, such that a part of it in this world is under the control of man, administering it according to his inclinations and ideals while providing for the other part as its otherworldly part! One can easily perceive the unity of the life and personality of man in both the worldly and otherworldly realms.

The salient features of secularism and the irreparable losses to the sublime values of humanity caused by the elimination of religion from man's mundane life

A brief introduction to extremism and dissipation, which have engulfed humanity throughout history, will show that mankind is rarely able to understand both, and if ever it does, it can hardly consciously avoid both extremes. The most serious and destructive extremism committed by man with regard to realities is that which is against his own self. This deviation, which always leads to the formulation of deviant ideas in other aspects of his life, is going to extremes in assessing his self. We must therefore believe that as long as the root of this precarious deviation remains in his being, it is certain that deviant ideas and inclinations will deprive him of a "intelligible life" in this world and in the hereafter. In order to elucidate this point, we shall hereby provide examples in this discussion:

1. Man sometimes has extreme views about his own self, regarding it as the universe's pick of the basket, and sometimes, bringing his self down as more dangerous than a preying beast![1]

2. In the past, "slavery" had been the most fundamental principle of life and the cornerstone of all facets of life, such as law, morality, religion, economy, politics, culture, and others! Nowadays, the concept of "freedom", which basically means emancipation from all religious and moral bounds, as well as,the other sublime human values has prevailed throughout (the so-called advanced) industrial societies. It is obvious that this extremism is the product of the earlier extremism or vice versa.

3. In the past, to be bound by the laws, duties and rights as well as extremist inclinations in the name of religion put some societies under so much pressure that even a window for free thinking could not be seen. Today, some people in society cannot even tolerate hearing religious expressions!

4. Psychology was once regarded as a head without a body and today it is treated as a body without a head. That is, yesterday, human knowledge about his soul plunged him into the halo of abstract notions, and now into physiological, biological and behavioral concepts about which no sufficient investigation has ever been made. As such, psychology deals with all issues except the essence of the personal "I".

5. Sometimes, extremism reaches the point in which one claims that economy has no importance in the conduct of human life. Another form of extremism propounds that the

---

1. What we mean by "sometimes" here includes two ways of going to extremes: (1) at one time, a person or people exaggerate in presenting or assessing a reality while at another time, he or they fall short of doing the same, and (2) a person or people exaggerate in presenting or assessing a reality while at the same time or at another time, another person or other people fall short of presenting or assessing the same reality!

essence of life and the all-embracing reason behind the development in human life is only economy and nothing else!

6. The pages of human history are replete with these optimistic and pessimistic forms of extremism. It is true that going to extremes in any of the various human dimensions, permeates his other dimensions on account of the strong relationship among them, but in two cases the permeation of both forms of extremism into other dimension has wrought the greatest havoc to man and humanity:

I. Going to extremes in presenting and appraising the "mind", "ego", "soul" and "personality".[1]

II. Going to extremes on the presentation and appraisal of religion which can cause derangement in knowing the salient features of all basic human values.

Now, we shall turn to the salient features of the "separation of religion and politics" approach and its irreparable losses.

Our discussion pertains to the second example and losses, in terms of importance, not inferior to the first case, which is deviant thought on the basic nature of man. We do not know whether the thinkers were aware of the havoc wrought by the entry of secularism into the lives of people—havoc caused by the elimination of basic human values, which led to man's alienation from the universe, fellow human beings, God, and above all, from himself.

Examples of Values Which Cease to exist after their removal from Human Life[2]

---

1 It can be said that committing the said extreme actions is equal to the deviation on the absolute nature of man.

2. What we mean by "being undermined or totally extinguished" is that since the prevalence of the secularist thought along this direction, we have faced most of the sublime fundamental and ideological human concepts and truths. That is, humanities—particularly the literary, artistic and moral culture of societies—deal with the said concepts and truths with much zeal and enthusiasm, but cannot present a convincing proof to substantiate these concepts' importance and merits. It seems that entire humanity must be grateful to the distinguished thinkers who identify the removal of religion from the root of those ideological truths and sublime human principles as the real cause of

1- Exposition of the essence of sensible and intelligible beauties: It is only religion which introduces the outward pole of beauty as a manifestation of Divine Beauty and advances the inward axis of beauty to acquire a manifestation of Divine Beauty. The outward pole is physical, such as a beautiful bunch of flowers, fountains, moonlight, elegant penmanship, a golden voice, and the azure sky.

The inward pole is real, such as sublime emotions, clemency, benevolence, and egalitarianism. Any person with the said traits possesses rational inward beauty, whose pleasure is more sublime than that acquired from outward manifestations of beauty. To provide an ultimate interpretation of the essence and main source of beauty, one should resort to the theory we offered earlier. And it is clear that by removing religion (whose basic foundation is the belief in God) from the equation, we will have no intelligible interpretation of beauty as Nī'ımī Ganjawī[1] says:

> Once the painter was ordered to depict the reality/ you got free of ignorance and I was no longer a cursed man

2. Justice in its true sense: We know that the meanings and extensions of justice are diverse because Divine justice in its actual sense emanates from His infinite wisdom. Legal justice signifies conforming an action or utterance to the prescribed law.

Justice in its moral sense denotes obeying the conscience to follow what is good and avoid wickedness, without relying and expecting any reward, or evading punishment. Justice, in its philosophical sense, connotes a lofty will manifested by the system of the universe. It is true that justice in its moral sense is a very desirable trait and the great sages of both the East and

---

inability to prove their importance and merits, courageously voicing out that in interpreting and justifying these truths, their main roots in particular, one must refer to religion.

1. Nī'ım al-Dın Abſ Muḥammad Ilyıs ibn Yſsuf ibn Zakč, better known as Nī'ımč Ganjawč (1141 – 1209): considered the greatest romantic epic poet in Persian literature. [Trans.]

the West have regarded it as one of the factors that contribute to human perfection, but when one analyzes the common conscience, he also perceives the pleasure from doing so. This is because seeking metaphysical pleasure also has an element of selfishness. Thus, it is the brigand for most of the people along the path of perfection. Then, justice in its moral sense stems from the common conscience, whose activities have a sublime manifestation and transcend pleasures and sufferings.

3. Personal freedom up to the sublime degree of freewill: Natural life wishes to preserve the human essence, attract sources of pleasure and repel sources of harm. This "natural self" has no work other than selfishly satisfying natural urges, and if a person fails to transcend the "natural self", even if he has the most beautiful outward appearance, he cannot bring the potential of the "sublime ego" to fruition. For this reason, all revealed religions have emphatic admonitions to transcend the "natural self" to achieve the "sublime ego".

In the words of the Commander of the Faithful 'Alī ibn Abī ±ịlib ('a),

> O servants of Allah! The best of Allah's servants in His sight is he who helps Allah with regard to himself (his self-building).[1]

To state the matter differently, without molding the "sublime ego," a person is an animal, nay, lower than that as Quran suggests:

> **They have hearts with which they do not understand, they have eyes with which they do not see, they have ears with which they do not hear. They are like cattle; rather they are more astray. It is they who are the heedless.**[2]

The basic factor involved in man's promotion from the "natural self" to the "human sublime ego" is exposing oneself to the divine radiations of Absolute Perfection which refers to God, the Exalted. This is because any privilege which is

---

1. Ibid., Sermon 87.
2. S£rat al-A'rịf 7:179.

considered the "goal of life" in this world is inferior to the "sublime ego".

The clearest proof of this claim is that if a person evaluates what he acquires of wealth, position, impressive mansion, wholesome assets, social status, and even knowledge and artistic talent, he will see that as compared to the greatness, and expanse of the "sublime ego", these things are insignificant.

Those who have a share of "personality" or the "sublime ego" know well that before obtaining it, every material and worldly goal seems so attractive. But, once it is obtained he will continue his journey to perfection until he reaches the radiations of Absolute Perfection. This Absolute Perfection refers to God who cannot be limited within the domain of "ego". Mawl¡n¡ Rūmī says,

> The deliciousness of milk and honey is the reflection of the (pure) heart: from that heart the sweetness of every sweet thing is derived.

> Hence the heart is the substance, and the world is the accident: how should the heart's shadow (reflection) be the object of the heart's desire?[1]

Real freedom (beyond the unrestrained liberty which is a product of such fatal formulas as "I want it; therefore it is right!") is so great that it will save him from the shackles of transitory worldly inclinations and not allow him to focus on "freedom" as the absolute goal of life. At the same time, it will guide him until he exposes himself to the radiations of Absolute Perfection.

It is through this journey to perfection that a person transcends "freedom" to achieve "freewill". And, by delivering "freedom" from the domain of material values, and self-centeredness, will transform it into God-centeredness, curb selfishness and turn it into a means of perfection of one's being. In human history, no influential personality has been able to really render service to humanity without attaining the lofty

---

1. Rumi's *Masnavi*, Book 3, lines 2265-2266, p. 249. [Trans.]

degree of freewill (doing good deeds and enjoying freedom along the path of goodness and perfection).

4. Sacrifices offered in the path of serving humanity: One of the essential features of secularism is opposing any type of self-sacrifice for the welfare of the people in society, particularly those altruistic acts that lead to one's suffering, persecution and even death. No loftier value can reciprocate this sublime human quality. That soul is great which, for the sake of saving the lives of others or their welfare, prefers to die an honorable death than to live a humiliating life.

5. Noble sense of unity of humanity: Since the beginning of social life and people's acquaintance with one another, there has been a noble sense of unity among mankind. This feeling exists in every person who is not an egoist. The activities of mundane life are founded on the edifice of egoism and an egoist only considers himself worthy to live; he does not have such a feeling nor even entertain such an idea in his mind.

This claim is based upon an eternal principle that the stronger the hold of materialism in a person, the more he is susceptible to contradiction and inconsistency. Therefore, attaining harmony and unity of the members of human race as well as transcend materialism is essential. The contents of the couplets below explain the above:

> When you see two of them meet together as friends, they are one, and at the same time, six hundred thousand.
>
> Their numbers are in the likeness of waves: the wind will have brought them into number (into plurality from unity).
>
> The Sun, which is the spirit, broke into rays in the windows, which are bodies.
>
> When you gaze on the Sun's disk, it is itself one, but he that is screened by (his perception of) the bodies, is in some doubt.[1]
>
> The souls of wolves and dogs are separate, every one; the souls of the Lions of God are united.[2]

---

1. Ibid., Book 2, lines 184-187, p. 23. [Trans.]
2. Ibid., Book 4, line 414, p. 51. [Trans.]

Separation (plurality) is in the animal spirit; the human spirit is one essence.

Inasmuch as 'God sprinkled His light upon them (mankind), (they are essentially one): His light never becomes separated (in reality).[1]

The human soul is like a single body while the animal soul is a solid earthenware.

None is aware of this enigma except the intellect, and none is knowledgeable of this secret except Allah.

What has the intellect to do with such transaction? What does a congenitally blind donkey to do with a cart?[2]

It can be noticed that Rūmī believes that the intellect, which relies on the sensory perceptions and submits to the "natural self", is incapable of perceiving the unity of human souls. In order to perceive this sublime reality, a sublime understanding, which can grasp the meaning of "God sprinkled His light upon them (mankind)" (*haqq rashsha 'alayhim nūrah*) is necessary. Hence, in order to attain such unity and perceive the enjoyment of the bounty of the Divine Light, the sublime immaterial aptitude of man must reach the level of his potential (*fi'liyyah*).

6. Answering sextuple questions concerning human quadruple ontological relationships (with himself, God, the universe, and his fellow human beings), i.e.:

- Who am I?
- Where have I come from?
- Where have I come?
- With whom am I?
- What have I come for?
- Where will I go?

It is impossible to give the ultimate answers to these sextuple questions without referring to religion.

7. The purity of conscience and its power: The secularists believe that people are capable of managing all the material,

---

1. Ibid., Book 2, lines 188-189, p. 23. [Trans.]
2. Ibid., Book 2, lines 188-190, in a longer version of the book. [Trans.]

psychological and spiritual facets of their lives, and do not need the elements beyond mundane life, and that there is no need of the purity of conscience for total control, it must be removed from life. This is because a clean conscience, which is the compass of the ship of human being in the ocean of existence, totally opposes self-centeredness, the basis of mundane life with the dual power of attracting pleasure and avoiding pain. How can the luminous human conscience, which is the direct messenger of God in the midst of people, work along with self-centeredness which is based upon "The end justifies the means", and "Since I like it, therefore, it is right"?

Two individuals—an extremely wicked and an extremely good—shall be identified by the presence or absence of conscience.

No being has as much diversity among its individuals as human beings. All human beings throughout history have shared the same internal and external organs; they were all called "humans". For the same human beings, which generally include both the lowest of the low and the nearest of the near have been extolled beyond limit,. Some have even regarded man as worthy of worship!

In his reply to my letter (about the contradiction existing on this issue), Bertrand Russell[1] wrote:

> Man can satisfy the sense of perfection and yearning for the Sublime Being (God) with humanitarianism!

For me, it is not clear whether or not Russell, who has unconditionally elevated man to be worthy of divine love and the status of divinity, had read about individuals such as Nero,

---

1. Bertrand Russell (1872 - 1970): a British philosopher, mathematician and man of letters. Initially a subscriber of idealism, he broke away in 1898 and eventually became an empiricist. His works include The Principles of Mathematics (1903), Principia Mathematica (3 vols., 1910-1913) in collaboration with A.N. Whitehead, Marriage and Morals (1929), Education and the Social Order (1932), An Inquiry into Meaning and Truth (1940), History of Western Philosophy (1945), and popularizations such as The ABC of Relativity (1925), as well as his Autobiography (3 vols., 1967-69). [Trans.]

Caligula, Attila,[1] Genghis Khan, Hulagu Khan, and Tamerlane who have had countless disciples in human history.

Yes, Nero had a pair of eyes, eyebrows, hands, and feet just like Socrates.[2] By the same token, the bodily limbs of Ibn Muljim Murịdī[3] and Imịm 'Alī ibn Abī ±ịlib ('a) had no difference at all in terms of anatomical constitution. But the inward nature of these two individuals, because of having or lacking a conscience, made them poles apart.

The infinite magnificence of the conscience defies any description except that it is a divine manifestation. Is it not an insult to humanity when we say that humanity must only use this trustworthy messenger of God to confess or claim in courts? In other words, should conscience be only a spare part in implementing a legal item?

8. In secularism, there is no need for any motive except providing for the needs of mundane life while implementing laws related to the realities of the second dimension (social mundane life, such as law, economics, etc.),[4]. What is needed are purely natural motives to benefit from the bodily members and continue their functions. For this reason, to abide with the laws of the said realities (legal code, economics, politics, and the like) is acceptable to the strong as long as doing so is profitable and not doing so is unprofitable, otherwise the existence and non-existence of those realities are the same for them. When a person, who believes in "eliminating religion from mundane life" says, that he respects the laws governing those realities, eother he is a hypocrite and makes use of this claim to advance

1. Attila (?–453), also known as Attila the Hun: the leader of the Hunnic Empire (stretching from the Ural River to the Rhine River and from the Danube River to the Baltic Sea) from 434 until his death, who was one of the most feared enemies of the Western and Eastern Roman Empires. [Trans.]
2. Socrates (circa 469-399 BCE): a Classical Greek philosopher and considered one of the founders of Western philosophy. [Trans.]
3. 'Abd al-Raịmịn ibn Muljim: the assassin of Imịm 'Al¢ ('a). [Trans.]
4. See the discussion on secularism (elimination of religion from mundane life) as having contributed to the derangement of personality (the human "I") in managing the human being.

his Machiavellian interest, or he definitely is an illusionist. We have heard the famous proverb that "The law is a cobweb" and strong animals like the lion, leopard and even the mouse are never caught in it.

9. In secularism, the necessity of revolutions and progressive movements by offering sacrifices even to the extent of giving one's life is meaningless and futile. This is because its goal is nothing but organizing mundane life. In this system, man himself is not discussed as a being capable of attaining essential excellence and perfection, for this must be sidelined on the same basis that religion is removed. It is for this reason that the contemporary legal systems, including those seemingly global ones, have no concern with the realities related to perfection (wisdom, virtue, etc.).

Legal provisions are usually based on the principle that human beings are brothers and equal in terms of nobility and honor! It is not mentioned that this equality is only in the superstructure of natural life, otherwise the difference among human beings in terms of morality, wisdom, nobility, and acquired honor is infinite. For example, one says,

> How I wish, all people have only one head and neck, and with only a single strike of the sword, I could have destroyed them.[1]

Another person says,

> **By Allah, even if I am given all the domains of the seven (stars) with all that exists under the skies in order that I may disobey Allah to the extent of snatching one grain of barley from an ant I would not do it.[2]**

10. In secularism, the value of responsibility and duty perishes in conforming life with the realities of the second dimension (such as law, economics, politics, and the like). We can witness human beings downgraded today, to the level of lifeless cogwheels. As admonished by the religions with divine origin and the great sages of both the East and the West, one

---

1. Ascribed to Nero.
2. Nahj al-Balịghah, Sermon 224. [Trans.]

can perceive his real value from the same sense of responsibility of the profiteers and egoists. Consider, for example, the following musings:

> *O duty! O great and high name! You are not pleasing and charming (because one has to exert effort to discharge you), but you ask people to obey, and you shake the will of some, bringing the self to what it abhors. You do not frighten it, but you only enact a law which penetrates into the self, and even if we do not obey it, willy-nilly, we respect it. And, all inclinations, although in the end one acts against it, submit to it.*
>
> *O duty! What is your due base, and from what did you originate? What can your noble racial root be found in, that, with utmost magnanimity of kinship it totally avoids inclinations, and the condition of compulsoriness of the real value of people, that they could give themselves, emanates from the same basis or root.*
>
> *Being part of the perceptible world, indeed, man goes beyond himself through that basis which connects him to something which only reason can perceive. That basis is indeed man's personality; that is, his autonomy and independence vis-à-vis the instrument of nature.*[1]

If the "elimination of religion from worldly life" approach had rendered only the blow of removing the spirit of responsibility, which emanates from man's perfect-seeking personality, it is enough ground for humanity to turn away from this approach and rescue the human personality from this perilous idea.

11. In secularism, due to the common grounding relation that is shared by all realities of second dimension with respect to their higher causes (like their being a means for the fulfillment of intelligible life), human personality remains partial in its process of evolution and nothing can repair this

---

1. Mu!ammad 'Al¢ Fur£gh¢, Sayr-e °ikmat dar Ur£p¡, vol. 2, p. 169 (originally in Persian).

partiality. How could a person who knows that no part of nature and no process in the universe is devoid of law, continue his life without law? Essentially related to his personality is intrinsic respect for the law, continuous efforts and endeavor for advancement and perfection, a noble sense of responsibility, and the unity of personality!

12. Fraternity and equality of human beings: After secularism alienatied them from one another, and subjected them to "self-alienation" by negating morality and religion from their lives, and went to the extent of plunging them into the dark pit of "Man is a wolf for man,"[1] can human beings still be presented as brothers to one another?! Have the framers of Western human rights answered this question?

13. Don't you know that by the denial of sublime human values and principles, all lines and words about the greatness, honor and dignity of man, written in millions of volumes of Eastern and Western books, are being falsified?! Man has incurred a wound no medicine can heal!

---

1. See the dedication to Thomas Hobbes' work De cive (1651). [Trans.]

Chapter 4
Islam and Secularism

A Survey of Some Muslim Writings on Political Issues[1]

It is of immense importance to conduct a historical survey, though a brief one, of the political ideas of Islam as its believers today constitute almost one billion and two hundred million out of the five and a half billion people populating the earth.[2]

Some scholars and translators of the history of political philosophy contend that "the origin of political philosophy and the source of the beliefs and ideas related to government and politics and the early political philosophies, which prevail in the contemporary world, is Ancient Greece. From there it was transmitted to Rome and from Rome to Europe during the Middle Ages until it prevailed throughout the world."[3] If they mean that no book has been written about the political philosophy of Islam, then it is not correct, because we have two types of researchers in political philosophy of Islam:

a) Most of the Muslim jurisprudents, philosophers and sages, devote a significant part of their research works to practical wisdom called "civil polity". Shahīd al-Awwal (Muḥammad ibn Jamīl al-Dīn al-Makkī)[4] has divided the

---

1. We have also discussed this topic in the commentary to the blessed instruction of the Commander of the Faithful ('a) to Malik al-Ashtar.
See Muḥammad Taqī Ja'farī, °ikmat-e U¥£l-e Siyīsē-ye Islīm: Tarjumeh wa Tafsēr-e Farmīn-e 'Alī ('a) beh Mīlik Ashtar (Political Philosophy of Islam: Translation and Commentary of Imīm 'Alī's Order to Malik al-Ashtar) (Tehran: 'Allīmah Ja'farī Institute, 1385 AHS (2006)). [Trans.]
2. Islam is the world's second largest religion. According to a 2010 study and released January 2011, Islam has 1.57 billion adherents, making up over 23% of the world population. According to the Pew Research Center in 2015 there were 50 Muslim-majority countries. [Ed.]
3. Bahī' al-Dīn Pīsīrgīn, Tīrēkh-e Falsafē-ye Siyīsē, vol. 1, p. 175.
4. Muḥammad Jamīl al-Dīn al-Makkē al-'īmilē (1334–1385) also known as

sections (*abw¡b*) of jurisprudence into four:
- Acts of worship (*'ib¡d¡t*),
- Contracts (*'uqūd*),
- Unilateral obligations (*īq¡'¡t*), and
- Politics (*siy¡sah*).

It is clear that Shahīd al-Awwal has divided jurisprudence into the aforementioned sections according the views of all jurisprudents (*fuqah¡*) and not according to his personal opinion alone.[1]

b) Books which have been written exclusively about political philosophy. Take, for example, the following titles into consideration:

- *Mak¡tīb al-Rasūl* compiled by 'Alī ibn al-°usayn Ahmadī. This volume includes different types of political decrees and religious-moral admonitions in Islam as narrated from the Holy Prophet (¥);
- *Al-Wath¡'iq al-Siyasiyyah* compiled by Dr. Mu¡ammad °amīd All¡h °aydar¡b¡dī. In this treatise, some political dimensions of Islam are traced from the Holy Prophet (¥);
- A considerable number of the sermons and letters of the Commander of the Faithful (*'a*) recorded in *Nahj al-Bal¡ghah* compiled by the late Sayyid al-Ra¤ī, particularly the blessed instruction to M¡lik al-Ashtar, an analysis and exposition of which has been made in one of the volumes of *Tarjumeh wa Tafsīr-e Nahj al-Bal¡ghah* ("*A Translation and Commentary on Nahj al-Bal¡ghah*");
- *Al-Ahk¡m al-Salt¡niyyah wa 'l-W¡l¡y¡t Jam' bayn al-Mas¡'il al-Shar'iyyah wa 's-Siy¡siyyah* written by Aq¤¡ 'l-Qa¤¡t Abū 'l-°asan 'Alī ibn °abīb al-Ba¥rī al-Baghd¡dī al-M¡wardī (died 450 AH);

Shah¢d al-Awwal: the first Islamic martyr from among the Sh¢'ah scholars and the author of Al-Lum'ah al-Dimashqiyyah ("The Damascene Glitter"). [Trans.]
1. Mu¡ammad ibn al-Makk¢, Dhikr¢ 'sh-Sh¢'ah f¢ A¡k¡m al-Shar¢'ah, p. 6.

- *Al-Khar¡j* authored by Q¡¤ī Abū Yūsuf ibn Ibr¡hīm;
- *Al-Amw¡l* written by Abū 'Ubayd al-Q¡sim ibn Sal¡m (died 224 AH);
- *Ma'¡lim al-Qurriyyah fī Ahk¡m al-°asabah* authored by Mu!ammad ibn Ahmad al-Qurshī, known as Ibn al-Ikhwah;
- *Al-Ahk¡m al-Salt¡niyyah* written by Abū Ya'l¡ Mu!ammad ibn al-°usayn al-Farr¡';
- *Kit¡b al-Fakhrī 'l-¡d¡b al-Salt¡niyyah wa 'd-Duwal al-Isl¡miyyah* authored by Mu!ammad ibn 'Alī ibn ±ab¡tab¡, known as Ibn ±aqtaqī;
- *Siy¡satn¡meh* by Khw¡jah Niz¡m al-Mulk;[1]
- *Al-Wal¡t wa 'l-Qu¤¡t* written by Kindī;
- *Al-Khar¡j wa ¯an'at al-Kit¡b* authored by Qudd¡mah ibn Ja'far;
- *Al-Siy¡sat al-Madīnah* by Mu!ammad ibn Mu!ammad ±urkh¡n al-F¡r¡bī;
- *¡r¡ Ahl al-Madīnat al-F¡¤ilah* written by Mu!ammad ibn Mu!ammad ±urkh¡n al-F¡r¡bī;
- *Akhl¡q-e N¡¥irī* authored by Khw¡jah Na¥īr al-Dīn al-±ūsī;[2]
- *Fiqh al-Siy¡sah* by Sayyid Mu!ammad °usaynī Shīr¡zī;[3]
- *Al-Im¡mah wa 's-Siy¡sah* written by Abū Mu!ammad 'Abd All¡h ibn Muslim ibn Qutaybah Daynūrī (died 213 AH);
- *Tanbīh al-Im¡mah wa Tanzīh al-Millah* authored by ¡yatullah al-'U"m¡ ¡q¡ Mīrz¡ Mu!ammad °usayn N¡'īnī;
- *°ukūmat az Na¨ar-e Isl¡m* by ¡yatull¡h ¡q¡ Sayyid Mahmūd

---

1. See its English translation, Ni"¨m al-Mulk, The Book of Government or Rules for Kings: The Siyar al-Muluk or Siy¡sat-n¡ma of Ni"¨m al-Mulk, trans. Hubert Darke (London: Routledge & Kegan Paul, 1960). [Trans.]

2. See its English translation, Na¥¢r al-D¢n ±£s¢, The Nasirean Ethics, trans. G.M. Wickens (London: George Allen and Unwin Ltd., 1964). [Trans.]

3. See its English translation, Sayyid Mu!ammad °usayn¢ Sh¢r¡z¢, The Islamic System of Government, trans. Z. Olyabek (London: Fountain Books, 2002). [Trans.]

±¡liq¡nī, a commentary on the late N¡'īnī's *Tanbīh al-Im¡mah wa Tanzīh al-Millah*;

- *T¡rīkh-e Siy¡sī wa Dīnī wa Farhangī dar Isl¡m*, 3 volumes, compiled by Dr. °asan Ibr¡hīm °asan;
- *Al-Muqaddimah* written by 'Abd al-Rahm¡n ibn Khaldūn;[1]

---

1. In order to prove that the sociopolitical realities of Ibn Khald£n in his Al-Muqaddimah are anchored in Islamic beliefs and that he has dealt with all these realities by referring to the primary Islamic sources, we can take into account his references to the Qur'anic verses, traditions (a!¡d¢th), and serious prayers at the end of most of the chapters of the book.

In his book, Dir¡s¡t 'an Ibn Khald£n, pp. 485-488, Ab£ Khald£n S¡§i' al-°a¥r¢ has discussed this subject and pointing out Ibn Khald£n's many citations of Qur'anic verses, traditions (a!¡d¢th) and supplications, he said: "In view of all these things, we deem it proper to declare that Ibn Khald£n was a man of correct faith uncontaminated by any doubt or skepticism about God and the religion."

Due to the importance of this issue, I considered it necessary to carefully examine all pages of the treatise. So I have studied all the instances of Ibn Khald£n's citation of Qur'anic verses and traditions as well as recitation of supplications. In out of 588 pages of the book, Ibn Khald£n has done so in 282 instances. In addition to the fundamental principles of social and economic philosophy, he has given consideration to Islamic sources and religious methodology, and we shall cite some instances as examples so as for the students of humanities, particularly economics, sociology and political science, as well as the researchers in all social sciences to know that the religion of Islam has given utmost importance to the said sciences, and at the same time, it has the highest principles of the said sciences in dealing with the individual and social lives of the members of society:

(1) The treatise Al-Muqaddimah commences with the following passage:

"Praised be Allah who is All-powerful and All-mighty. He holds royal authority and kingship in His hand. His are the Most Beautiful Names and Attributes. His knowledge is such that nothing, be it revealed in secret whispering of left unsaid, remains strange to Him. His power is such that nothing in heaven or on earth is too much for Him or escapes Him. He created us from the earth as living, breathing creatures. He made us to settle on it as races and nations. He gave us sustenance and provisions from it. Our mothers' wombs and then houses are our abode. Sustenance and food keep us alive. Time wears us out. Our lives' final terms, the dates of which have been fixed for us in the Book [of Destiny], claim us. But He lasts and endures. He is the Living one who does not die. Prayer and blessings be upon our Chief and Master, Mu!ammad, the Arab Prophet, whom the Torah and the Evangel have mentioned and described; for whose birth the world that is was already in labor before Sundays followed upon Saturdays in regular sequence and before Saturn and Behemoth had become separated; to whose truthfulness the pigeon and spider bore witness. Prayer and blessings be also upon his family and the men around him who, by being his companions and followers, gained wide influence and fame, and who by supporting him found unity while their enemies were weakened through dispersion. Pray, O Allah, for him and them, for as long as Islam shall continue to enjoy its lucky fortune and the frayed rope of unbelief shall remain cut! Manifold blessings be upon them all!" (translation adapted from Ibn Khaldun, The Muqaddimah: An Introduction to History, trans. Franz Rosenthal (New Jersey: Princeton University Press, 2005), p. 3)

(2) It is written in page 2, thus: "And I beseech God to purify my actions by His mercy and He is sufficient for my existence and He is the best Counsel."

(3) Errors in history are caused by nothing except one's greediness to hear amazing things and easily transmit the same orally without any investigation and assessment... and in this way, this erring historian would put Qur'anic verses in ridicule and invent baseless and amusing stories until he would stray away from the path of God. And Ibn Khald£n cites these two Qur'anic verses:

"Should he learn anything about Our signs, he takes them in derision." (S£rat al-J¡thiyah 45:9)

"Among the people is he who buys diversionary talk that he may lead [people] astray from Allah's way without any knowledge." (S£rat Luqm¡n 31:6)

There is no doubt that the mind of a thinker who would quote Qur'anic verses and traditions in approximately 250 instances in a 580-page treatise and quote a verse or recite a supplication at the end of most of the chapters is nothing but a manifestation of his faith in Islam and his vast research in social, economic, political, and mystical philosophy as well as the fundamentals of sciences and others. So far, ample studies about Ibn Khald£n's Al-Muqaddimah have been conducted by thinkers of both the East and the West, among which are the following:

(1) Ab£ Khald£n S¡§i' al-°a¥r¢ dealt with Dir¡s¡t 'an Ibn Khald£n at the index of his book;

(2) Falsafah Ibn Khald£n: Al-Ijtim¡'iyyah by Dr. ±¡h¡ °usayn (Cairo, 1952);

(3) Ibn Khald£n: °ay¡tuhu wa Tur¡thahu 'l-Fikr¢ by Prof. Mu!ammad 'Abd All¡h 'Ann¡n (Cairo, 1933);

(4) Falsafah Ibn Khald£n by Dr. 'Umar Farr£kh (Beirut, 1942);

(5) R¡'id al-Iqti¥¡d ibn Khald£n by Dr. Mu!ammad 'Al¢ Nish¡t (Cairo, 1944);

(6) Muh¡¤ar¡t 'an Ibn Khald£n by Prof. Mu!ammad al-Kha¤r °usayn (Cairo, n.d.);

(7) Ibn Khald£n f¢ 'l-Madrasat al-'¡daliyyah by Sayyid 'Abd al-Q¡dir al-Maghrib¢ (Damascus, n.d.);

(8) Ma'a Ibn Khald£n by Prof. A!mad Mu!ammad al-°awf¢ (Cairo, 1952);

(9) Al-Ta'r¢f Bi-Ibn Khald£n wa Rihlatahu Sharqan wa Gharban (Cairo, 1951);

(10) Ibn Khald£n by Prof. Fu'¡d Afr¡m al-Bast¡n¢ (Beirut, 1928);

- *Falsafeh-ye Siyịsī-ye Islịm* authored by Dr. 'Askarī °uqūqī;
- *Al-Islịm wa 'l-°a¤ịrat al-'Arabiyyah* by Kurd 'Alī;
- *Al-Islịm wa 't-Takịmul al-Ijtimị'ī* written by Shaykh Mahmūd Shaltūt;
- *Al-Siyịsah Min Wịqi'a 'l-Islịm* authored by Sayyid ¯ịdiq Shīrịzī;
- *Al-°a¤ịrat al-Islịmiyyah* by Adam Mitch (?), translated by Muịammad 'Abd al-Hịdī Abū Raydah;
- *Tamaddun-e Islịm dar Gharb (Islamic Civilization in the West)* written by Gustave Le Bon;[1]
- *Tịrīkh-e Tamaddun-e Islịmī* authored by Jurjī Zaydịn;
- *Al-Fikr al-Islịmī wa 'l-Mujtama'a 'l-Mu'ị¥ir fī Mushkilịt al-°ukm wa 't-Tawjīh* by Dr. Albahī;
- *Al-Islịm al-Na¨m al-Insịnī* written by Dr. Mu¥tafị Rịfi'ī;
- *Al-Fikr al-Islịmī wa 't-Tatawwar* authored by Fathī 'Uthmịnī;
- *Andīsheh-ye Siyịsī dar Islịm-e Mu'ị¥ir* by °amīd 'Inịyat;
- *Falsafeh-ye Siyịsī-ye Islịm* written by Dr. Abū 'l-Fa¤l 'Izzatī;
- *Al-Lawịmi' al-Ilịhiyyah*[2] which is an important discourse by Fị¤il Miqdịd;
- *'Awị'id al-Ayyịm* authored by Mullị Ahmad Narịqī;[3]

---

(11) Muntakhabịt Min Ibn Khald£n by Dr. Jam¢l ¯al¢b and Dr. Kịmil 'Ayyịd (Damascus, 1934);

(12) Ibn Khald£n: Khamsah Ajzị' Manịhil al-Adab (Beirut: Maktab ¯ịdir, 1949).

Research works about Al-Muqaddimah have been also done in a number of European languages including French, German, English, and Italian.

1. This most probably refers to Gustave Le Bon's La civilisation des arabes (The Civilization of Arabs) (1884). [Trans.]

2. In Al-Lawịmi' al-Ilịhiyyah f¢ 'l-Mabịịith al-Kalịmiyyah, p. 264, Fị¤il Miqdịd says, "Religion and government are complementary and one cannot be beneficial without the other. Wisdom dictates that these two truths must be fused into a single body, and if a religious authority does not express opinion about the exigency of time and governance for the justification and leadership of society, it is a defect on the purport of religion."

3. Mullị Aịmad Narịq¢, 'Awị'id al-Ayyịm, pp. 185-206 (originally in Persian).

- *Kitjb al-Siyjsah* by Qudjmah ibn Ja'far;
- *Adab al-Sultjn* written by Abū 'l-°asan 'Alī ibn Na¥r;
- *Kitjb al-Siyjsah al-Kabīr* authored by Ahmad ibn Sahl Abū Zayd al-Balkhī;
- *Kitjb al-Siyjsah al-¯aghīr* by Ahmad ibn Sahl Abū Zayd al-Balkhī;[1]
- *Kitjb al-Dawlah* written by Abū Ishjq Ibrjhīm ibn al-'Abbjs al-¯awlī;[2]
- *Siyjsat al-Mulūk* authored by Abū Dalaf al-Qjsim ibn 'Īsj ibn Ma'qal.[3]

How can a civilization emerge and achieve a significant height of advancement and progress without having a rational political system?![4]

In the early years of the advent of Islam, and even in the succeeding centuries, a specified code of laws had not been framed because human life in Islam has a very significant reason, which the Muslim religious authorities know, and that is, the unity of all dimensions of human life (economic, political, legal, moral, artistic, etc.).

It is for this reason that the political discourses compiled in distinct book forms, or available to the Muslim thinkers and scholars as a section in jurisprudence (*fiqh*), are in reality the schema of one of the dimensions of the Islamic school of thought. The importance of the political dimension of man in Islam, will be pointed out to some extent in this book. According to the tradition, "Whoever wakes up without having any concern for the affairs of Muslims is not a Muslim", a lack of participation in organizing the social lives of people is a deviation from the way of Islam. Islam has the best formula to organize and manage the rational lives of people.

---

1. Ibn Nad¢m, Al-Fihrist, p. 135 (originally in Arabic).
2. Ismj'¢l Pjsh¢ al-Baghdjd¢, Kashf al-²un£n, vol. 1, p. 2 (originally in Arabic).
3. Ibn Nad¢m, Al-Fihrist, p. 130.
4. In his book Adventures of Ideas (1933), Alfred North Whitehead says, "Two pure and original civilizations have flourished in history; namely, the Islamic civilization and the Byzantium civilization."

All the known Qur'¡nic verses on the exigency of justice ('adl) and fairness (qist) (15 verses on justice and 18 on fairness) and those that affirm removing impediments to intelligible life to achieve "freedom", are sufficient to establish the importance given by Islam to the man's political dimension in life. Some Qur'¡nic verses indicate that the most important purpose behind the apostleship (ris¡lah) of the prophets of God is the emergence of justice and equity. For example:

> *Certainly We sent Our apostles with manifest proofs, and We sent down with them the Book and the Balance, so that mankind may maintain justice.*[1]

As a matter of fact, the importance given to the issues of political philosophy of Islam does neither have a detailed scientific and jurisprudential framework nor it is practically observed. Why?

First of all, it must be borne in mind that the governments and the rulers who have held the reigns of government according to the Sunnī school of thought used to deal with the issues in Islam according to the Sunnī notions of politics. In most Muslim societies until the recent time, the Shī'ah school of thought had no practical power in political matters, so the jurisprudents (fuqah¡) and authorities did not feel the need to discuss the political issues. However, they have been examined in some sections of jurisprudence, philosophy and theology, thereby, categorically affirming the vital importance of thinking about governing society. I have dealt with some of these subjects in the commentary on the blessed instruction of Im¡m 'Alī ('a) to M¡lik al-Ashtar in the book °ikmat-e U¥ūl-e Siy¡sī-ye Isl¡m (The Wisdom behind the Political Principles of Islam).

Islamic Sources on the Integrity of Religious Laws

1- If the worldly aspects of life, like the spiritual aspects, were not an integral part of religious laws, all the religious admonitions, emphases and instructions to uproot corruption on earth would not have been revealed. Take, for example, the

---

1. S£rat al-°ad¢d 57:25.

following two verses:

> ... *those who break the covenant made with Allah after having pledged it solemnly, and sever what Allah has commanded to be joined, and cause corruption on the earth— it is they who are the losers.*[1]
>
> *Indeed the requital of those who wage war against Allah and His Apostle, and to try to cause corruption on the earth, is that they shall be slain or crucified, or have their hands and feet cut off from opposite sides or be banished from the land. That is a disgrace for them in this world, and in the Hereafter there is a great punishment for them.*[2]

The Noble Qur'¡n, has given the order to uproot corruption on earth 41 times in different forms. It goes without saying that if religion had nothing to do with matters pertaining to mundane life, the moral and legal emphases of the Qur'¡n on fighting against corruption would have been meaningless, because people usually understand the abomination of corruption and know that it is impossible to live amidst corruption and the corrupt.

The idea that the religious order to fight against corruption is meant for a mental case, does not hold water, because most agents of corruption and their followers do not regard their acts as a form of corruption. In fact, the egoists imagine that what they do is something meritorious!

Throughout history, we encounter hundreds of false interpretations and justifications of corruption through which its agents exonerate themselves for their wicked acts. And in many cases, they describe their filthy acts, bloodshed and transgressions of rights as campaigns against corruption!

Religion maintains that it is the function of a sound mind and pure nature to determine what constitutes corruption and who its agent is,

---

1. S£rat al-Baqarah 2:27.
2. S£rat al-M¡'idah 5:33.

as in determining other things, and not by those who consider themselves rightful even if they have annihilated half of humanity.

2- The emphatic order to compete in good works (*khayrɪt*), as this Qur'ɪnic verse shows:

> *Everyone has a cynosure to which he turns; so take the lead in all good works.*[1]

There are two important points in this noble verse:

- The word *khayrɪt* embraces all types of goodness— individual and collective, material and spiritual, worldly and otherworldly. Anyone who thinks that the word *khayrɪt* only includes that which is otherworldly is either ignorant of Arabic language or someone who resorts to the "logic of rationalization" in order to advance his own interest.[2]

- The same important rule we have mentioned in interpreting the first item is also applicable here. That is, in most cases, a person or a group regards as good whatever he or it likes out of selfishness, though it may be a wicked act or thing, whereas, the divine religion's admonitions and orders are based upon "real goodness".

3- The permission to utilize useful things on earth for subsistence and organization of life:

> *O mankind! Eat of what is lawful and pure in the earth.*[3]

This point has been highlighted in the Noble Qur'ɪn 16 times. Human beings who live consciously in this world— believing there is harm in consuming certain food and drinking items, refrain from doing so—should also do the same with regards to actions, utterances and any connection with the

---

1. S£rat al-Baqarah 2:148.
2. The logic of rationalization refers to the use of certain propositions in order to support one's claim or interest although such propositions are incapable of doing so.
3. S£rat al-Baqarah 2:168.

world of nature. They should not consider themselves "free" and "open" to do or say anything in their quadruple ontological relationships. Yet, given the probable harm or unpleasantness of an action, utterance or even thinking something, they do not even exercise rational precaution. It is based upon this rule that God says, "Whatever I have provided on earth is for your utility except if there is harm in doing so (physical or spiritual harm)."

4- Financial obligations are meant to organize the material dimension of life; for example, zakjt, khums[1] and [other] known [financial] obligations are prescribed in a bid to eradicate poverty. Prevention of *kanz* (accumulation and amassing of gold, silver and other essential minerals as well as hoarding and embezzlement of wealth), usury (*ribj*) and encroachment upon the property of orphans is also intended for the same purpose. In keeping with these obligations, rights have been prescribed. The poor and needy are entitled to receive *zakjt*. Similar are the rights of those who are entitled to receive *khums* and other known financial obligations. The indigents of society also have the right to utilize withheld treasures. That is, the Muslim ruler is duty-bound to order the utilization of gold and silver which has been withheld at the expense of society's welfare.

> *Charities are only for the poor and the needy, and those employed to collect them, and those whose hearts are to be reconciled, and for [the freedom of] the slaves and the debtors, and in the way of Allah, and for the traveler. [This is] an ordinance from Allah, and Allah is all-knowing, all-wise.*[2]

This decree has been made obligatory by God, the All-wise and All-knowing.

> *Know that whatever thing you may come by, a fifth*

---

1. Khums: a kind of religious levy, equivalent to one fifth of taxable income. [Trans.]
2. Sfrat al-Tawbah (or Barj'ah) 9:60.

of it is for Allah and the Apostle, for the relatives and the orphans, for the needy and the traveler, if you have faith in Allah.[1]

...and in whose wealth there is a known right for the beggar and the deprived...[2]

Those who treasure up gold and silver, and do not spend it in the way of Allah, inform them of a painful punishment."[3]

Rivalry [and vainglory] distracted you until you visited the graves."[4]

Allah brings usury to naught, but He makes charities flourish.[5]

Do not approach the orphan's property, except in the best [possible] manner.[6]

5- Abidance with the terms of contracts as obligatory:

... and those who fulfill their covenants, when they pledge themselves...[7]

And fulfill the covenants; indeed all covenants are accountable.[8]

And do not cheat the people of their goods.[9]

6- Law of retaliation (qi¥¡¥); 7- Penal law (hudūd); 8-Blood-money and other fines (diy¡t); 9- Last will (wa¥iyyah);10-Questions on inheritance (irth); 11-The prohibition of accumulating wealth through illegitimate means; 12-Jih¡d; 13-Self-defense; 14-Marriage (nik¡h); 15-Divorce (tal¡q); 16-Trading and transactions; 17-Giving exact measures and weights; 18-The

1. S£rat al-Anf¡l 8:41.
2. S£rat al-Ma'¡rij 70:24-25. [Trans.]
3. S£rat al-Tawbah (or Bar¡'ah) 9:34.
4. S£rat al-Tak¡thur 102:1-2.
5. S£rat al-Baqarah 2:276.
6. S£rat al-An'¡m 6:152.
7. S£rat al-Baqarah 2:177.
8. S£rat al-Isr¡' or Ban¢ Isr¡'¢l 17:34.
9. S£rat al-A'r¡f 7:85; S£rat H£d 11:85.

prohibition of hoarding (i¦tik¡r); 19-The prohibition of selling weapons (except defensive arms) to hostile people; 20-Debt (dayn) and pertinent matters; 21-Mortgage (rahn); 22-Guarantee and surety (¤im¡nah); 23-Peace and reconciliation (¥ulh); 24-Proxy and deputation (wik¡lah); 25-Renting (ij¡rah); 26-Partnership (shirkah); 27-Trusteeship and safekeeping (am¡nah); 28-Competition for exercise and wellbeing; 29-The prohibition of usurpation (gha¥b); 30-Confession (iqr¡r); 31-Judgment and testimonies; 32-The prohibition of ignorance in direct encroachment with respect to property and other aspects of life; 33-Pious endowment (waqf); 34-Gift and donation (hibah); 35-Economic rules and principles; 36-Legal rules and principles; 37-Political rules and principles; 38-Defining the relationship with non-Muslim minorities, communities and nationalities; 39-Organizing medical and health affairs; and 40-Organizing, altering or formulating things, which become part of life with the passage of time.

It is for this reason that we can divide Islamic jurisprudence into the following sections:

- Jurisprudence pertaining to the acts of worship ('ib¡dah);
- Jurisprudence pertaining to personal matters;
- Jurisprudence pertaining to transactions, contracts and unilateral obligations;
- Jurisprudence pertaining to morality;
- Jurisprudence pertaining to politics and governance;
- Jurisprudence pertaining to mysticism and gnosticism;
- Jurisprudence pertaining to technology, industry and craftsmanship;
- Jurisprudence pertaining to international relations;
- Jurisprudence pertaining to culture;
- Jurisprudence pertaining to management and administration;
- Jurisprudence pertaining to jih¡d and defense;
- Jurisprudence pertaining to sciences;
- Jurisprudence pertaining to discoveries and inventions;

- Jurisprudence pertaining to penal law;
- Jurisprudence pertaining to other laws;
- Jurisprudence pertaining to the judiciary;
- Jurisprudence pertaining to injustice and oppression;
- Jurisprudence pertaining to undesirable acts and practices;
- Jurisprudence pertaining to doing what is good;
- Jurisprudence pertaining to medical issues and questions;
- Jurisprudence pertaining to the future and prospective issues; and
- Jurisprudence pertaining to whatever happens in the world

Jurisprudential principles and rules based upon primordial discernments and rational propositions and fundamentals, which elucidate all rights and obligations in life in this world and the hereafter[1]

The jurisprudential rules which refer to general propositions that justify human life in the material and spiritual domains and can be applied to many particular cases; for example, the rule of "neither loss nor harm" (*l¡ ¤arar wa l¡ ¤ar¡r*) and the principle of the exigency of transactions. In acting upon these propositions, the mujtahid and the muqallid are the same. That is, they are both obliged to abide by them.

Having said this, however, in the rules of the principles of jurisprudence, only the jurisprudent (faqīh), after conducting a research and proving them, benefits from them in proving universal propositions in jurisprudence.

The principles and rules cited in jurisprudence can be generally divided into two:

1. The principles and rules provided for in the primary sources; for example, the rules of "negation of difficulty and trouble" (nafī 'asar wa haraj) and "neither loss nor harm" as provided for in this Qur'¡nic verse:

---

1. These principles and rules have been discussed in the section "The Scope of Religion".

Allah does not desire to put you to hardship.[1]

2. The principles and rules inferred by reliable proofs; for example, the preponderance of what is more important (ahamm) to what is important (muhimm) in cases of contradiction.

In jurisprudence, the ways of knowing realities differ in the modes of discovering them but all of them are either supported by the perception of pure nature, such as yaqīn (certainty) and qata' (suspension of judgment), or rational. Rational rulings such as exigencies that revoke the rulings' requirement, and data whose being discovered is completed by the Legislator, such as Qur'¡nic verses whose indication of the reality is abstract and traditions whose issuance (being authentic) is not definite. However, by complementing their proofs through another means, their potential of revealing legal realities is rational.

Meanwhile, the principles that are cited to remove any confusion in doubtful cases, such as the principle of disavowal [of the polytheists] (bar¡'at) and the principle of preponderance of eliminating harm over gaining profit, are rational propositions although their being proofs can also be consolidated by the endorsement of the Islamic legislator.

In view of their functional scope in jurisprudence, jurisprudential rules can be generally divided into two:

- General rules that can be implemented in all sections (abw¡b) of jurisprudence
- Particular rules that can be cited in some sections of jurisprudence.[2]

When one turns to these general and particular rules, he can draw two significant conclusions upon a close inspection of them:

1- To manage human life both in the worldly and otherworldly domains, Islamic jurisprudence has not resorted

---

1. S£rat al-M¡'idah 5:6.
2 The reader can find the examples of these general and particular rules on pages 134 to 156.

to some artificial principles rather it has sought to have intelligible life as its guiding principle and orient itself toward it.

2- Islamic jurisprudence is also founded on the transcendent codes of Islamic morality and this helps it to sustain itself both in the domains of pioneering and adherence. It is pioneer in the sense that it answers the permanent needs of human life and it is adherent in that it is open to new changes. The scope of its openness covers all domains of innovations unless those which contradict the very nature of a purposeful life.

°ĩkimiyyah and °ukm in the Qur'ĩn

In order to prove that revealed religion is not alien to politics, rule and human worldly life, it is essential to study about °ukm from the Qur'ĩnic viewpoint. Sayyid Murtaͅ Zubaydī, a great Arabic lexicographers, has mentioned the following points while elaborating the word °ukm:

"°-k-m (حكم) with ͅammah vowel (u) of the *h*ĩ' letter (ح) means decree (qaͅ') (in the sense of insh*ĩ*' or origination) in a thing in the sense that such a thing is so or not so, whether such decree obliges a person or not. This is the opinion of the lexicographers on the meaning of °ukm and some of them have been more specific by saying, "°ukm means decree on the basis of justice. This has been mentioned by Azharī." Qaͅĩ' refers to its general meaning which is creation of an obligation or recommendation, or, in relation to a thing. Zubaydī, who has earned the honorable title "Master of Language" (imĩm al-lughawī), has undertaken comprehensive studies of this word (°ukm) and its derivatives, but in no instance has he ever given "knowledge" ('ilm) as the meaning of °ukm.[1]

"°ukm includes hikmah (wisdom), and every hikmah is °ukm but not the opposite."

This is because the meaning of hikmah expressed by the theosophers and Zubaydī is, "°ikmah means knowing the

---

1. Tĩj al-'Arͣs fͨ Sharͥ al-Qĩmͣs by Muͥibb al-Dͨn Abͣ 'l-Fayͤ Sayyid Murtaͅ Zubaydͨ, vol. 8, p. 354 (originally in Arabic).

truths of things as they are, and acting upon what they require." °ukm is one of the distinctive manifestations of hikmah, and if a man of wisdom, notwithstanding all the conditions for removing hostilities and managing the social life of people, refrains from ruling, he will be regarded as misguided from the viewpoint of the religious law. If it is used to purely mean knowledge, gnosis or wisdom, this is exceptional, and mean an essential preliminary to the "real °ukm" (the formulation of an obligation or recommended act or their opposites with regard to a thing), and not °ukm itself.

Qur'¡nic Verses which Contain the Word °ukm and Some of Its Derivatives

These verses are of six kinds:

1) Verses indicating °ukm as emanating from God. There are 55 verses related to this group.Take, for example, this passage:

> *Indeed Allah has judged between [His] servants.*[1]

°ukm in this category of verses means adjudication and sovereignty, and not knowledge or wisdom, although the Absolute Knowledge and Wisdom of God are requisites of His sovereignty and adjudication.

2) °ukm here applies to the prophets of God ('a), as this passage shows:

> *But if you judge, judge between them with justice.*[2]

°ukm in this sense (adjudication and judgment) is used 14 times in the Qur'¡n.

3) °ukm here refers to the decrees issued by people, as indicated in this verse:

> *... and, when you judge between people, judge with fairness*[3]

4) °ukm here originates from the Heavenly Book, as suggested by this passage:

---

1. S£rat Gh¡fir (or al-Mu'min) 40:48.
2. S£rat al-M¡'idah 5:42.
3. S£rat al-Nis¡' 4:58.

And He sent down with them the Book with the truth,
that it may judge between the people concerning that
about which they differed.[1]

This category can be observed in 3 verses in the Qur'¡n, and
the "sovereignty of the Divine Book" means the settling of
hostilities and removal of differences through the prophets ('a),
by considering the contents of the Book.

5) There are 3 verses of the Qur'¡n in which the word °ukm
can be interpreted in its popular sense (adjudication,
sovereignty and origination of do's and don'ts) as well as in the
sense of knowledge and wisdom:

My Lord! Grant me [unerring] judgment, and unite
me with the Righteous.[2]

In 3 verses of the Noble Qur'¡n, the said two possibilities
exist.

They are the ones whom We gave the Book, the
judgment and prophethood.[3]

'O John!' [We said,] 'Hold on with power to the
Book!' And We gave him judgment while still a child.[4]

Some have imagined that the °ukm God has endowed to
Prophet Yahy¡ (John the Baptist) ('a) could not mean °ukm in its
popular sense on the ground that, prior to the age of puberty, a
person cannot exercise sovereignty. The reply is clear. Just as
God bestowed the asset and position of prophethood and the
acceptance of the Heavenly Book to Prophet 'Ïs¡ (Jesus) ('a) a
few days after his birth, so He bestowed the asset and aptitude
of °ukm in its popular sense (adjudication, sovereignty and
promulgation of do's and don'ts) to Prophet Yahy¡ ('a). In the
second verse above (Sūrat al-An'¡m 6:89), the probability of
°ukm in its popular sense is far stronger than °ukm as
knowledge and wisdom, because they are implicit in the Book

---

1. S£rat al-Baqarah 2:213.
2. S£rat al-Shu'ar¡' 26:83.
3. S£rat al-An'¡m 6:89.
4. S£rat Maryam 19:12.

and prophethood. The purport of the verse is ruling, adjudication and promulgation of do's and don'ts through the Book and prophethood, as indicated in these two other verses:

> *And He sent down with them the Book with the truth, that it may judge between the people concerning that about which they differed.*[1]

> *We sent down the Torah containing guidance and light by which the prophets judged.*[2]

6) It consists of Qur'¡nic verses containing both °ukm (judgment) and 'ilm (knowledge). For example:

> *We gave judgment and knowledge to Lot."*[3]

> *We gave its understanding to Solomon, and to each We gave judgment and knowledge.*[4]

> *When he (Moses) came of age and became fully matured, We gave him judgment and knowledge.*[5]

> *When he (Joseph) came of age, We gave him judgement and [sacred] knowledge.*[6]

If °ukm really meant knowledge ('ilm) and gnosis (ma'rifah), the word 'ilm in the said verses would have been redundant.

If ever there is an instance in the Noble Qur'¡n where the word °ukm means knowledge and gnosis, this is to show the similarity between the meaning of °ukm (promulgation of do's and don'ts) which pertains to one's actions, and that of gnosis and realities which pertains to perception and understanding. °ukm in the sense of *hikmah* (wisdom) includes theoretical and practical wisdom, and °*ukm* in its popular sense is one of the most distinctive manifestations of practical wisdom.

There are other verses in the Qur'¡n explicitly stating the

---

1. S£rat al-Baqarah 2:213.
2. S£rat al-M¡'idah 5:44.
3. S£rat al-Anbiy¡' 21:74.
4. S£rat al-Anbiy¡' 21:79.
5. S£rat al-Qa¥a¥ 28:14.
6. S£rat Y£suf 12:22.

definite role of religion in the different aspects of human life. For example:

> *Certainly We sent Our apostles with manifest proofs, and We sent down with them the Book and the Balance, so that mankind may maintain justice.*[1]

It is clear that the establishment of justice and the observance of the Balance and law are meant for the organization of the different facets of life.

The very important conclusion we can draw from this discussion is that °ukm in the sense of adjudication, governance and promulgation of divine decrees is one of the distinctive features of the prophets of God and their genuine successors. And this principle is repugnant to the secularist way of thinking. In this regard, there are two important issues worth studying and investigating:

1. °ukūmah refers to the wisdom and knowledge of the political issues and economic life of people, and nothing else.

This point implies that the common statesmen following the Machiavellian approach in administering their respective countries are not really worthy of governing the society because the motive of organizing the activities is based on the purely instinctive inclinations, and not anchored in the principles of the theoretical and practical wisdom, "the fundamentals and principles of the intelligible life".

In selecting the goals and motives of such organizations and passing them through the filter of discreet forms of selfishness—whether for themselves or their subjects called "citizens," they have nothing to do with wisdom as well as rational and inalterable values. In the same manner, in selecting the means for achieving those selected goals, they neither understand wisdom nor are concerned with any value. Of course, it is possible for these statesmen to somehow possess theoretical wisdom and statecraft, but it is clear that such

---

1. S£rat al-°ad¢d 57:25.

realities are actually political activities by statesmen that are like neutral onlookers but without any right to enter the arena of political activity. It is for this reason that whenever a statesman is interpellated, he seeks refuge in the impenetrable fortress of "Sir, this is politics!" thereby slinecing the destitute ignoramuses.

2. Governance cannot be a kind of totalitarian rule and control over the people, let alone be a so-called religious guardianship and leadership!

It is needless to say that statecraft and politics do not imply the theoretical and practical wisdom as indicative of real wisdom; rather, the ruler or statesman must rule and supervise by utilizing them. He must formulate and promulgate the do's and don'ts in both the material and spiritual domains while keeping in mind the elements and motives of "intelligible life" in society. History shows that the rulers can be divided into just and tyrannical rulers.

It goes without saying that the term h¡kim (ruler) is also laden with the concept of "command" (the term w¡lī). These two terms are essentially not laden with despotism, egoism and self-centeredness, but rather depend on the person of the ruler, commander or guardian. We amply encounter the phrases "just or unjust governors and rulers" in Islamic resources. Of course, to align each of these phrases to those who deprive the people of their freewill and human dignity, degrade and debase them, is strongly rejected and condemned by the political wisdom of Islam.

Why Rulers and their Subjects confuse °ukm and °ukūmah

To begin with, one needs to distinguish between the factors causing this confusion among the rulers and those that lead the laity to get stuck in that confusion. The causes of confusion in the concepts of °ukm and hukūmah in the minds of the people are diverse, because in some societies in history, mankind has not been able to distinguish the different meanings of °ukm and hukūmah and has therefore submitted to despotic and unjust rule. The factors causing it are the following:

1. Inability to resist oppressive powers, so that people can not afford to express any verbal or practical opposition;

2. Egotism, carnal desires and hedonistic inclinations led to pleasure-seekers, who subscribed to the school of "Let us enjoy and make the most of the present moment" and "Strive in whatever way possible to maximize pleasure, for death is in the offing"!

3. The destitute who look for their daily bread for survival and a hut to rest in, do not pay attention to the °ukm or hukūmah being good or bad. Those who can remember the clash between the Constitutionalists and the Monarchists[1] say, "At the time, many people were being asked, 'Which group do you belong, the Constitutionalists or the Monarchists?'They would reply, 'We belong to the group of the family-oriented. We cannot understand what you say, and do not pointlessly bring about the death of people!"

Some people hold that governance is nothing but absolute command and control; that is, the ruler is above any responsibility or duty while the people are mere subjects and subordinates of the ruler! It is clear that such °ukm and hukūmah do not exist in Islam because it strongly opposes it. °ukm and hukūmah, in whatever rational sense they are understood—must have the power to command people to follow them— cannot be called mere knowledge of the ways

---

1. Instigated by a proclamation issued by two religious authorities (¡yatull¡h al-'U¨m¡ Mu!ammad K¡¨im Khur¡s¡n¢ and ¡yatull¡h al-'U¨m¢ 'Abd All¡h M¡zandar¡n¢) which reads, "The constitution of each country limits and conditions the will of the ruler and the offices of government so that the divine ordinances and common laws based on the official religion of the country are not transgressed," what has become known as the Constitutional Movement, Constitutional Revolution or simply Constitutionalism (1905-11) took place due to the chaotic situation in Iran at the end of the nineteenth century and the beginning of the twentieth century, the popular protest over the tyranny of the governors and agents of the dictatorial regime and the unruly officials of the government, the weakness and ineptitude of the then king Mu¨affarudd¢n Sh¡h, and finally the rising awareness among the people and revolt of the clerics and 'ulam¡'. Years of struggle by the people culminated in the victory of the Constitutional Revolution in 1906. [Trans.]

and means of statecraft. It is important to clarify the confusion surrounding the concepts of °ukm and hukūmah to prove that benefiting from sublime human character and the universal religion of God is essential, and this is impossible with the "removal of religion from worldly life" approach.

Should political philosophy be sought for in Ancient Greece and only then post-Renaissance centuries?

No one would doubt that Islamic civilization would have been impossible without rational and practical political philosophy. So, it is necessary for the analysts of political philosophy to refrain from this baseless short cut (the political philosophy of Greece and Rome to the political philosophy of the recent periods), and also to investigate the political philosophy of Islam. This error has also been committed by most historians of philosophy and analysts in the history of science. As we can observe, with regards to the history of science and philosophy, these thinkers suddenly jump from Greek science and philosophy and then deal with them in the period after the Renaissance! They overlook a considerable share of Islam in the said two branches of knowledge, and this myopic view undermines the credibility of their views on these very important subjects. They must know that the phrase "Dark Ages" for the Middle Ages is only applicable to the West and during the same centuries (particularly from the latter part of the second century up to the fifth century AH) science was flourishing in Muslim countries and some Eastern communities.

Both the ancient and modern systems of political philosophy, anchored in secularism, are incapable of solving political problems.

There are different views about the ancient and modern systems of political philosophy. Some authorities are of the opinion that the basic difference between the ancient and modern political mindsets is that the ancient political views took into account all human rights and privileges for the entire human society. In reality, the duty of the government establishment is to justify and implement this policy and not focus more on individual welfare, rights and freedom.

It is very difficult to exactly determine the difference between the political philosophy of the ancient world and the modern world. The intrinsic progress of people has a very long history, although its origin, quality and quantity are extemely diverse in human societies. According to Whitehead, the meritorious services rendered by the Hebrew prophets to freedom are very great. Can civilization ever be conceivable without the members of society having the sense of innate individual identity, honor and dignity? Whitehead identified slavery and liberty as the main difference between the ancient and modern political views. He says:

> *Now, with respect to the political factions in the ancient world, nothing has yet been settled. Every problem, which Plato[1] discusses, is still alive today, yet there is a vast difference between ancient and modern political theories, for we differ from the ancients on the one premise on which they all agreed. (Slavery was the supposition of premised theorists then. Freedom is the presupposition of political theorists now.)*
>
> *For both sets of thinkers, God has been a great resource: a lot of things, which won't work on Earth, can be conceived as true in His sight. Ancients and Moderns, in respect to this question, face directly opposite directions.*

In order to be certain as to the nature of this difference in the ancient and modern political mindsets, one must closely study social relations of people and their cultural, class, economic, religious, and moral conditions. Without this research, our views will be nothing but mere guess and imagination. Keeping in mind the difference between the two infrastructures of political philosophy (ancient and modern)

---

1. Plato (428/427-348/347 BCE): a Classical Greek philosopher, mathematician, writer of philosophical dialogues, and founder of the Academy in Athens, the first institution of higher learning in the Western world. Along with his mentor, Socrates, and his student, Aristotle, Plato helped to lay the foundations of natural philosophy, science, and Western philosophy. [Trans.]

and the basic problems in each of them, the said viewpoint is worth examining and reconsidering. Moreover, one must also closely examine the quality and quantity of individual liberty in the political realm of ancient Greek society.

Chapter 5
The Relationship of Governance and Politics with Divine Laws

Are governance and politics outside the realm of divine duties and laws?

In secularism, governance and politics lie outside the realm of universal divine duties and laws. If we take glance at human history, we can see that all the governments that have ruled over societies originate from a natural need based on empirical principles and rules. This phenomenon is like the natural need of all animals for their own habitats in an environment, which can provide the things they need for their subsistence. The human race provides such a change for itself. Therefore, governments have no relationship with metaphysical realities and are devoid of inalterable divine dimensions. From the viewpoint of transcendental wisdom (hikmat-e 'ịliyah), however, in order to organize all aspects of the "intelligible life," the system of government must also have a divine dimension. The explanation of the context of this type of government is given in the following discussion.

In whatever advanced form it may be, any system of government can have natural as well as divine dimensions.

Just as there are different levels of human individual life, there are also different levels of collective life and systems of government. The main types of human life are as follows:

1. Purely natural life: this means managing one's animal nature. In this type of life, all the human faculties and powers — ranging from the simple perception and imagination up to the most important mental, rational and conscientious activities — are under the control and utility of the same "natural self". No matter how advanced it may be, this type of life cannot be rationally proved, for it cannot provide the answer to the sublime goal of life, just as it cannot have a reasonable defense

against the struggle for existence. In this arena, the champions are the self-centered, powerful ones. If the system of government—even in its most advanced form—would revolve around the axis of the "natural self", whose primary distinctive feature is egoism, it does not need the involvement of divine factors because they impede this system of government, which must go against those factors.

2. Natural-divine life: this form of life implies that initially the human beings strive to solve their problems by benefiting from nature and their fellow human beings by virtue of natural laws, and secondly, they organize their life according to the attainment of the lofty goal of life, which is entry into the Axis of Sublime Perfection. In this type of life, involvement of a divine factor becomes necessary in the sense that without such involvement, it is impossible to answer the six questions which can be deduced from this Qur'¡nic verse:

> *Indeed we belong to Allah, and to Him do we indeed return.*[1]

By the same token, without the involvement of a divine factor, which religion possesses, no rule or law can answer the fundamental questions of man pertaining to the quadruple relationships. As the author of °ikmat wa °ukūmat says,

> *Government or system of statecraft, whatever advanced form it may assume, is a very primary concept and natural experiment...*[2]

This is like the system of life of ants and bees based upon their respective laws of instinct and natural peculiarities. The only difference is that the systems of human life are far more complex, extensive, elaborate, and intricate, because human beings have faculties and powers such as general perceptions, rational abstractions, thinking and intellection, constructive competitions, discovery, and creativity- anchored in ingenuity, and the like. No matter how systematic the abovementioned

---

1. S£rat al-Baqarah 2:156.
2. Mahd¢ °¡'ir¢, °ikmat wa °uk£mat, n.p. [Trans.]

animals may be, their life is limited and beyond improvement, development and enhancement. Inspite of having all those faculties and potentials, if human life revolves around the axis of egoism and justifies its activity with the laws of sheer nature, without benefiting from the divine rays that transcend matter and materiality, it is essentially the same animalistic life we have mentioned earlier. In the same vein, politics and government can also be divine-natural, as in the case of the luminous path of the prophets ('a).

3. Intellectualism: what we mean by this kind of life is the use of reason in all aspects of life. Nowadays, this kind of life is usually associated with the West, and many Westerners claim it. The basis of the logical soundness of this kind of life is that all affairs of human life, which include the theoretical and practical intellect, are brought to fruition. It seems that tracing all the affairs of life to the intellect has not yet been realized fully in any society and it can be said that such substantiation is impossible. For example, which conventional theoretical or practical intellect can afford to affirm the real value of justice, human dignity and rational freedom in the arena of "might is right" and "survival of the fittest"?! All societies that claim to be following the rational approach in the sociopolitical domain of life consider themselves original proponents of ideological realities.

We can observe the most illustrious example of this support in approximately 20 cases in the introductory paragraphs of the Universal Declaration of Human Rights which contain the preliminary provisions and value-laden terms. The introductory paragraphs of the Universal Declaration of Human Rights are as follows:

> "Whereas recognition of the inherent dignity and of the equal and inalienable rights of all members of the human family is the foundation of freedom, justice and peace in the world,

> "Whereas disregard and contempt for human rights have resulted in barbarous acts which have outraged the

conscience of mankind, and the advent of a world in which human beings shall enjoy freedom of speech and belief, and freedom from fear and want has been proclaimed as the highest aspiration of the common people,

"Whereas it is essential, if man is not to be compelled to have recourse, as a last resort, to rebellion against tyranny and oppression, that human rights should be protected by the rule of law,

"Whereas it is essential to promote the development of friendly relations between nations,

"Whereas the peoples of the United Nations have in the Charter reaffirmed their faith in fundamental human rights, in the dignity and worth of the human person, and in the equal rights of men and women, and have determined to promote social progress and better standards of life in larger freedom,

"Whereas Member States have pledged themselves to achieve, in co-operation with the United Nations, the promotion of universal respect for and observance of human rights and fundamental freedoms,

"Whereas a common understanding of these rights and freedoms is of the greatest importance for the full realization of this pledge,

"Now, therefore, THE GENERAL ASSEMBLY proclaims THIS UNIVERSAL DECLARATION OF HUMAN RIGHTS as a common standard of achievement for all peoples and all nations, to the end that every individual and every organ of society, keeping this Declaration constantly in mind, shall strive;

by teaching and education to promote respect for these rights and freedoms; and, by progressive measures, national and international, to secure their universal and effective recognition and observance, both among the peoples of Member States themselves, and among the people of territories under their jurisdiction.[1]

Most of these paragraphs have expressed support for the values of life. The value-laden terms and phrases used in the entire preamble and other provisions of the Universal Declaration of Human Rights are as follows:

> *Man as an honorable being", "inherent dignity of man", "members of the human family", "fraternity and equality", "friendly relations", "spirit of humanity", "equal rights", "freedom", "peace", "justice", "the highest aspiration of the common people", "reason and conscience", "life", "belief", "faith of the United Nations", "universal respect", "sense of common understanding", "barabarous acts", "rebellion" "strive" "better standards of life", and, "proper observance of moral imperatives.*[2]

In the aforementioned kind of life, the (so-called "rational") government and politics, some universal propositions are assumed to be presuppositions on the basis of which life, government and politics function. That is, in order to prove the realness of their demands and activities, the people, and rulers, invoke those presuppositions, which might have inherent defects that cannot be remedied.

The best example of such presuppositions is democracy, which has been accepted as a fundamental principle by countries and their rulers and administrators, and is used to interpret and establish social, political, cultural, legal, economic, and similar propositions. As such, life, government and politics being "rational", does not mean that all their issues can really be interpreted through the intellect's indisputable principles and axiomatic rules.

In a bid to prove this claim, it is sufficient to pay attention to the six leading issues, which, scientifically and rationally, exist under the outward levels of the democratic system.

---

1. United Nations' 1948 Universal Declaration of Human Rights, "Preamble," available online at http://www.un.org/en/documents/udhr. [Trans.]
2. Ibid.

The Democratic System of Life, Government and Politics, and Its Sextuple Problems

Before stating these six problems, one needs to remind that no conscious man of reason ever doubts that next to the blessing of life, human freedom is the highest bounty and excellence bestowed by God, the Glorious, to human beings. A person bereft of freedom is a person bereft of identity and personality, and sheer plaything in face of natural forces and under the yoke of egoist powerful individuals. It is clear that such a person is a moving creature for whom life is a burden he must carry. He has a borrowed identity and fragmented personality for which he must ask permission, at every moment, from natural forces and egoist powerful individuals. Hence, we categorically say that anything that deprives a person of freedom commits the same crime of depriving him of his life, or at least, putting it in derangement.

1. Are people's desires reasonable at all times, and does egoism have no pivotal role in democracy?

2. Is every phenomenon considered the desired aspiration of the people and the rulers, throughout history, really meant for the real wellbeing of the people and the rulers? If it is so, how can the wars, bloodshed, oppression, and treaty violations motivated by power, position and wealth, throughout history, be justified? Moreover, how can the periods of slavery, the foundation of all cultural, legal, political, and moral issues, be justified?

3. Shrewd inculcations to let certain things or persons appear desirable or undesirable, influence the views and opinions of people accordingly, and in simpler and clearer terms, "an artificial supply for an artificial demand" comes into being. Given this, can one still talk about real democracy?

4. Throughout human history, eloquent and elegant slogans, terms and expressions have far-reaching and profound impact upon conditioning the minds of people. In view of the fact that the motive or goal of the sloganeers is not the exact content of those slogans, and that they express them through an extreme

and utopian optimism, what can be done?

> The road is smooth, and under it are pitfalls: amidst the names there is a dearth of meaning.

> Words and names are like pitfalls: the sweet (flattering) word is the sand for (the sand that sucks up) the water of our life.[1]

It is appropriate to open before your eyes an index of the deplorable plight of mankind in contrast to the sweet, beautiful and charming words:

O freedom, O anti-chains, O the best means of giving breathing space to man, what burdensome chains have been tied to human feet in your name!

O justice, what acts of oppression and tyranny have been committed in your sacred name and kept human society disunited, and far from harmonizing its way of life with your principles!

O right, O the beginning, the origin and the conclusion of the universe, how many falsehoods have they embellished with your name, and how they have deprived you of humanity!

This is the perpetual state of affairs of the weak. The egoist power holders have, through charming slogans and words, silenced them and changed their lives into a lifeless movement.

> Thou beguilest me with the Name of God in order that thou mayst expose me to shame and confusion.

> The Name of God enthralled me, not thy contrivance: thou madest the Name of God a trap: woe to thee!

> The Name of God will take vengeance from thee on my behalf: I commit my soul and body to the Name of God.

> Either it will sever the vein of thy life by my stroke, or it will bring thee into a prison as (it has brought) me.[2]

5. Like law and culture, if we divide politics into two major types (pioneer and adherent), democracy will be categorized as "adherent", and not "pioneer", accordingly. To elucidate this,

---

1. Rumi's *Masnavi*, Book 1, Ramaнin¢ Manuscript, p. 24, lines 16-17. See Rumi's *Masnavi*, Book 1, lines 1060-1061, pp. 115, 117. [Trans.]
2. Ibid., p. 148, lines 9-11. See Rumi's *Masnavi*, Book 1, lines 2337-2340, p. 251. [Trans.]

one needs to give a brief definition of the notions of "adherent" and "pioneer".

In the abovementioned cases (law, culture, politics, and the like), "adherent" means that there is no principle beyond the conventional natural life for man's spiritual growth and advancement. "Pioneer" implies that one must follow a certain set of sublime principles because without doing so, it is impossible to achieve any spiritual growth and progress. "Pioneer law" implies that it is the human beings themselves who identify what is good and bad for life, accept certain propositions as legal provisions, and act upon them in the domain of their lives. No person or power has the right to determine the legal rights of the members of society. "Advanced law" is that part of the principles which ensures the progress and perfection of man's identity as well as organizes his natural life.

It is needless to say that no legal, moral, cultural, political, or economic system can be purely "adherent" or "pioneer" because the rational, conscientious and empirical perception of human individuals plays a very vital role in identifying and practically addressing the concerns of their lives. For this reason, Islam has set the human intellect, heart (spirit) and experience as proof, and indispensable in identifying the objects of concern, except in very few instances. It follows that as far as the subjects, phenomena and addressing the genuine needs of human life are concerned, Islam has an "adherent" dimension—whether it is in realm of law, morality, politics, or economics.

Law, ethics, culture, and politics that can set the goal-oriented life of man in the Axis of Absolute Perfection and provide the answer to his sextuple fundamental questions, must definitely follow a set of "pioneer" principles in dealing with his quadruple ontological relationships. For example, acquiring a sublime character, keeping in constant contact with God, the Glorious, and responsibly exploiting the bounties of the earth in which he lives. If we look at politics only within the prism of the democratic system then democracy means that the people are free in whatever they think, whatever they want and whatever means they use to achieve an end except in cases where it arbitrarily affects the life of other members of society. This is the same "adherent politics" which imprisons humanity in the age of the cave-dwellers though it may have been adopted the world over. By following "adherent politics," man cannot take a step beyond the reach of selfishness, whereas, his goals for perfection are definitively divine and metaphysical.

6. Evolutionary movements and transformations in history have been initiated by a few individuals or an insignifant minority (quantitatively speaking). If these approaches and movements were entrusted to the skills and inclinations of the majority, humanity could not have taken a single step forward. There is no instance at all in which the majority of people, in a primitive society, directly rose up and made some discoveries and inventions, or delivered society from ignorance and misery, thereby, bringing the elements of progress into existence.

7. The following reads a Platonist's mind on democracy:

> The more Plato would think about this matter—this folly which is called 'democracy'—the more he would be astounded. It is the democratic system, which relies on the carnal desires and inclinations of the public in electing political leaders. The reason behind Plato's astonishment is that in trivial issues such as addressing our need for a pair of shoes we do not rely on anybody except a skilled shoemaker. Yet, how can we accept anyone who has many voices (or many voices support him) to rule? When we get sick, we want a proficient doctor who is highly skilled in medicine, and "not a good-looking and eloquent doctor.[1]

That politics is a specific field, which requires certain expertise, is not inconsistent at all with the need to harmonize politics and government with man's divine dimension.

---

1. Plato, Jumh£riyyat (Republic), trans. °ann¡ Khabb¡z, "Preface," p. xvi (originally in Greek as translated to Persian).

In proving that statesmanship is a special art, there is a very good parable reported from Plato. He is quoted to have said:

> *Statesmanship is the art of weaving. One must witness how a skilled weaver would initially turn wool into thread, and then how he would twist threads together in a particular scheme and way. Afterward, he would hand them over to his weaving factory and finally he would bring out from that factory a beautiful textile which could be used as man's garment... The art of statesmanship is similar to the craft of weaving, as it can unite groups of free and separate individuals, organize them and build their harmonious relationship with such accuracy and dexterity that they become an elegant and decorated piece of cloth covering the whole country.[1]*

Then, the author of °*ikmat wa* °*ukūmat* (wisdom and governance) comments on Plato in the following words:

> *Upon this philosophical parable of Plato, as well as the previously discussed account of Aristotle, it becomes clear that the art of statesmanship, like handcraftship, is a practical skill. In terms of its direct connection with the needs of individuals and citizens and the daily happenings in the country and its relations with other countries, near and far, is like a garment, which must have cohesion, harmony and unison. A statesman must know the universal moral precepts and theoretical pure sciences, acquire inward traits and excellences, such as wisdom (practical wisdom), bravery and modesty, which can be summed up in justice. Then, he must practically and sagaciously have extensive knowledge of the actual particular matters and changing realities about his country, preserve harmonious relations among the citizens and maintain a friendly neighborhood with other countries, so that he can discharge this practical responsibility satisfactorily. The basic element of statesmanship is reflecting on the rational and religious tenets, principles and rules which are not consistent*

---

1. Mahd¢ °¡'ir¢, °ikmat wa °uk£mat (Wisdom and Government), pp. 77-78 (originally in Persian).

with theoretical reason. His main responsibility is to identify the internal and external issues of the country and its changing geopolitical realities, which are generally outside the realm of higher rational thinking or theoretical reason. However, since practical reason always connects knowledge and action, the intelligible and the tangible, the general points of theoretical reason with the particular and minor points of practical reason, the statesman must also know his ideals from the philosophers and moral thinkers. The moral ideals must be perfectly compatible with the actual particular concerns and issues of the country.[1]

There are some important issues to examine here as to the latter comments on Plato:

First Issue: In this parable, Plato has presented a dimension of the statesman's actual functions in a very elegant figurative fashion.

This dimension refers to the physical appearance of a society, which a professional statesman has brought into being through his political skill. Thus, this parable by Plato does not describe and elaborate all his beliefs on the nature of politics, the salient features of a statesman, and the purpose behind political activities, which is to prepare the people for the attainment of the sublime goal of their lives.

Second Issue: This parable does not reflect all the beliefs of Plato on government and politics.

That Plato compares statesmanship with good weaving, which must have cohesion, unity and unison for the people, does not reflects all of his ideas. It is certain that the statesman must not interfere in the inner, spiritual and ideological state of affairs that the citizens have or must have. If the statesmen of a country do not know who the individuals that they have woven, cut and sewn are and how they can be, are actually painting on the roof of a room which either does not exist or is not suitable for that painting.

---

1. Ibid., pp. 78-79.

But we know that the totality of Plato's ideas on politics and government are acceptable to the divine religion. The righteous men of wisdom, who regard the blossoming of all dimensions—material and spiritual—of man as necessary, base their ideas on these very principles, and we shall touch on this point below.

Third Issue: Keeping in mind the totality of Plato's ideas about politics and government as well as the education of the members of society, one cannot say that this great personality, like Aristotle, is among those who agree with secularist ideas.

Since the ideas of Plato about government and politics are among the most important views on politics utilized by most political philosophers, both in the past and in the present, it is necessary to make a summary of his ideas in this discourse.

Jules Barthélemy-Saint-Hilaire,[1] who was among the most authoritative philosophers in understanding and interpreting the ideas and beliefs of Aristotle and Plato in the West, has mentioned the fundamental elements and pillars of Plato's political philosophy in the following manner:

It must be noted that the reason behind giving an elaborate account of the fundamental elements of Plato's political philosophy is that every political philosophy scholar justifies Plato's views due to its immense importance in validating his own opinion. Yet, it is not sufficient to separate the children from that which may undermine their innocence. In the same manner, it is not sufficient to mold the children's intellects with the light of cogent knowledge and make virtue acceptable to them by means of advice, admonition, and giving parables. Instead, beyond that, the principles of religion which nature has ingrained in their hearts must flourish within. Those principles of religion from which firm beliefs spring are principles, which connect man to God—the God who is the First, the Middle and the End-point of everything.[2] It is God, who is the Real

---

1. Jules Barthélemy-Saint-Hilaire (1805 – 1895): a French philosopher, journalist, statesman, and possible illegitimate son of Napoleon I of France. [Trans.]
2. See Plato, The Laws, Book 4, "Reply 56 of Athenian to Cleinias," trans. Dr.

Criterion of justice for the people He has created, and belief in His existence is the foundation of all laws. These are the essential beliefs, which must be the standard of educational training of the children. These are the same transcendent rules, which must be inculcated into the minds of the citizens by the legislator, if ever he is a man of wisdom. These beliefs are simple inasmuch as they are useful. These beliefs can be identified with three basic propositions: God, His supervision of the universe, and His justice, which is immune from giving favor to any party. Without these beliefs, man will get lost in the midst of the waves of incidents in this world. That person denies himself as long as he does not know where he comes from and what the sacred ideal is which his self must willingly follow and rely on. As for justice—so long as this rule is not the focus—there is no fixed rule, because justice, which is the one that gives life to the state and its government cannot be implemented except by God, in whose Eternal Essence justice is integrated. It is appropriate, therefore, for us to take action many years before the beginning of upbringing and training, to instill these sacred beliefs into the minds of the children. In fact, the law itself must not be lax in bringing to fruition those beliefs by means of being contented, but focus on those who forget those beliefs due to their inner weakness or moral corruption.

Any upringing or mode of training, which is not religious is defective and invalid. Any state whose citizens do not pay attention to these very important issues is on the verge of destruction. It is not correct to say that statesmen, who are unaware, imagine that they have to utilize religion sometimes for their rule. This is not so, because religion is needed for the identity of societies and states—in fact, it is above common needs. The need for religion is more than its function of organizing life. Of course, by having both essential and utilitarian dimensions [of religion], it can also be effected in

---

Muḥammad °asan Luṣf¢, p. 129: "God, as the old tradition declares, holding in his hand the beginning, middle, and end of all that is, travels according to His nature in a straight line towards the accomplishment of His end."

organizing and ensuring the welfare of society. In various forms of human intellection, religion is the interpreter of pure nature and the most profound agent expressing realities. Man treats as holy all divine truths (such as the prophets and the saints (awliy¡')), as they honor pious fathers as blessed sources of all good, particularly of virtue and sound reason.

The state, as perceived by Aristotle, is constituted by people who are equal and free. The people collectively benefit from their own works, understanding and awareness, and all of them nurture the divine seeds ingrained in them. By virtue of the pact of brotherhood, they are related to one another and for the preservation of their country's government, they obey their illustrious leaders, who are tactful and prudent. These are the leaders, elected by the people to rule over them. These are the leaders, who have developed and undergone their training for virtues and all the sciences related to the discharge of their functions. They entrust their noble lives to the sacred creatures of God.

There is no need for the state, which is formed for the maintenance of internal harmony to constantly express its desire for harmony to its neighboring states. It must always be ready to face the aggression of any other state, and through regular rigorous training, its defenders must constantly resist the enemies, regardless of their number. Peace, not war must be the sole motive behind its patriotism and various military trainings and preparations, as done by famous communities and nations in history.

It should refrain from aggression against others just as it cannot withstand any internal revolution or violent movement. As the peaceful, prudent state decides to refrain from oppressing others, it shares half of the goal of other states in arming themselves; that is, given the presence of justice in applying force and enjoining virtues, it has no motive other than defense when attacking tyrannical enemies.[1]

---

1. Aristotle, A Treatise on Government, "Introduction" by Barthélemy-Saint-

After depiction of the basic elements of Plato's political philosophy, Barthélemy-Saint-Hilaire continues:

> These are the basic elements of Aristotle's politics. Is this philosophy not full of truth, greatness and ample benefit? Is there anything obsolete in this upright and prudent state policy? Is this policy something delusional? Can it be said that this policy cannot be applied except to Greece where Plato lived? They are the same noble truths that have immortalized his political ideas. It is the same truths that have made this philosopher the validator of the philosophers' and statesmen's ideas. In most cases, people call this philosophy "Platonic Dreams" and sometimes, some intellectual scholars even reject this label, making a mockery of it. These sensible objections and allegation against "dreams" cannot be regarded as a criticism of this philosopher who pioneered these ideas and conveyed them to mankind. Instead, this "criticism" aptly clarifies the point that justice, reason and virtue are empty rhetoric for people and that these allegations and derisions against Plato's sociopolitical beliefs are tantamount to the denial of human primordial nature, history and society.[1]

The concluding statement highlights the most devastating tragedy in human history, and that is, the lack of importance given by people in various societies to justice, reason and virtue, and even regarding them as empty rhetoric. Of course, the esteemed translator should add "common" to "people" because to believe that the common people do not give importance to the three concepts, regarding them as empty rhetoric, is a sort of error in judgment. To state that, "these allegations and derisions against Plato's sociopolitical beliefs are tantamount to the denial of innate human nature, history and society" is a most vital and constructive outcry any person has ever expressed to his fellow human beings.

Fourth Issue: The author says, "The basic element of

Hilaire in French, translated into Arabic by Aḥmad Luṣfṭ al-Sayyid, pp. 20-22.
1. Ibid., p. 22.

statesmanship is reflection on the rational and religious tenets, principles and rules which are not consistent with theoretical reason. In fact, the main responsibility of the statesman is to identify and know the internal and external issues and affairs of the country and its changing geopolitical realities which are generally outside the realm of higher rational thinking or theoretical reason."

In this regard, this question comes to the fore: can people be persuaded to lead an "intelligible life" even without necessary and sufficient familiarity with the rational and religious tenets, principles and rules as well as belief in the most important and essential of them? This is because the statesman does not tell anything about the causes of anything that previously transpired in society, is currently happening, or may possibly happen in the future. Instead, by discerning or perceiving them, he would choose, issue judgment and, in a sense, bid and forbid. Can an intelligent, just and wise statesman find out the best of goals amidst a plethora of events in various periods, choose the ways and means suitable for the said goals, and promulgate the appropriate laws for the people, without knowing the rational and religious tenets, principles and rules (at least within the country under his jurisdiction)?

In view of the necessity to persuade human beings to lead an "intelligible life" and to prepare them for the achievement of the Supreme Telos of this form life, the existence of a lofty spiritual station, alongside professional political activity, is indispensable.

Statesmen should sincerely coordinate with the spiritual station at all times in all societies, leading the society toward the best of goals. This harmony does not imply that the statesman and the holder of a spiritual station have to divide and partition man into two dimensions (physical and spiritual) and each of them take charge of one dimension. It means that the two dimensions of a single reality, which is the "intelligible life" of man, shall be managed by the spiritual and political stations without any contradiction and incompatibility. The psychologist and the physician takes charge of one dimension of man although the importance of psychotheraphy, as far their respective areas are concerned, is greater than that of medical science, which is concerned with man's physical health, whereas, the former is concerned with the soul, mind, self, personality, and identity. These two groups cannot divide the human being into two parts and say, "I have nothing to do with the physical dimension of man" or, "I have no business with his soul, mind, personality, and identity." Don't you think that man's exit from the scene of real life and entrance into the barren plains of egoism, self-centeredness, illusions, coining of terms, and finally nihilism is the result of such fragmentation of the human personality? Unfortunately, it is.

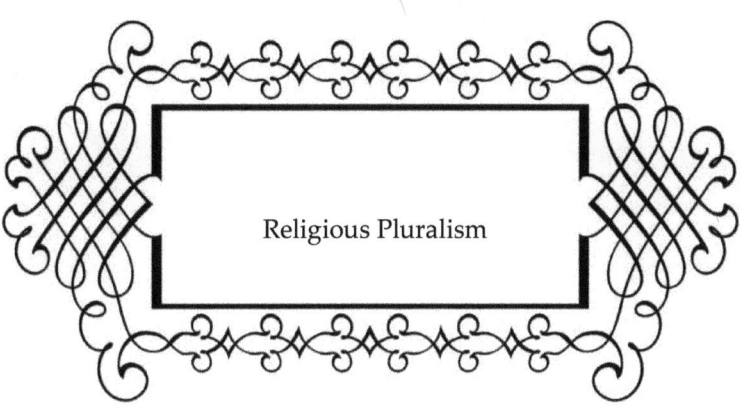

Religious Pluralism

Interview on Pluralism

Q1: Thank you very much indeed for your participation in this dialogue, what is the definition of 'religious pluralism' and which one of its various types are acceptable?

Jafari: Before embarking on the subject, we must pay close attention to existing cultures of the developed societies in technology, and the justifiable use of some terms taken from them. What is meant is the permission to use all scientific terms, for every word is introduced into a society from outside. If the said term is more expressive in conveying an intended meaning, no intelligent person can prohibit the use of the term unless the society can coin an appropriate word from its own vocabulary. However, if the society has an appropriate term or word to convey the desired meaning, imitating other societies is not permissible. Imitating other communities is an outwardly 'scientific' camouflage to advance anti-cultural objectives. Or, it may be caused by a sort of self-defeatism generating abjectness within the scientists and scholars of that society. In the Farsi or Arabic speaking communities, for instance, the term *mantiqī* (meaning 'logical') is a well accepted, well understood and a well entrenched word. Now, the use of the word 'logical' in such communities has no other motive except a sort of self-defeatism. Also, the use of the phrase, "natural child" instead of "illegitimate child", or "born out of wedlock", as somehow value-laden, is not correct from our point of view. In the same manner, the use of the phrase "natural death" for suicide (although the killing of the weak by the strong is also a natural phenomenon) is equally wrong. What is correct is to call it a "crime". The use of the term "pluralism" which conveys the meaning of multiplicity, and even diversity in a sense is similar to the use of "logical" in place of the indigenous word mantiqī, (Of course, knowing words of every language has its own advantage and sometimes essential, but this is a different story.)

Meanwhile, religious pluralism can be accepted in the sense

that in the beginning, individuals treat certain principles as similar to common thematic principles in a religion, or accept them as their definite and indisputable principles. Then, come the questions: "Which is better for the realization of such-and-such principle, religious sources, feelings, or intellection?" In this regard, how can one perceive and arrive at any conclusion? How should one apply them? If such merit exists in it, what is the way to learn and benefit from it?" These and similar questions are points that may show the extent of plurality or pluralism. However, since the discussion starts with a thematic principle and the purport of "existence" is juxtaposed to that of "non-existence", pluralism no longer has a double affirmative (muha¥¥alī) meaning and cannot accommodate any rivalry. On the one hand, it negates another and on the other, it mutually opposes such a trend. In reality, we must have commonalities, which must be assumed to mean commonalities, and in them there must be rivalry. If there is no commonality, which discussion will be termed investigative conversation? And which rivalry can be conceived? For example, which rivalry can be conceived between theism and atheism? Similarly, what kind of rivalry can exist between a form of secularism, which holds that this world is a passageway toward eternity, and another form, which maintains that this world is the final abode, i.e. the ultimate destination? One accepts values as intrinsic while the other treats them as utilities.

Q2: In your analysis, what relation can religious pluralism have with sectarian pluralism? In this regard, what point can be deduced from such Qur'¡nic verses as,

To you your religion, and to me my religion? [1]

Jafari: The relationship between pluralism in religions and pluralism in sects is a relationship between general and particular because the general concept of religion embraces all religions and is wider than the scope of religion, which includes sects. An example of religion in its general sense is the

---

1. Surat al-K¡fir£n 109:6. [Trans.]

Abrahamic Faith, which consists of the three world religions of Judaism, Christianity and Islam. Religious pluralism means the possibility of believing in any of the said religions while sectarian pluralism is like the various theological and jurisprudential beliefs in any of the sects under consideration.

In this discussion, we must pay attention to a very important point and that is, what is meant by pluralism? Are the people's ideological stances on any of the religions within the circle of a universal faith, and on any of the sects within the circle of a specific religion equal? Can one abandon his professed religion and incline toward another religion? In view of the thematic (basic accepted) principles and essential features of every religion—which have been established for each of its followers as essential beliefs to be believed—this option is invalid and not viable. If the truths, which have been acknowledged as fundamental principles and essential features, are logical and based upon solid proof, they become principles that interpret and explain the life of the religious person. Therefore, if there is any possibility of relinquishing them and resorting to another set of principles and salient features, in reality the spiritual life of the said person is undermined. If it means the option of removing regional, historical and cultural elements from each of the religions within the realm of the universal faith, or from the sects within a religion, this option is completely logical, though requiring extraordinary mental or psychological ability and effort. The excellent outcome of these two types of removal is the acceptance of the universal divine religion revealed to Prophet Noah and Prophet Abraham ('a) by God for man. And, all religions and faiths associated with the said religion have manifested, after passing through the stage of Judaism and Christianity, its perfect form, which is Islam in its comprehensive sense.

Regarding the degree of validity of Qur'ınic verses such as *"To you your religion, and to me my religion"*, *on the acceptability of pluralism in Islam, it must be stated that if the*

audience of the address, "O faithless ones!"[1] are the polytheists,
then definitely "To you your religion", because this verse is a
denial of polytheism, one of the most fundamental ideological
pillars of Islam. The meaning of "To you your religion" is not to
be construed as an affirmation of polytheism but rather, it
signifies stern reproach with regards to the persistence and
obstinacy of the polytheists.God says in the words of His
Apostle, "You persist and remain obstinate in your polytheism
and faithlessness, never relinquishing it, and this is your stance."
This does not accept polytheism. For example, God says:

> *As for the faithless, it is the same to them whether you
> warn them or do not warn them; they will not have
> faith.*[2]

This does not mean that their lack of faith is acceptable from
the Islamic perspective. Neither does it mean cessation of
hostility, nor does it refer to the religions of the People of the
Book (*ahl al-kitῑb*)[3] as been unconditionally accepted by the
Prophet (¥) for coexistence. In the Qur'ᵢnic verse, *"Indeed, with
Allah the religion is Islam"*[4] "Islam" (*al-islᵢm*) is not stated in the
indefinite form (*islᵢm*) for in it is restriction. Of course, until the
advent of the religion of Islam, *islᵢm* assumed many diverse
forms. However, since the Abrahamic faiths have undergone
changes and alterations prior to Islam, what is meant by *al-islᵢm*
is its specific meaning which has manifested in the form of the
Muᵢammadan Islam.

Q3: Is acceptance of pluralism based on the epistemological
interpretation of our relation with truth?

Jafari: In the earlier discussion about the Law, Way and Truth
(*sharῑ'ah, tarῑqah and haqῑqah*), which is a sort of pluralism, we
have said that the plurality and contradiction initiated between
the three are baseless, and some of the so-called theoretical and

1. Sᵣrat al-Kᵢfirᵣn 109:1. [Trans.]
2. Sᵣrat al-Baqarah 2:6. [Trans.]
3. People of the Book (ahl al-kitᵢb): the respectful title given to the Jews and
Christians in the Qur'an. [Trans.]
4. Sᵣrat ᵢl 'Imrᵢn 3:19. [Trans.]

practical mystics have deprived us of the "near truth" by showing something far from the truth. At the very moment of awakening, we are in tune with the melody of existence and we are bed-fellows of the truth, yet the ocean of truth is boundless. With the foremost step into the boundless ocean of truth, we achieve aloofness from aridness.

The first *All¡hu akbar* (Allah is the greatest) after the awakening is a wave of the truth and there is no partition between them. It is true that this very first step in itself has another dimension, which prepares us for the succeeding stages, but this in itself is in the state of truth.

When a person stands firm in seeking nearness to Allah (*qurbatan illall¡h*), this in itself is entry into the truth, but when he is situated in the midst of the immense waves of truth, there is no end in sight. Such is the union with truth. We attain the truth but the extent of such truth is infinite. We cannot accept the notion that, "It is not important to have attained the truth but that we are on the ways of truth". Instead, it must be stated, that we surge and the truth is boundless. The mystics are not supposed to deprive humanity by saying that one has to tread the path for seventy or eighty years in order to attain the truth, while even now, pristine truth is in one's possession. In the past, we read this statement from John Dewey: "Considerable amounts of our cognitive interests perish out of our hands only on account of keeping a distance between ourselves and the truth."

Meanwhile, there is another meaning of pluralism which is very important. In reality, this pluralism does not mean belief in diverse truths, but it rather means abstraction of unity from diverse truths, which exist in human worldview, science and knowledge. Cognition of such unities is obtained from synthetic thoughts. At this level, we may accept pluralism as essential for abstracting a synthetic unity.

But as Russell says, "My effort is to reach the ultimate particles of knowledge" and he sets it forth through an analytical way, Mr. Russell must be asked, "Does human knowledge have no synthetic state?" Analysis and scrutiny are great, nay essential. It is good for us to know the last elements of synthesizing our knowledge and where to start. Yet, it is obvious that we also want synthetic knowledge. Through pluralism and synthesis, we have left humanity wandering between scattered parts of relative universals and the whole set of existence.

In the comparison I have done between the Islamic psychology ('ilm al-nafs) and contemporary psychology in a conference in Rūzbeh Hall, I pointed out that 'ilm al-nafs is more inclined to the synthetic method, announcing [the existence of] the magnificent edifice of psychology, nay humanities as a whole, but does not give due importance to the parts and components. Therefore, in the sphere of its activity, it is dull, monotonous and tedious! But today's psychology is good with respect to the parts and components but it has also some dullness and monotony. In spite of having a considerable amount of good components, it does not give importance to the synthetic state and a pluralism naturally governs it, and it is not clear which unit must be their unifying factor! It does not discuss and examine the "self" with such magnificence! This is while all knowledge related to the human mind and even the main roots of this knowledge pertains to the "self", without which one cannot arrive at the ultimate explanation of the "self". Although it is said, that a split personality is a kind of illness, expertise shows this plurality as essential. However, there is no need of closing a door so that in his limited span of life, man cannot know who he is, where he has come from, where he has come, with whom he is, where he is heading, and what he has come for. The psychologists felt compelled to pursue the analytical method and sensed it as a forced necessity, so that a person in one field of science had no knowledge of a much related field.

Q4: What are the examples of the stated thematic principles or the commonalities in the realm of sociopolitical discourses? In which discourses can we discuss pluralism? What will the sociopolitical implications and repercussions be on accepting this meaning?

Jafari: The thematic principles, which in acceptability come second to the axiomatic principles, mean that the proposition of a field of science has been accepted as definite and indisputable. By considering them, the issues related to the said field of science are affirmed or negated, as the case may be, but scientifically affirming them takes place in another field of science. There are two components in mathematics, viz. number and conventional mathematical symbols. Number is the core element of mathematics. The existence of this reality is an established fact for the mathematician. He is not concerned with providing proof of the existence of number because for him it is something accepted and axiomatic. He is engrossed with his mathematical activities. Examples of conventional mathematical symbols are those of the four operations (addition, subtraction, multiplication, and division) of whole, fractional, radical, and other numbers.

In the domain of religious and sociopolitical issues, there are also some thematic principles which are being followed; for example, transmigration and the prohibition of slaughtering animals in Hinduism and the lack of sanctity of animal meat in Islamic jurisprudence. Other examples are all those political principles accepted in a society but need to be established in philosophy or another field of science; for example, the alleged separation of church and state or the fusion of the two, and inalterable cultural elements of society, which are accepted as thematic principles. This is while their correctness must be proved somewhere else, and thus, they cannot be applied in other societies.

Now, we shall embark on answering this question: In which discourses can we discuss pluralism? We must say that since thematic principles in every religion, sect or sociopolitical system are treated like correct essential propositions by their respective followers, one cannot expect these principles to be rejected, because rejecting such thematic principles is more or less tantamount to abandoning an element of the said religion, sect, or sociopolitical system. What is possible in such cases is to conduct an indepth study and examination of the sources of such thematic principles and their proofs in the sciences or schools of philosophy from which the said principles are derived and deduced. The acceptance of the said principles will depend on conformity with their proofs.

Meanwhile, what can be said regarding the last portion of your question is that we must not strive hard that this discussion of pluralism and its relevant subjects immediately yield result in political culture because given the insufficient preliminary points, one cannot arrive at any conclusion. In political culture, it is categorically said, "We are dealing with variables." Even if the statesman has certain inalterable ideological principles, he may disregard them in political practice, otherwise he would be included among the immature, and he always follows the majority (what is deemed expedient and desirable for many people at any given time). This is prevalent in conventional politics, and we take into account the Machiavellian way of thinking. There is no fixed stance other than what the statesman has set before as his objective, whether unity will be maintained in pursuing this objective or not! More than anything else, one must reflect on the commonalities and merits to see which things we can present to humanity as commonalities and which things can be offered as merits.

Q5: If we limit pluralism from the interreligious realm to the intrareligious realm, i.e. if we discuss plurality in the existing perceptions within a religion (just as this is our main objective in this discussion), how can you examine it and what is your ultimate analysis?

Jafari: Sometimes, this plurality and diversity has an actual effect on society. For example, some individuals opposed Ayatullịh Mīrzị Shīrịzī's[1] religious edict (fatwị) of prohibiting

---

1. ịyatullịh Mḉrzị °asan Shḉrịzḉ (d. 1312 AH/1894): the mujtahid who declared in December 1891 that "the use of tobacco is unlawful (ịarịm) and tantamount to war against the Imịm of the Time ('a)" after the production and marketing of tobacco in Iran had been made the monopoly of a British company. In obedience to his declaration, all of Iran boycotted tobacco, forcing the cancellation of the

tobacco, came forward for sometime and expressed it. It is clear that such differences are caused by the multiplicity of views on jurisprudential bases, but sometimes the effect of plurality does not appear in society, yet it occurs in the minds of individuals within the circles of discussion. In the second assumption, presenting and examining diverse views do not pose any problem at all, provided that divulging them does not cause agitation in the minds of people. In the first assumption, however, once there is interpretation, decision must naturally be made. In the level of the veracious experts, this has been settled and the authority of such decision is established. In order to impart the truth to the people, it is necessary to discuss it at the societal level. We made it a condition that discussing various opinions must not cause agitation because considering their mental state, the people really want a peaceful life. Disrupting this tranquility not only loses this kind of pleasure but also leads to disorder in the religious, moral, and even legal-political culture. Concerning freedom of expression, it must be asked, "What does he want to say? To whom does he want to say it?" For one who is not an expert or an illiterate, will the freedom of expression cause anything other than anxiety and additional pain? This notion [of freedom] originated from the extreme views of freedom-worshippers such as John Stuart Mill.[1] Are all the people in the West like Hegel or Kant, and all people in the East like Mullį ʿadrį, who can distinguish a truth from among thousands of falsehoods? The masses are not authorities and they are not well-informed. Once the discussion is disclosed in public, doubt will be created in their minds. Discussions in this proposal must be academic in form and published in specialized journals. Thereafter, their results—if ever definitely

---

concession in early 1892. See Hamid Algar, Religion and State in Iran in 1785-1906: The Role of the Ulama in the Qajar Period (Berkeley and Los Angeles: University of California Press, 1969), pp. 205-215; Nikki Keddie, Religion and Rebellion in Iran: The Tobacco Protest of 1891-92 (London: Frank Cass, 1966). [Trans.]

1. John Stuart Mill (1806-73): a British philosopher, civil servant and an influential contributor to social theory, political theory, and political economy. [Trans.]

established—should be put into practice. I asked Mr. Mayer, "Why did you Germans, who have insightful philosophers, kneel down to positivism?" He said, "Nowadays, Europe—or Germany—has no philosophers; it has philosophy workers!" Will the intellect allow us to put forward hundreds of theoretical issues to philosophy workers? Never, let alone to the common people. Yes to innovation and novelty, but not to the derangement of the people's minds.

It is said that today philosophy and basic human sciences are no more interesting for students in the universities. With respect to law, politics, culture and others, the society has its own way and is treading another path. Just because of the attractiveness of baseless novelty, why one must be anxious for any definite reason at all?

> *Oppressor is the nation who has blinded the eyes*
>
> *Destroyed the whole world just because of some views.* [1]

Certainly, a student who has spent many years in the university and then settles down will not easily submit to a few attractive words spoken by you and me. If we are concerned with the plight of humanity, this is no way. For the lower class and even the poor average people, all individuals are authorities! This is especially so if these individuals are eloquent and can stir their emotions. I have totally no problem with review and reconsideration of even the most fundamentally accepted issues. In the words of Khw¡jawī Kirm¡nī,

> *The residents of your land are experiencing a new momen in every moment*
>
> *The wayfarers of the path of your love are every moment in a new world.*

At every moment, you may be with a teacher, but with whom? In which environment? About which subjects? There are certain conditions necessary for any search or competition. It requires a paved ground; otherwise, we will become like the Westerners who have been subjected to contradictions, but

---

1. Rumi's *Masnavi*, Book 1.

refrained from conducting research about social sciences and opened the gate for technology.

Voltaire says, "I am such an advocate of freedom that I am willing to die for the sake of what you would freely express, although I would not agree with it." What does the latter part of this statement mean? Apparently, it is elegant, but it is actually the last nail driven into the coffin of human principles, because under the imaginary nature of freedom and the need for information and talent, an astute writer can formulate elegant and deceptive statements and hand over helpless society to the powerful! Will Mr. Voltaire also commit suicide for this?!

Q6: Is it possible, that by presenting different views in a society, in the beginning, society would be deceived and face many problems along the way, but, because of the improved level of awareness, after sometime, people would distinguish the good from the evil and follow the right path?

Jafari: In essence, all issues which are put forward as new ideas are not "real", especially philosophical, social science and ideological issues, in which personal taste and mastery of words and expressions have enormous impacts in drawing the attention of common people. For this reason, their damage may possibly be irreparable. Our contemporary time has plunged into futility because of the mushrooming of baseless views expressed in attractive words. They are a few individuals who are lovers of the truth. In today's mechanical societies—in which technology encompasses all our existence, and individuals easily succumb to problems in life—how much opportunity can they have? I consider it problematic and even impossible. How can we take into account the lives of individuals? Of course, if this issue is necessary, the educators need to think of the way to address it and what the course of action should be. That is, here the necessity for specialized activities is put forth. How surprising it is! Is the importance of social sciences not equal to that of a headache relieving tablet which requires the prescription of biochemists and physicians before it can be consumed? That is, different understandings must enter the scene after the experts have given their opinion on it. Of course, when it becomes clear that the current official view in society is erroneous, we must not allow the society to be sacrificed before the altar of errors. It must be candidly declared that the said view is erroneous. The courage to do so can also be gleaned from the importance of the truth. However, for us to conduct the discussion openly from the beginning is not correct. One would say something while the other would express its opposite, and if two contradictory or seemingly contradictory views are expressed, a new idea must independently enter the scene to deal with the contradiction, and in the words of N¡¥ir Khusrū,

When someone express his dark mind in sophisticated terms
Soon you think that he is a great thinker of the highest status.

We say that you must give importance to the human soul in the same manner that extra care and expert opinion must be given to a prescription for the consumption of a pain-relieving tablet. So, this is a gesture of concern for the "intelligible life" of human beings which must not be taken as a plaything. A person who entertains doubt in the foundations of his ideological life can no longer truly render service to his society. In fact, he can no longer think correctly about his identity. A youngster who is not certain of the principles upon which his life is based, the goal of his life, and the essence of humanity—words come out of his mouth and notions get instilled in his mind similar to what does not come out of the mouths or gets instilled in the minds of even the founders of nihilism. This is not censorship of knowledge but rather concern for humanity. Hence, there is no contradiction in logically dealing with this subject while not taking human life as a plaything.

Q7: Is this analysis based upon a religious principle, a scientific conduct of the Prophet (SAW), or as a rational understanding?

Jafari: It is a rational understanding of the definite subjects of Islamic sources to logically protect the human soul from agitation, indecisiveness and inattention to the sublime goal of existence and life. In our opinion, responsible freedom has the flavor of real life. We do not have absolute freedom especially if the destiny of people is at stake. In these cases, pragmatism is correct in holding that one must also take the outcome into account; one must not be only in love but also seriously know what he wants.

Some of Qur'¡nic verses and traditions point out that if you misguide a person, you are responsible for his soul! If you do something so that the poor fellow can never be guided, you have annihilated him. Carefulness in this set of juristic laws, which strongly prohibit initiating the factors of misguidance (such as blasphemous books), keeping and promoting them, except for good utilization, confirms that freedom in presenting non-Islamic beliefs must be based upon rational motives. In the noble verse,

> *That is why We decreed for the Children of Israel that whoever takes a life, without [its being guilty of] manslaughter or corruption on the earth, is as though he had killed all mankind, and whoever saves a life is as though he had saved all mankind.*[1]

On the basis of reliable proofs, the exegetes have considered taking a life and saving a life beyond the manifestations of physically taking and saving a life—and in a sense, worse than it. In his famous strophe-poem, Gibran Khalil Gibran[2] says,

> *Anyone who steals a flower shall be reproached and humiliated while the one who grabs a piece of land is treated as a hero and champion! Anyone who kills a person shall be penalized while the one who commits mass murder draws nobody's attention!*

Criminals of the human soul are famous under attractive titles such as "abled writer," "free thinker," "intellectual," and "thinker". Sometimes, even the grandiloquent word "philosopher" is displayed in the showcases of a society, most of

---

1. S£rat al-M¡'idah 5:32.
2. Gibran Khalil Gibran (1883-1931): a Lebanese American artist, poet, and writer who is the third best-selling poet of all time, behind Shakespeare and Lao-Tzu. [Trans.]

whose members are deprived of profound pieces of knowledge. This is while these criminals are incapable of anwering essential questions of philosophy! Now, if the subject were such that all those who expressed their views would sincerely come to the scene and the differences and competitions were constructive, fatal clashes would not have brought into existence great problems, and with the goal of "constructive competition," no person would have persisted with his claim for no reason at all. Presentation of contrasting and differing views was prevalent during the early period of Islam. We may take into account ±abarsī's[1] Al-Ihtijjj and the like. We can see how views and beliefs could be freely presented in the presence of the Im¡ms ('a) and scrutinized. Im¡m al-Ri¤¡ ('a) would put forward very sublime scientific and philosophical issues, but only with 'Imr¡n ¯¡bī and not for the common people who could not possibly discern the dialogue between the master and his student.

At any rate, by having two very vital principles of "rational collective life," we move forward while always supporting the presentation of religious diversities with those who are worthy of delving into those diversities:

> *So give good news to My servants who listen to the word [of Allah] and follow the best [sense] of it. They are the ones whom Allah has guided, and it is they who possess intellect.*[2]

The principle of coexistence with the basic commonalities in the natural Divine Faith:

> *Allah does not forbid you in regard to those who did not make war against you on account of religion and did not expel you from you homes, that you deal with them with kindness and justice.*[3]

---

1. A¦mad ibn 'Al¢ ibn Ab¢ ±¡lib al-±abars¢ (d. circa 620 AH): a great Sh¢'ah scholar, jurisprudent, traditionist (muhaddith), and historian of the sixth and early seventh century AH. Among his works are Al-I¦tijjj, Al-K¡f¢ f¢ 'l-Fiqh, T¡r¢kh al-A'immah and Kit¡b al-¯al¡h. [Trans.]
2. S£rat al-Zumar 39:17-18.
3. S£rat al-Mumtahanah 60:8.

***

> *Say, 'O People of the Book! Come to a word common between us and you: that we will worship no one but Allah, and that we will not ascribe any partner to Him, and that we will not take each other as lords besides Allah'. But if they turn away, say, 'Be witnesses that we are muslims'.*[1]

Q8: In conclusion, in moving toward the ideal culture, what indicators do you think can be presented in the domain of sociopolitical discourses?

Jafari: By taking into account two holy verses of the Noble Qur'in,

> *And their affairs are by counsel among themselves,*[2]

and

> *"And consult them in the affairs, and once you are resolved, put your trust in Allah. Indeed Allah loves those who trust in Him,*[3]

Keeping in view the fact that knowing and deciding the subjects of life are in the hands of the people and that in determining the subjects of life the Islamic jurisprudence system is "adherent" and not "advanced". The role and position of people in the subjects is foremost, and considering that consulting the experts and authorities is agreed upon in society, in conforming the laws to the subjects as well as in secondary laws, the people's participation and their investigation and acceptance are of immense importance. As such, in general, the ideal culture in Islam signifies explanation and management of the "intelligible life" of human beings in both the individual and collective realms for the best possible goodness in both the material and spiritual dimensions. The things that have an "advanced" feature in the said two realms are the inalterable principles which

---

1. S£rat ¡l 'Imr¡n 3:64.
2. S£rat al-Sh£r¡ 42:38.
3. S£rat ¡l 'Imr¡n 3:159.

Allameh Muhammad Taghi Jafari

(1923-1998)

About the Author

Muhammad Taghi Ja'fari (born 1923, Tabriz, Iran, and died 1998) was a contemporary sage and an expert in philosophy and Islamic knowledge. Ja'fari was familiar with Western culture and also with the needs of modern human being and the contemporary culture. He was indeed an original and innovative thinker.

One of the most important innovations of this honorable master was that he, like Allameh Tabatabaei and Sayyed Muhammad Bagher Sadr, used the methodology of comparative studies for introducing Islamic knowledge to a generation who was thirsty for truth. Indeed, Ja'fari has left us a collection of invaluable works on Islamic teachings, philosophy of arts, aesthetics, literature, mysticism, the study of the *Nahjulbalaghah*, psychology, human rights and pedagogy.

In addition to being an expert in philosophy, in Islamic mysticism and in *Fiqh* (jurisprudence), Ja'fari was familiar with the works and the ideas of classical Western philosophers such as Socrates, Plato, and Aristotle. He was also versed in the works of modern philosophers including Descartes, Leibniz, Hume, Kant, Hegel, and contemporary philosophers such as Balzac, Dostoevsky, Tolstoy, Hugo, and modern-day physicists including Max Planck, and Einstein.

Ja'fari's epistemic geometry comprises of the knowledge of the mind, the revelation and the heart, tradition and modernity, physics and metaphysics, law and aesthetics. While the first three sources were the main pillars of his thinking, the expressions of his thoughts were nonetheless the result of dialogues made on the different bases of this epistemic geometry, which – due to their up-to-date nature – made his works novel and attentive to the debates on the difficulties of the "modern human" and the "modern life".

Ja'fari's 15-volume *Rumi: the Man and His Ideas, an Interpretation, Criticism and Analysis of Rumi's Masnavi* and his 27-volume *Translation and Interpretation of the Nahjulbalaghah* have a distinct place in his body of work. In terms of the clergies' principles, attending to Rumi's *Masnavi* was a heresy, or disliked to say the least. Moreover, writing commentaries on the *Nahjulbalaghah* was considered as a virtue, not a science. Scholarship was, and still is seen as footnoting on important books on *fiqh* (jurisprudence). It was in such an environment that the honorable master instilled *Masnavi* back in the minds of students and academicians. By comparing Rumi's sublime and amorous assertions with those of French and Russian thinkers and scholars, with whom Iranian intellectuals are more familiar, he once again took Rumi's *Masnavi* back into Iranian homes, in which households were more acquainted with Western culture. Afterwards, by writing an exegesis on the *Nahjulbalaghah,* entitled "A Manifesto on Wisdom, Mysticism and Politics," he familiarized the younger generation with an Islam devoid of superstition, factionalism and backwardness, an Islam based on the mind, revelation, justice and love. We can consider Ja'fari as the vanguard in writing commentaries on Rumi's *Masnavi* and the *Nahjulbalaghah* in the contemporary era, to whom all the later commentators are indebted.

According to Allameh Ja'fari, love and the mind are the two wings that make humans fly towards the absolute truth. The mind and revelation, science and religion, the mind and *shari'a* (Islamic law) are all compatible and do not contradict one another. Of course, the mind is the solid pillar of knowing (episteme). In his thoughts on the political principles of Islam, he saw justice, compassion, mercy, tolerance, serving the people, and reliance on consultation (*Shura*) and also on people's decisions as the basis of Islamic governance.

In terms of personal character and ethical manner, despite his high stature, Ja'fari was humble and modest. Unlike some learned scholars, he did not consider himself as someone who knew everything; there was no trace of arrogance and contemptuousness in him. Throughout his productive life, he preferred the trappings of science by devoting himself wholeheartedly to the cultivation of intellectual life.

He passed away on 15 November, 1998 suffering from a cancer disease in London. He was buried in Dar-Al-Zohd, by Imam Reza's Holy Shrine in Mashhad.

The Allameh Jafari Institute

www.ingramcontent.com/pod-product-compliance
Lightning Source LLC
Chambersburg PA
CBHW051608120626
46551CB00014B/1709

9 781990 451935